X.25 and Related Protocols

Uyless Black

1951 - 1991
40 YEARS OF SERVICE
IEEE COMPUTER SOCIETY
A member society of the
Institute of Electrical and Electronics Engineers, Inc.

X.25
and Related Protocols

X.25

X.25

Uyless Black

1951 - 1991
IEEE Computer Society Press

The Institute of Electrical and
Electronics Engineers, Inc.

X.25 and Related Protocols

Uyless Black

1951 - 1991
40 YEARS OF SERVICE

IEEE COMPUTER SOCIETY
A member society of the
Institute of Electrical and Electronics Engineers, Inc.

IEEE Computer Society Press
Los Alamitos, California

Washington • Brussels • Tokyo

IEEE Computer Society Press Monograph

Library of Congress Cataloging-in-Publication Data

Black, Uyless D.
    X.25 and related protocols / Uyless Black.
        p. cm.
    Includes bibliographical references and index.
    ISBN 0-8186-8976-5 (case). — ISBN 0-8186-5976-9 (microfiche)
    1. Computer network protocols. 2. Packet switching (Data transmission) I. Title.
    TK5105.5.B568 1991   91-6511
    004.6'2—dc20   CIP

Published by the
IEEE Computer Society Press
10662 Los Vaqueros Circle
PO Box 3014
Los Alamitos, CA 90720-1264

IEEE Computer Society Press Order Number 1976
Library of Congress Number 91-6511
IEEE Catalog Number EH0333-5
ISBN 0-8186-5976-9 (microfiche)
ISBN 0-8186-8976-5 (case)

Additional copies can be ordered from

IEEE Computer Society Press	IEEE Service Center	IEEE Computer Society	IEEE Computer Society
Customer Service Center	445 Hoes Lane	13, avenue de l'Aquilon	Ooshima Building
10662 Los Vaqueros Circle	PO Box 1331	B-1200 Brussels	2-19-1 Minami-Aoyama
PO Box 3014	Piscataway, NJ 08855-1331	BELGIUM	Minato-ku, Tokyo 107
Los Alamitos, CA 90720-1264			JAPAN

Technial Editor: Jon Butler
Editorial production: Catherine Harris and Anne Copeland MaCallum
Copy Editor: Thomas Culviner
Cover Design: Joseph Daigle
Printed in the United States of America by Braun-Brumfield, Inc.

 THE INSTITUTE OF ELECTRICAL AND ELECTRONICS ENGINEERS, INC.

This book is dedicated to some long-time friends:

Jack and Louise Norris

Gene and Billie Keith

Acknowledgments

I would like to express my thanks to the following individuals and organizations for ideas and suggestions used in this book: The engineers at Bell Northern Research (BNR) have been most helpful in sharing ideas on their X.25-based products. AT&T also provided me with valuable information on their networks. Both Bell Labs and BellCore personnel provided excellent suggestions for the book.

Several years ago, I worked with Peer Networks in Santa Clara, California, during the development of their products. David Chung and Randy Presuhn gave me several ideas about packet networks that have found their way into this book.

During some recent lectures in London and Amsterdam, I developed several ideas for the X.25 internetworking chapter, and I thank the delegates for our brainstorming sessions on internetworking X.25 and ISDN.

I have been consulting and lecturing on X.25 for about 10 years. Much of the material in this book really stems from input from hundreds of clients and seminar delegates who attended my lectures. Although they go unnamed, they deserve a byline on the cover.

I owe thanks to my European seminar partner, IBC Technical Services Ltd., for scheduling and coordinating my talks in Europe, and to the Information Engineering Institute, for supporting my efforts in North America and the Far East. A special note of thanks goes to Helen Savill and her staff at IBC for their friendship to me and their support of the European X.25 lectures.

The IEEE Computer Society Press reviewers who reviewed the manuscript that led to this book were quite important to the finished product. Their perspective resulted in a better book. My editor, Jon T. Butler, also has my thanks for his faith and patience. To the reviewers: thanks for holding my feet to the fire!

Preface

During the past several years of working with X.25 systems, I found that many people have expressed a need for documentation that explains X.25 operations. The X.25 source documents published by the standards organizations are viewed by some as too terse and lacking in sufficient tutorial explanations about X.25. Others view the documents as too complex for the lay reader to comprehend. This problem was not readily apparent to me since I work with X.25 protocols frequently, and use only these source documents for my work.

For those people who have the technical background necessary to understand the CCITT X.25 Recommendation, the problem remains of reading a stack of other related specifications, because X.25 has now found its way into many diverse systems such as local area networks, PBXs, and ISDNs.

The CCITT recommendations and the ISO standards that deal with X.25 and related protocols are not intended to be tutorials. They are intended to be concise and succinct descriptions of the X.25 operations. As such, they are indispensable for network designers, engineers, programmers, and other technically-oriented personnel. But they do not suit the needs of people who need only a general view of these protocols.

Therefore, my goals in this book are twofold: (a) to provide a tutorial view of X.25 and the other protocols with which X.25 operates, and (b) to provide a convenient reference guide to these protocols.

The book is organized at different levels of detail to suit the individual reader. A considerable amount of detailed information is provided about X.25 itself. In turn, overviews are provided of the related protocols.

Each chapter beginning tells the reader about the nature of the chapter and its level of detail. The same approach is taken with several topics within the chapters. This is to help readers select portions of the book best suited to their needs.

Notwithstanding, some protocols related to X.25 are given a longer treatment than others. Discussions with clients, vendors, and seminar delegates revealed that a number of readers need detailed information on several widely used standards, but are content with knowing, in a general way, how the others fit into the X.25 picture.

This book should not be used as the sole document for learning about and using X.25. There is no substitute for the actual source document. For a detailed view of X.25, the reader is urged to obtain and study the CCITT X.25 Recommendation.

The requisite knowledge for reading this book is a basic familiarity with data communications terms and concepts.

Contents

Chapter 4   X.25 and the Data-Link Layer   **51**

Chapter 5   The X.25 Network Layer   **83**

Chapter 6   X.25 Facilities   **131**

Chapter 7   X.25 Companion Standards   **161**

Chapter 8   Internetworking X.25 with Other Systems   **179**

Chapter 9   The PAD Standards   **213**

Chapter 10   X.25's Future   **227**

Appendix A   Examples of Packet Networks   **233**

Appendix B   A Tutorial on Link Protocols   **241**

List of Illustrations

xvi

Chapter 5

Appendix C

Appendix D

List of Tables

The X.25 Network

Goals of Chapter 1

The goals of this chapter are to provide the reader with a brief history of the development of X.25 and a discussion of why X.25 is so prevalent in the packet network industry. We also examine some advantages and disadvantages of using X.25. The basic concepts of packet networks are examined, as well as several key terms associated with X.25.

Readers familiar with the general concepts of X.25 may skip this chapter. Readers unfamiliar with the topics cited above should read the entire chapter.

Introduction

In the late 1960s and early 1970s, many data communications networks were created by companies, government agencies, and other organizations. Each organization designed and programmed these networks to meet their business needs. Organizations had no reason to adhere to any common convention for their data communications protocols, because each organization's private network provided services only to itself. Consequently, these networks used specialized protocols tailored to satisfy the organization's requirements.

During this period, several companies and telephone administrations in the U.S., Canada, and Europe implemented *public data networks* conceived to provide a service for data traffic that paralleled the telephone systems' service for voice traffic. They are known today by several other names: public packet networks (PPN), public packet-switched networks (PPSN), and packet-switched data networks (PSDN).

The public network vendors had to answer a major question: How can the network best provide the interface for a user's terminal or computer to the network? The problem was formidable because each terminal or computer vendor had developed its own set of data communications protocols. Indeed, some companies, such as IBM, had developed scores of different protocols within their own product line.

X.25 came about largely because people working on these nascent networks recognized that a common network interface protocol was needed—especially for the network owners.

Imagine the expense and complexity of maintaining a public network sad-

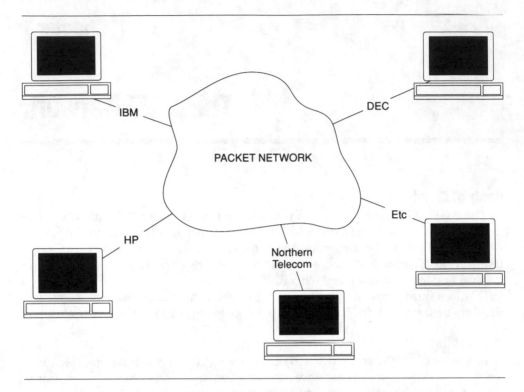

Figure 1-1. Problems with Multivendor Network Interfaces

dled with providing a protocol conversion routine for *each* unique user device (see Figure 1-1). The situation would be something like our local telephone company being forced to accommodate different dialing schemes, ringing tones, etc., for every company that entered the marketplace to sell telephones. Therefore, limiting a data network's interface options makes very good sense.

Thus, X.25 was conceived with the goal of establishing a limited set of interface conventions to a data communications packet network (see Figure 1-2). It was developed primarily from the impetus and direction of several telecommunications organizations, especially the European telecommunications administrations. However, the original document was based on proposals from Datapac (Canada), and Tymnet and Telenet (U.S.), three new packet-switching networks.

Since its inception, the recommended standard has been expanded to include many options, services, and facilities. X.25 is now the prevalent interface standard to wide area packet networks.

X.25 was first published in 1974, when CCITT issued the first draft of X.25 (the "Gray Book"). It was revised in 1976, 1978, 1980, and again in 1984, with the publication of the "Red Book" Recommendation. The latest release is the 1988 "Blue Book."

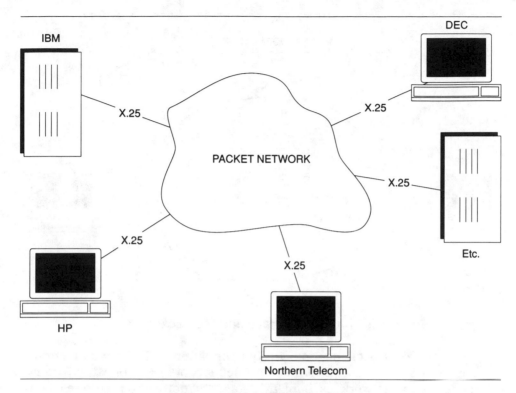

Figure 1-2. The X.25 Interface

Until 1988, X.25 was revised and republished every four years. In 1988, CCITT announced its intention to publish revisions to X.25 (and all its recommendations) more frequently if the changes warranted it.

X.25 is called the *X.25 Recommendation* by CCITT. The organization uses this word to avoid the impression that its specifications are required, which might present significant problems for its members. Also, CCITT avoids using the term *standard*, although many people use it. This book uses the term *recommendation*.

X.25 Configurations

X.25 defines the procedures for exchanging data between a user device, identified as *data terminal equipment* (*DTE*), and a network node, identified as *data circuit-terminating equipment* (*DCE*) (see Figure 1-3). Its formal title is *Interface Between Data Terminal Equipment and Data Circuit-Terminating Equipment for Terminals Operating in the Packet Mode on Public Data Networks.* In X.25, the DCE represents the network's interface to the user DTE. The DCE does not perform all the DCE operations that are cited in X.25. Typically, a network packet switch performs these operations and makes them available at the DTE-DCE interface.

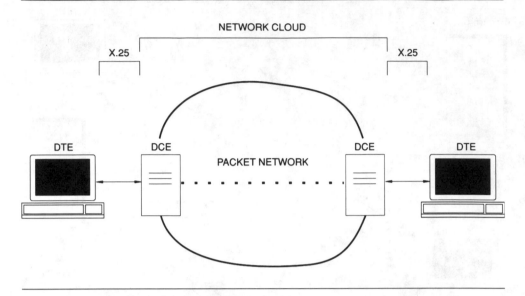

Figure 1-3. The X.25 Interface and the Packet Network

The principal idea of the X.25 Recommendation is to provide common procedures between a user DTE and a packet network DCE for establishing a connection to the network, exchanging data with another DTE, and releasing the connection. The procedures include such functions as identifying the packets of specific user terminals or computers (with *logical channel numbers* or LCNs), acknowledging packets, rejecting packets, providing for error recovery, and controlling flow. X.25 also includes some very useful facilities, such as charging the transmitted packets to the receiving DTE, rather than the transmitting DTE.

Interestingly, the X.25 Recommendation contains no routing algorithms. Features such as fixed or dynamic packet-routing schemes within a network are left to specific vendor implementations, because they are internal to a vendor's product. Consequently, the term "X.25 network" does not mean that the internal operations of the network use X.25. Rather, it means the interface to a packet data network is governed by the X.25 protocol. This is not to say that X.25 cannot be used inside a network. Indeed, several networks also use the recommendation to define certain operations between the packet nodes within the network cloud.

Why Use X.25?

Like any other communications protocol, X.25 has its advantages and disadvantages, and they will be examined in this book. But the enquiring reader may already be wondering why X.25 would be of any value.

There are several reasons for using any standard. We will focus on X.25, since it is the subject of this book. First, the adoption of a common standard among vendors provides an easy way to interface different vendors' products. Second, the X.25 standard has gone through numerous revisions and is relatively mature. It has seen considerable use since 1980, and several systems were implemented as early as 1976. Consequently, the changes and adaptations in the 1988 document reflect substantial industry-wide experience with packet network interfaces. Third, a widely used standard such as X.25 can decrease network costs, since off-the-shelf software and hardware are readily available. Fourth, it is easier to write a request-for-proposal to a vendor stating the network must conform to X.25 than to write a lengthy specification document. Fifth, a transmission link using conventional line protocols (for example, High Level Data Link Control or HDLC) provides for error recovery and data accountability only on one link between the DTE and the network (and perhaps on the links between the packet-switching nodes within the network). X.25 provides a higher level of support by defining many operations that enhance the reliability of data transfer between each sending DTE and its DCE (the entrance packet node to the network) and each receiving DTE and its DCE (the exit packet node from the network). In other words, it gives considerably more end-to-end support than a link protocol like HDLC.

In these introductory remarks, we should also note that many systems use X.25 as a DTE-to-DTE interface. Others use it to manage such resources as peripheral devices, applications programs, databases, and even the "windows" on a workstation CRT screen. Even though X.25 was not written for a non-DCE interface, the industry has adapted it as such, because it is available and it offers numerous functions to support a user-network connection. Chapter 7 describes the DTE-to-DTE implementation and explains an ISO specification for this configuration.

A widely used convention (such as X.25) for network connection enables one vendor's equipment to communicate with equipment from other vendors (if all use the convention). But use of a network interface like X.25 does not mean equipment made by different manufacturers can exchange meaningful information. Levels of protocol other than X.25 are required for end-to-end communications. These protocols are the users' or vendors' responsibility; they are discussed briefly in Chapter 2.

On the down side, the four-year revision cycle for X.25 strikes some people as too frequent for achieving stability in communications product lines. Some manufacturers have also said that the increasing number of functions and services being written into X.25 is making it too large and complex for effective and efficient use. Furthermore, X.25 is often criticized because it is not well-suited to certain environments such as transaction-based, point-of-sale applications. As we proceed, we will examine these pros and cons with more detailed analysis.

Logical Channels and Virtual Circuits

X.25 DCEs and DTEs use statistical time-division multiplexing to transfer the users' traffic into and out of the network. The DTE and the network are jointly responsible for combining (multiplexing) multiple user sessions onto a single communications line. In other words, instead of dedicating one line to each user, the DTE and DCE interleave the multiple users' bursty traffic across an X.25 interface (the interface is between the DTE and DCE). The user perceives that a line is dedicated to the user's application, but is actually sharing it with other users.

The multiplexing of more than one user onto the physical communications line is one aspect of an important feature of X.25 called the *virtual circuit*. Here, virtual means that a user perceives the availability of a dedicated, physical resource when, in practice, the resource is a multiplexed end-to-end (DTE-to-DTE) connection that can be shared by other users.

X.25 uses the term *logical channel* to describe one aspect of this concept, but the terms "virtual" and "logical" are often used erroneously to convey the same meaning. It is better to define these terms more precisely, as well as the term *physical circuit* (see Figure 1-4):

- *Physical circuit:* The communications link between two devices such as DTEs and the network switch. The telephone lines often form the physical circuit.

- *Virtual circuit:* The *end-to-end* connection or relationship (through a network) between two user devices (DTEs). Since intermediate packet switches are used to route the data through the network, the virtual

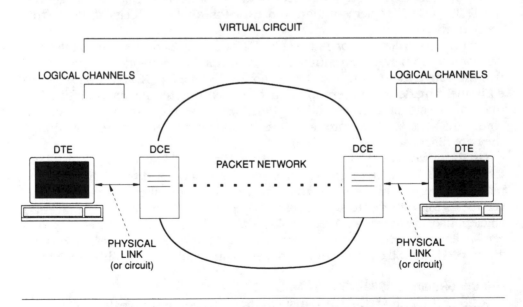

Figure 1-4. Logical Channels with Virtual Circuits

circuit usually consists of multiple physical circuits between the switches, which collectively make up the virtual circuit. The network is responsible for maintaining the end-to-end connection of the users.

- *Logical channel.* The local connection relationship between the user DTE and the network; the connection between the user device and the packet exchange. The logical channel has significance only at the DTE and DCE interface on *each* side of the network. Therefore, a logical channel exists on each side of the network cloud. The network *maps* the two logical channels to a virtual circuit.

Switching and Routing in Networks

We learned earlier that X.25 does not define the operations within the packet network. Nonetheless, a grasp of the rudimentary aspects of switching and routing is helpful in understanding how certain network operations affect X.25 and vice versa. This section provides an overview of some of the more widely used packet-switching and routing techniques.

Many networks have hundreds of computers and terminals that must communicate with each other. A computer or terminal cannot have a direct (point-to-point) connection to every other component. For example, a relatively small network of 500 components would require 124,750 individual communications links; the conduits underneath the city streets would overflow with the wires needed for larger communications systems.

One solution is to place switches on the transmission path. The user stations are not connected directly to each other. Rather, they communicate with each other by sending data through a switch (or set of switches). The switch relays the data to the receiving computer terminal, telephone, or some other component. Ideally, the user thinks a point-to-point link is in use and the intervening switches remain "transparent" to the communications process.

A data communications switching system uses one or a combination of the following switches (and X.25 is used on the first and third types of networks): *circuit switches, message switches,* and *packet switches.*

Circuit Switching

In circuit-switching technology, a *direct* connection is created through the switches that reside between the communicating stations. Originally, it was designed for voice traffic, which needs a dedicated line for conversation between two people. It can be compared to having a transmission wire (or wires) attached directly between two stations. The direct connection serves as an open "pipeline" for voice or data transfer, permitting the two end users to use the pipeline as they see fit.

However, the two users do not have direct wires through a circuit-switched network. Instead, the intervening switches have electronic connectors that "couple" the communications links directly to each other.

Even though circuit switching provides the lines (links) for the traffic flow between user devices (DTEs), such operations as error checking, session establishment, and traffic flow control are the responsibility of the users. Simply stated, the telephone company does not provide these features unless the user purchases them through a separate contractual arrangement. Consequently, a circuit-switching network is often the foundation for a data communications network, and additional features are provided by a "value-added carrier," the network vendor, or the user organization. Other data-switching methods (e.g., message and packet switching) often install leased telephone circuits to provide the basic transfer medium. Then they add other functions and facilities to the circuit-switched facility.

Before we leave this subject, note that modern circuit-switching systems no longer use direct physical couplers between two users. Digital circuit switches actually provide indirect connections that make transfers from the input line to memory and the output line. Notwithstanding, these systems are designed to give the user the perception of a direct connection.

Message Switching

Message switching is designed specifically for data traffic. As with circuit switching, the communications lines are connected to a switching facility, but the end users do not have a direct physical connection to each other. Rather, the message is transmitted to the switch, and stored on direct access media (such as disk) for later delivery. The term *store-and-forward* is associated with message-switching networks.

In large networks, specialized computers are used for the message-switching operations. The computer receives the message and, according to traffic conditions and message priority, stores the data unit on a number of files (queues) on disk. If the traffic load in the network and the priority of the message permit, the switch retrieves the message, examines the header to determine the destination address, and routes the message to its recipient.

Packet Switching

Packet switching has become the prevalent switching technique for data communications networks. It is used in such diverse systems as private branch exchanges (PBXs), local area networks (LANs), and even multiplexers.

Packet switching is so named because a user's data (such as messages) are separated and transmitted in small units called packets (see Figure 1-5). Each packet contains the fields needed for the network to identify the packet, the destination switch, and/or the destination DTE.

Each packet occupies a transmission line only for the duration of the transmission; the line is then made available for another user's packet. Thus, packet switching uses statistical multiplexing techniques and takes advantage of the intermittent (bursty) transmission characteristics common to many user applications and workstations.

Packet size is limited so that packets do not occupy the line for extended periods. Therefore, a packet network environment supports bursty (asynchro-

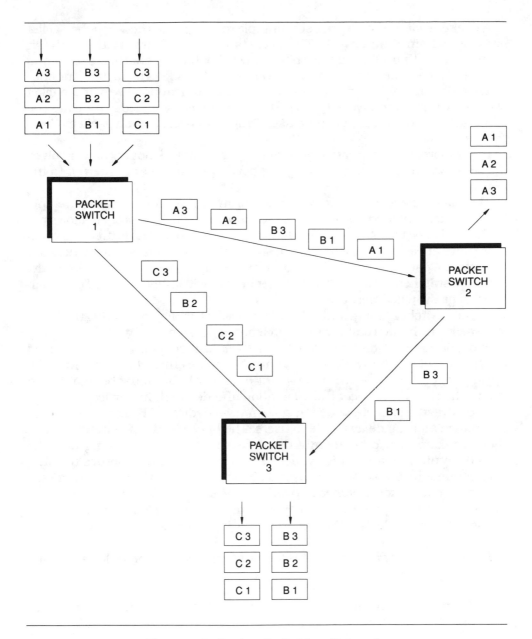

Figure 1-5. Packet Switching Networks

nous) traffic quite well. Notwithstanding, the modern packet network is designed to support continuous, high-volume traffic, as well as asynchronous, low-volume traffic. Each user is given a variable transmission capability based on throughput and response time requirements.

A packet-switched network uses multiple routes (paths) between the packet switches within the network. The packets are routed across the paths in accordance with traffic congestion, error conditions, the shortest end-to-end path, and other criteria. In some networks, a user's packets for an ongoing end-to-end session are routed across different communications lines and packet switches within the network. The packets are then reassembled at the exit node of the network for the receiving end user. In other networks, each packet follows the same path.

It is important to emphasize once more that X.25 does not become involved in these switching operations; they are beyond its scope and internal to the network.

The packet network topology is different from that of message switching. First, packet-switched networks use more switches. This approach allows the traffic load to be distributed to other switches. Second, at least three and often more lines are attached to the switches. This arrangement allows the network to route the packets around failed or busy switches and lines. Consequently, a packet-switched network gives the user better availability and reliability than a message-switched network.

Packet switching also provides an attractive feature for connecting the DTEs for a session. In a circuit-switched (telephone) system, the time to set up a connection is often lengthy (sometimes, several seconds). First, a switched telephone call requires a destination number to be entered (dialed). Next, all physical circuits between the intervening circuit switches must be established before the call can connect the origination and destination parties.

In contrast, a packet-switching system uses dedicated leased lines, which are immediately made available to users. The lines require no circuit setups; they are connected permanently through the network. Assuming that the virtual circuit is created quickly, dedicated circuits should improve the slow connect time that is sometimes associated with circuit-switched networks.

However, a packet-switched network can be slower than a circuit-switched network. Network performance depends mainly on design soundness and traffic load—regardless of the underlying switching method.

In summary, the primary reasons for the widespread use of packet switching are

- Shared channels and ports among multiple users to enhance resource use

- Increased data transmission integrity with the ability to bypass failed or busy links and congested or failed switches

- Balanced bidirectional traffic flow on each circuit in the network

- Improved response time for users

Another Look at Logical Channels

Let us return briefly to the discussion of X.25 logical channels (refer again to Figure 1-4). Most packet networks use the logical channel concept to identify the users connected to the network. Upon establishing an initial connection to a network, each user selects a logical channel number that is used to identify the connection (some users may have preassigned numbers).

The users can be connected to and disconnected from the network on the basis of this unique logical channel number without affecting other users. Since each user is known by a number, software-driven tables can be changed easily to reflect the changing network user connections, as they are "brought up" and "taken down" in the network.

For example, let us assume that user A is identified by logical channel number 7, and user B is assigned logical channel number 44. These users could be sharing the same physical line that connects their sessions to the network. Nonetheless, user A could ask for a disconnection by sending a "clear request" packet to the network that contains logical channel number 7. This operation does not affect user B, whose connection is being managed under logical channel number 44.

The user is unaware of much of this activity. As we shall see in Chapter 5, the user's major tasks in the X.25 connection setup are (a) to provide an identification to the network of the called DTE (and, in some networks, the calling DTE); and (b) to include a logical channel number with the connection setup packet. Then the network's task (actually, the network administrator's task) is to translate (map) the calling and called DTE identifiers and logical channel numbers into network-specific addresses and packet routes within the network.

Cost Comparisons of Media and Switching Methods

Public packet networks are not the best approach for all data transmissions. Generally, low-volume users can use public telephone dial-up lines and incur fewer costs than with a comparable session in a packet network. The dial-up option is especially attractive for short sessions. At the other end of the spectrum, high-volume users are better served with leased circuits (from the standpoint of costs), because most packet networks price their services according to the volume of packets transmitted. Consequently, a high-volume user typically incurs significant charges from the packet network. Studies show that packet networks are usually more economical for the user who transmits traffic in the mid-volume range. (The definitions of traffic volume depend on each network and the application; each organization must decide what it considers to be low-volume, mid-volume, and high-volume traffic.)

Figure 1-6 illustrates these points. The dial-up and packet network "cost lines" show a variable cost in relation to the amount of use. Dial-up costs are based primarily on time of connection, and packet network costs are based primarily on volume. The "cost line" for dial-up service favors the low-volume user, but heavier use of dial-up options becomes more expensive than either a leased line or packet network. The packet cost line favors the mid-volume user,

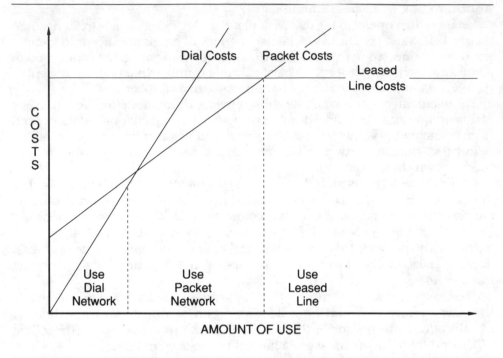

Figure 1-6. Choosing the Service Based on Cost

but after a point, the packet network becomes more expensive than the leased line. Of course, the leased line costs are independent of time of use and the volume of packets transmitted.

Many organizations choose a combination of these options and acquire the media and service that offer the most attractive cost advantages for a particular application. Aside from considerations of traffic volume versus costs, some users choose X.25-based packet networks because of the rich functions in the X.25 Recommendation.

Inside the Network Cloud

The illustration in Figure 1-3 shows the "network cloud." It is drawn so that no details (such as the switches in Figure 1-5) are shown. As we learned earlier, X.25 does not define the internal operations within the network cloud. Nonetheless, a general understanding of how data are transmitted through a packet-switched network is helpful, because some machinations inside the cloud affect X.25 actions.

Routing Schemes

Major concerns in most packet network designs are how control is maintained, how routing directories are managed, and how routing decisions are made. A brief tutorial on these concepts follows. The hierarchy below is diagramed in Figure 1-7:

- Routing control
    Centralized
    Distributed
- Routing directory
    Full
    Partial
    None
        Flooding
        Random
- Routing decisions
    Fixed: Made before network session begins
    Session-oriented: Made upon a logon into the network
    Adaptive: Made during the network session

Network routing is usually categorized as *centralized* or *distributed* routing. Centralized routing requires a network control center to determine the routing of the packets. The packet switches have limited functions and are not very "intelligent," usually lowering the cost of operating the switches. However, centralized control is vulnerable to central site failure. Consequently, network control centers (NCCs) are usually duplicated (duplexed). Centralized routing is also vulnerable to bottlenecks at central sites, and care must be taken to ensure that the central site can handle the routing tasks.

Distributed routing requires more intelligent switches. However, it provides more network resilience, because each node makes its own routing decisions

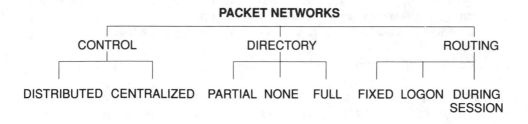

Figure 1-7. Packet Switching Tree

without regard to a centralized control center. Distributed routing is also more complex, as we will see shortly.

Use of Routing Directories

Most packet networks use a routing directory or table. The directory instructs the switches to transmit a packet to one of several possible output lines at the switch. Typically, a directory will use one or a combination of three approaches:

- *Fixed (or static) directories* change at system generation time. They remain static for each user session.

- *Session-oriented directories* change with each user session, but are static for an individual session once the session is established.

- *Adaptive or dynamic directories* may change during a user session.

Figure 1-8 shows how a routing directory can be used. The directory contains values that represent the number of intermediate switches (nodes) between the originator of the traffic (source) and the receiver (destination). With this approach, the packets are routed to the adjacent switch closest to the final destination. For example, a packet at node A destined for node G would be routed to node C, because node C is closer to the destination than the other alternative, node B.

Typically each packet switch maintains its own routing directory. In this example, each switch routes the traffic as follows (we highlight node A):

1. Access the directory to determine the adjacent nodes (source to destination = 1). Therefore, node A examines row A (as the source) and finds it is one hop away (noted by the value 1) to nodes B and C.

2. Route the packet to the adjacent node on the shortest path to the destination. Node A then accesses rows B and C to determine how far (how many hops) they are from destination G. Since B is four hops away from G, and C is two hops away from G, A routes the packet to C.

3. Repeat steps 1 and 2 until the packet has reached its destination.

Figure 1-9(a) shows another widely used packet-switching technique called adaptive (or dynamic) routing. In this example, node D is sending a packet to node A. To determine the best path between the two switches, a routing table at node D is examined. The final destination (FD) entry of A reveals that the packet is to be routed to packet switch C. Even though the path through node E is "shorter" in the number of nodes and links traversed, the estimated delay for D to E to A is 9 units of time (D → E = 3 and E → A = 6, for a total delay of

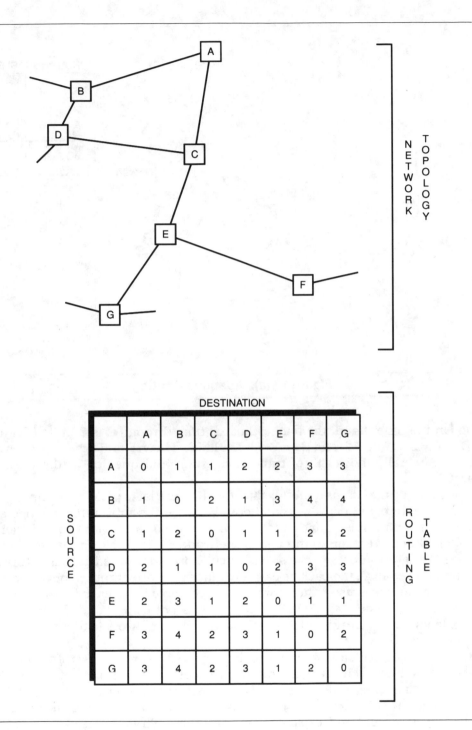

Figure 1-8. Routing Based on Fewest Number of Nodes

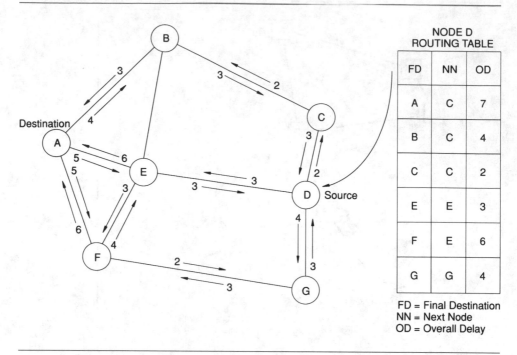

NODE D
ROUTING TABLE

FD	NN	OD
A	C	7
B	C	4
C	C	2
E	E	3
F	E	6
G	G	4

FD = Final Destination
NN = Next Node
OD = Overall Delay

Figure 1-9(a). Adaptive Routing

9). On the other hand, the total estimated time through C is 7 units of time (D → C = 2; C → B = 2; and B → A = 3). The link between E and A is experiencing delays (usually the result of traffic congestion and queuing at the packet switch).

Each node maintains a routing directory (table) that is periodically updated to reflect changing network conditions. Because the tables may change at almost any time, it is possible that the packets associated with two end users might take different routes through the network. For example, in Figure 1-9(b), node C might route its packets to D, then E, in order to reach A. If network conditions change, the packets can take different paths through the network. If this technique is used, the network is responsible for packet reassembly at the receiving node. As we shall see, X.25 does not concern itself with these problems, but certain features of X.25 can assist the network in the sequencing operations.

The shortest path and minimum delay approaches are only two of a number of options used in choosing the route to the destination. Many networks use other routing criteria such as throughput considerations, queue lengths at the nodes, and requirements for secure links. Appendix A has more information on packet routing and explains some routing techniques used by several organizations and companies.

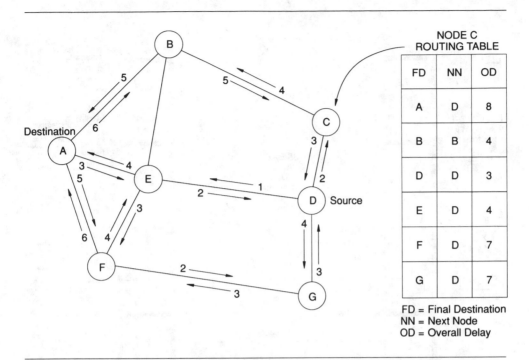

NODE C ROUTING TABLE		
FD	NN	OD
A	D	8
B	B	4
D	D	3
E	D	4
F	D	7
G	D	7

FD = Final Destination
NN = Next Node
OD = Overall Delay

Figure 1-9(b). The Packet Network Conditions Change

The Relationship of X.25 and Network Routing

As discussed earlier, X.25 does not specify the routing techniques used by the network. Nonetheless, the structure of the X.25 packets and the contents of the address fields in the X.25 packets often influence how the vendor determines the route of the packets to the destination. As we will see in later chapters, X.25 does not use any source and destination addresses in its *data* packets. Therefore, a network that uses adaptive routing must append addresses or routing information to the X.25 data packets for the traversal through the network. X.25 is not concerned with this nontrivial task, but the network manager must devise an internal network addressing scheme to support the operation. We return to this important point in Chapter 5.

Packet Networks and X.25 Terminology

The uninitiated reader may become confused about X.25 and network interfaces, because the protocol is used with several types of interfaces. This section should help you gain a general understanding of these interfaces. Be aware that it is an overview and an introduction to the chapters that provide more detailed information. Figure 1-10 is used during the discussion.

As we learned earlier, the conventional X.25 interface lies between the user device (the DTE) and the network packet exchange (the DCE).

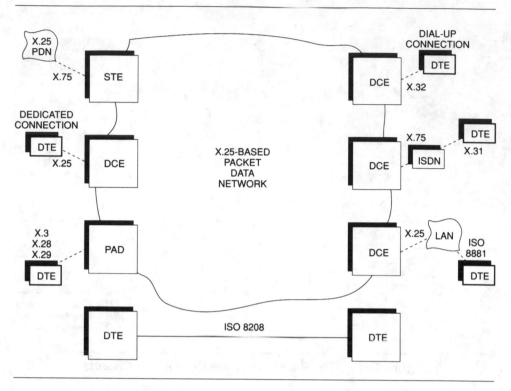

Figure 1-10. X.25 Interface Options

The packet network also provides a network interface for a DTE with a *PAD* function (packet assembly/disassembly). The user DTEs, such devices as asynchronous terminals or asynchronous personal computers, do not support the sophisticated X.25 logic needed for the network interface. Therefore, a PAD transports the user data to and from the network by placing the data inside the X.25 packet. With this approach, the user device can use its own protocols (usually simpler and less costly).

Another network interface option is the interconnection of two or more packet networks or packet exchanges to support the end users' session. This type of connection is supported by an *STE* (signaling terminal exchange). The STE could be (and often is) a packet switch with additional software. This software is coded to support the X.75 Recommendation. Many networks are interconnected by other methods (for example, the Internet Protocol, IP), but this book focuses on X.25-related protocols.

Yet another approach is an X.25 interface with an Integrated Services Digital Network (ISDN). With this configuration, the two networks communicate with the X.31 protocol. The interface device supports the connection of the X.25 station through the ISDN node to the packet network. It is called a *packet handler.*

X.25 systems are designed for use on a nonswitched, dedicated channel (between the DTE and the network). The X.32 Recommendation is available for users who need a dial-in capability into the network. It specifies a procedure for authenticating the user to the network before beginning the X.25 session.

Figure 1-10 shows another specification that defines a protocol for using X.25 on local area networks, the ISO 8881 standard. It uses an *IWU* (internetworking unit) to provide a gateway between the local network, the X.25 station, and another local network or X.25 node.

X.25 is also now used in many nonnetwork interfaces. For example, direct DTE-to-DTE communications are common today. The ISO 8208 standard defines the procedures for using X.25 in this nonnetwork interface.

For a summary of the major packet network interface support devices, see Figure 1-10 and the following list (these specifications are discussed in more detail later in the book):

- *PAD (packet assembly/disassembly)*: Provides packet network interface support to DTEs that have no packet logic. Uses the X.3, X.28, and X.29 specifications. See Chapter 9.

- *STE (signaling terminal exchange)*: Provides packet network interface support to DTEs in other packet networks or between packet exchanges. Uses the X.75 specification. See Chapter 8.

- *Packet handler*: Provides a gateway between an X.25 station through an ISDN node to an X.25 network. Uses the X.31 standard. See Chapter 8.

- *DCE (data circuit-terminating equipment)*: Provides packet network interface support to DTEs with full packet logic capabilities. Uses the X.25 specification. May also use X.32 for an X.25 dial-up port. See Chapters 5 and 6.

- *IWU (internetworking unit)*: Provides gateway functions between X.25 and local area networks. Uses the ISO 8881 specification. See Chapter 8.

Conclusions

The X.25 Recommendation is one of the most widely used data communications network interfaces. Its use has eased the task of interfacing dissimilar vendor products with each other and with packet networks. This chapter has focused on the basic terms and concepts associated with packet networks and X.25 network interfaces. It has also introduced the terms logical channel and virtual circuit.

We now have enough information to examine other aspects of X.25 and packet networks. The next step is to focus on the architecture of X.25, which is based on layered protocols and (to a more limited extent) the Open Systems Interconnection (OSI) Model.

Layered Protocols, OSI, and X.25

Goals of Chapter 2

The goals of this chapter are to introduce the reader to the general concepts of the OSI Model and to the documentation tools used in OSI and X.25. The layers of X.25 are discussed in their relation to the OSI layers. We also examine the concepts of connectionless and connection-oriented networks, and explain how X.25 uses (or does not use) these important concepts.

Readers conversant with OSI and layered protocols may wish to skip to the section titled "The X.25 Layers."

Layered Protocols

The X.25 Recommendation is organized around the concept of layered protocols. In addition, X.25 uses a number of principles and concepts found in the Open Systems Interconnection Model (OSI). OSI and layered protocols have become quite prominent in data communications, and are found in many other standards and recommendations.

The International Standards Organization (ISO) began work in the late 1970s on the Open Systems Architecture. The OSI, as it is now called, was published as a model for the design of computer communications systems. Other organizations—CCITT, IEEE, ANSI, and EIA—participated in the development of this important standard. Several of these efforts have found their way into the X.25 specifications.

The OSI Model and many data communications networks are designed around the concept of *layered protocols*, consisting of techniques to meet the following goals:

- Decompose a complex system into smaller, more comprehensible parts (layers).

- Establish standard (and limited) interfaces between the layers.

- Achieve symmetry in the functions performed at each layer in a system: Each layer in a computer performs the same function(s) as its peer layer in other computers.

- Establish a means to predict and control changes made to logic (software or microcode).

The basic idea of common standards (for layered protocols) is to develop a common set of conventions for use between vendors' products. Of course, a particular user may not be satisfied with a standard. But at least an accepted set of standards provides a reasonable point of departure, if a common protocol does not meet a specific need.

Communications between Layers

Figure 2-1 shows the basic terms associated with layered protocols. A layer is a *service provider* to a *service user*. The OSI Model states that the user is situated above the layer providing the service to the user. The user may be an applications program (such as a spreadsheet package), a workstation (such as a PC), or even a protocol entity in the adjacent, upper layer.

The layer may offer several service functions, for example, code conversions such as ASCII to/from EBCDIC, and mapping functions such as assigning X.25 logical channel numbers from the DTE addresses. These service functions are also called *entities*.

The basic idea is that each layer adds a value to the services provided by the layers below it. Consequently, the top layer, which interfaces directly with the end-user application, is provided with the full range of services offered by all the lower layers.

The actual services invoked at a layer are dictated by the upper layers

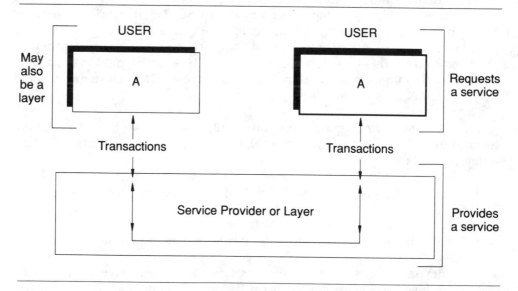

Figure 2-1. The Layer as a Service Provider

passing requests (transactions). In Figure 2-1, users A and B communicate with each other through a lower layer. Keep in mind that these users reside in the next layer up. The lower layer performs the actions requested by the users and typically passes transactions up to a user or users as a result of these actions. If A wishes to send data to B, it sends the data to the lower layer service provider. It is the task of the lower layer to transport the data to user B, and user A need not be concerned with the mechanisms needed. Indeed, it is desirable to keep lower layer operations transparent to the user, so the lower layers can be changed with minimal effect on the upper layers.

Figure 2-2 illustrates several terms and concepts used at the interface between the service users and providers. Four transactions are invoked to and from the layers: *request, indication, response,* and *confirm.* (Some sessions do not require all transactions.) These transactions are called *primitives* and contain additional parameters to convey information to and from the layers. A process such as a user application or terminal invokes a function from the service provider by sending it a request primitive. This service request may be affirmed by the service provider returning a confirm primitive. If the service is going to provide a function for another user (in this case, user B), the service provider must send an indication primitive to B. As Figure 2-2 shows, user B can send a transaction to the service provider with a response primitive.

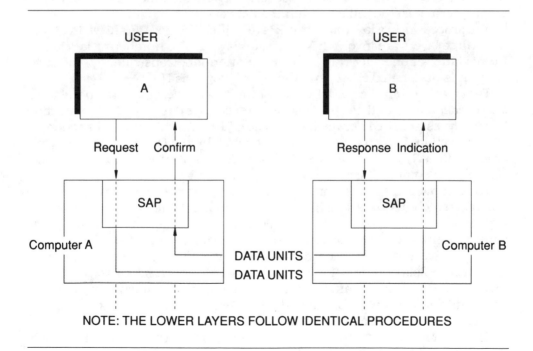

Figure 2-2. OSI Terminology

In summary, the OSI primitives perform the following functions:
At user A:

- *Request:* Primitive by service user to invoke a function.

- *Confirm:* Primitive by service provider to complete a function previously invoked by a request primitive.

At user B:

- *Indication:* Primitive by service provider to invoke a function or indicate that a function has been invoked.

- *Response:* Primitive by service user to complete a function previously invoked by an indication primitive.

The service provider connects to users through *service access points* (*SAPs*), and the users must know the associated SAP that is to receive the specific service from the service provider. In effect, a SAP is the address or identifier of the specific service function (the X.25 addressing scheme and the use of SAPs are discussed in more detail in Chapter 5). The SAP can be the address of a user terminal, a user application, or anything agreeable to the user and the network administration. Several X.25-based networks create the SAP by concatenating three addresses together: a country code, a network identifier within a country, and a specific user identifier within the network.

The procedure in a layered network is to request services as shown in Figure 2-3. Three layers are involved: N + 1, N, and N - 1. The numbering is relative. In this illustration, layer N is the focus of attention. Consequently, the layer above it is designated N + 1, and the layer below it is N - 1.

The layers and entities with the same numbers are designated as *peer layers* and *peer entities*. For these peer entities to exchange data, a logical connection is usually established between them. The OSI Model calls this connection an (N)-connection. It is an association established by the (N)-entity between two or more (N + 1)-entities. As we shall see, X.25 uses the concept of logical channels to obtain (N)-connections between users.

To see how these ideas work, let us assume the peer layers reside in two different computers (although a single computer could perform the same function). We also assume the user computer and the X.25 network node contain peer layers. These layers are designated as N layers and communicate through the exchange of N-headers and N-trailers (fields of control information). These fields control the communications between the two machines. Ideally, the machines can be built by different manufacturers and still communicate effectively, because the headers and trailers evoke the same operations at each machine.

The OSI Model stipulates that the control fields should be exchanged only between *peer* layers of the two computers (see point 1 in Figure 2-3). It further stipulates that the primitives are exchanged only between the adjacent layers

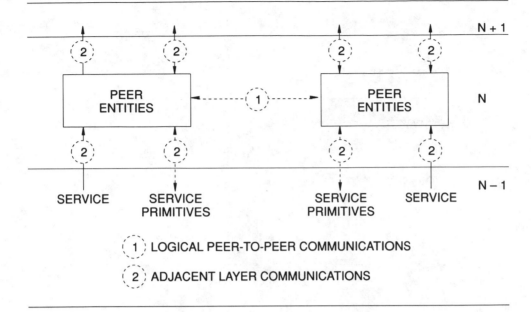

Figure 2-3. Layer Communications

(see point number 2 in Figure 2-3). In effect, the primitives contain the necessary information to enable the layer entities to create the correct values in the fields within the headers and trailers.

Three major components (other OSI components are beyond this discussion) are involved in the layers. Their names and functions are as follows (see Figure 2-4):

- The *SDU* (service data unit) consists of user data and control information created at the upper layers, which is transferred transparently by layer N + 1 to layer N, and subsequently to N - 1. The SDU identity is preserved from one end of an (N)-connection to the other. That is, the peer layer receives the SDU from its peer layer in another computer in an unaltered form.

- *PCI* (protocol control information) is information exchanged by peer (the same) entities at different sites on the network to instruct an entity to perform a service function (that is, the headers and trailers we just examined).

- The *PDU* (protocol data unit) is a combination of the SDU and PCI.

When the PDU from layer N + 1 passes to layer N, it becomes the SDU to that layer. The SDU at layer N has a PCI added to it, and it becomes the N-layer PDU.

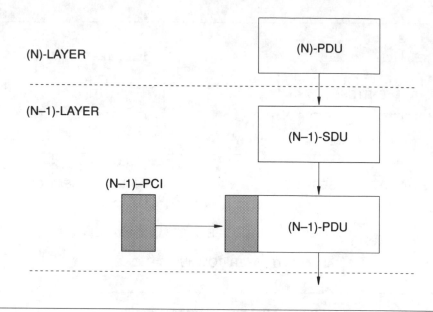

Figure 2-4. Mapping between Layers

Thus, a full protocol data unit is passed through each layer. In effect, this is simply adding a header at each layer. Remember, the header is used by the peer layer entity at another node of the network to invoke a function. Also, remember that the process repeats itself through each layer, although *each layer uses different PCIs to invoke different functions.*

The term *packet*, used in the X.25 Recommendation to describe the X.25 network protocol data units, is hereafter used interchangeably with the term protocol data unit.

Primitives and Time-Sequence Diagrams

A time-sequence diagram is a useful way to view the operations of the primitives (see Figure 2-5(a)). In later chapters, this technique is used to explain several X.25 features. The relative positions of the arrows on the vertical lines show the order of events. The vertical lines are time lines. In between the time lines is the service provider, which could be a layer or an entity within a layer. The arrow positions in this figure show that the indication primitive is issued after the request primitive, and the response primitive after the indication primitive.

The OSI reference model allows many time-sequence scenarios (X.25 uses a more limited set). For example, in Figure 2-5(b), the confirm primitive could be returned independently of a response primitive from the remote user. In this case, the local service provider provides the confirmation without regard to the

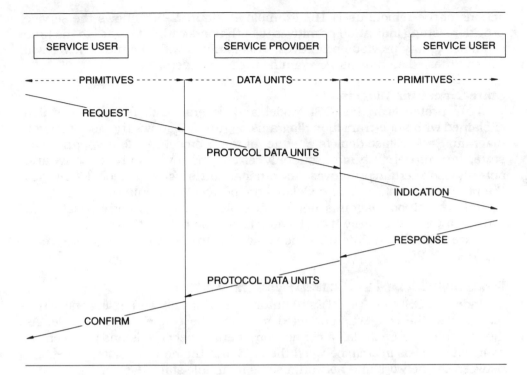

Figure 2-5(a). Primitives and Time Sequence Diagrams

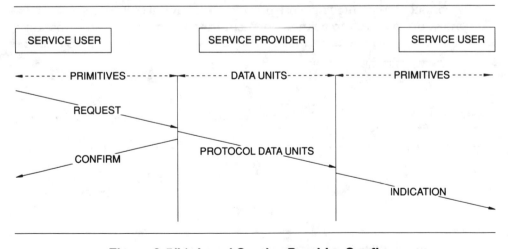

Figure 2-5(b). Local Service Provider Confirms

actions of the remote user. The example in Figure 2-5(c) shows the service provider issuing indication primitives to both users without regard to the time sequence of any previous primitives. This is noted with the tilde (~). We will expand these diagrams as we examine the X.25 layers.

State-Transition Diagrams

Many protocols in the OSI Model and several X.25 features are also explained with state-transition diagrams. Figure 2-6 shows the use of such a diagram. Each ellipse depicts a "state" of the protocol. While in a particular state, the protocol entity may issue only certain primitives, and can receive and act only upon certain primitives. Any other action is logically inconsistent with the protocol specification and violates the protocol convention.

State-transition diagrams impose discipline on the protocol's logic and provide a means to verify its behavior. They also help with writing protocol software. We will use state-transition diagrams to describe the logic of several aspects of X.25.

Connection-Oriented and Connectionless Networks

Under the OSI concept, DTEs communicate with a network using one of two techniques: the connection-oriented mode or the connectionless mode. As illustrated in Figure 2-7(a), a connection-oriented network is one in which no connection exists *initially* between the DTE and the network. The connection between the network and network user is in an idle state.

For the DTEs to communicate through a connection-oriented network, they must go through a handshake called a connection establishment. During this process, the users and the network may negotiate the services to be used during the session. Once the connection is established, data are exchanged in consonance with the negotiations. Eventually the DTEs perform a connection release, after which they return to the idle state.

The connection-oriented network provides substantial care for the user data. The procedure requires an acknowledgment from the network and responding user that the connection is established; otherwise, the requesting DTE must be

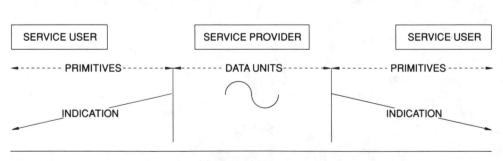

Figure 2-5(c). Service Provider Invokes Indication Primitive

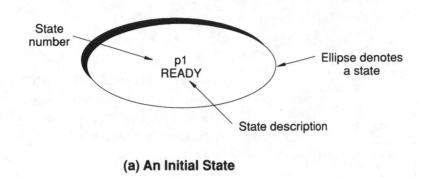

(a) An Initial State

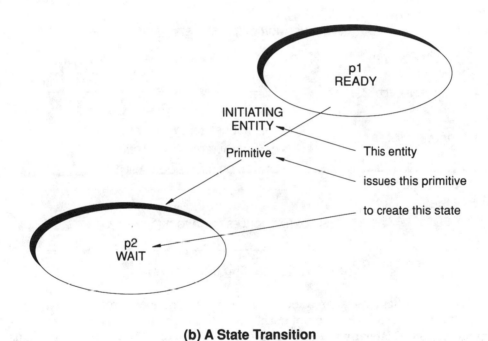

(b) A State Transition

Figure 2-6. State Transition Diagrams

informed why the connection request was not successful. The network must also stay aware of the DTE/DTE connection. Flow control (i.e., making certain that all the data arrive correctly and in order, and do not saturate the user computers in the various parts of the network) is also required of the network.

Error checking and error recovery are performed by connection-oriented networks. They are designed to recover from problems with lost packets, misrouted packets, and out-of-sequence packets.

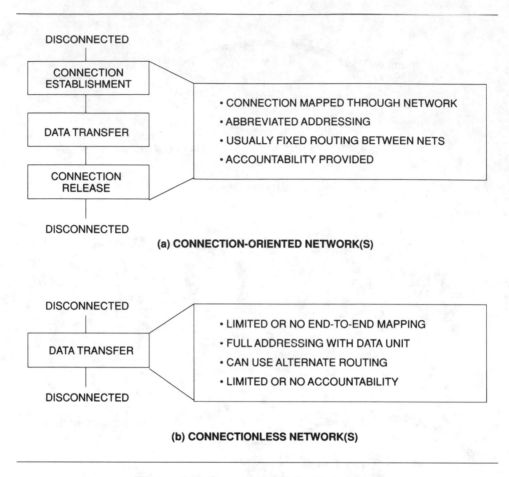

Figure 2-7. Connecting into Networks

The connectionless (also called *datagram*) network goes directly from an idle condition (the two DTEs are not connected to each other) to the data-transfer mode, followed later by the idle condition. The major difference between this network and the connection-oriented network is the absence of the connection establishment and release phases. Moreover, a connectionless network has no end-to-end acknowledgments, flow control, or error recovery.

X.25 is a connection-oriented protocol. It requires the exchange of call-establishment signals before data can be transferred between the users. (Certain options of X.25 allow the exchange of data to accompany the call-establishment packets.) Once the call is established, X.25 remains aware of the ongoing communications between the two end users. It provides for flow-control procedures, and requires that the network sequence the packets. In later chapters, we will return to this aspect of X.25.

A network may use a mixture of connection-oriented and connectionless techniques. Indeed, some organizations that must transfer data between networks use X.25 as the user-to-network interface and then implement a connectionless network protocol at the gateway between the networks. These concepts are described in the chapter on X.25 and internetworking (Chapter 8).

The OSI Model

The ISO and CCITT developed the OSI Model to define many of the operations of data communications networks (see Figure 2-8). The model has received worldwide attention and has been implemented in many vendor products. In this section we take a general look at the OSI layers and then examine how X.25 fits into the OSI Model.

The OSI Layers

The lowest layer in the model is called the *physical layer*. Its functions are activating, maintaining, and deactivating a physical circuit between a DTE and a modem, multiplexer, or similar device. The layer also identifies the bits (as 0s or 1s). Many standards are published for the physical layer, and Chapter 3 explains its use in X.25.

The *data-link layer* is responsible for the transfer of data across the communications channel. It synchronizes data to delimit the flow of bits from the physical layer. It also delineates the bits between the protocol data units and ensures that the data arrive safely at the receiving station. Its flow-control measures ensure that the receiving machine does not become overburdened with traffic. One of its

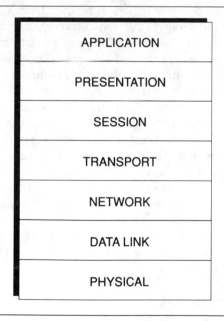

Figure 2-8. The OSI Layers

most important functions is detecting transmission errors on the link (channel) and recovering from lost, duplicate, or damaged data. The X.25 data-link layer is discussed in Chapter 4.

The *network layer* specifies the operations of the user DTE with the network. These procedures are known as the *network interface*. This layer also specifies the operations of the DTEs with each other (through the network) and is responsible for routing (although X.25 does not contain any routing specifications). The X.25 Recommendation includes part of the network layer, as discussed in Chapters 5 and 6.

The *transport layer* is the interface between the data communications network and the upper three layers. It gives the user options in obtaining certain levels of quality (and cost) from the network (i.e., the network layer), and keeps the user isolated from the physical and functional aspects of the packet network. It also provides for end-to-end integrity of the transfer of user data. X.25 does not encompass the transport layer or any services in the other upper layers. However, because of the data-recovery mechanisms available in this layer, it should be used above the X.25 layers. It is designed to recover from X.25 resets, clears, and restarts. Chapter 8 provides an overview of X.25's relationship to the transport layer.

The *session layer* is the user interface to the transport service layer and provides an organized means to exchange data between end-user applications. The users can select the applications program synchronization and control needed from this layer. For example, users can establish an alternate two-way dialogue or a simultaneous two-way dialogue between the applications. Synchronization procedures can be established to recover from file- and data-transfer problems. An important function of the session layer is its provision for a "graceful close" between the user applications. This service ensures that all data are received before a connection is released at any of the lower layers.

The *presentation layer* ensures that user applications can communicate with each other, even though they may use different representations for their protocol data units. The layer preserves the data syntax. For example, it can accept various data types (character, Boolean, integer) from the application layer and negotiate an acceptable syntax representation with its peer presentation layer. It also can describe data structures in a machine-independent way, coding data from an internal format of a sending machine into a common transfer format, and then decoding this format to a required representation at the receiving machine.

The *application layer* supports an end-user application process. The layer contains service elements to support such application processes as job management, file transfers, electronic mail, and financial data exchanges. The layer also supports the virtual terminal and virtual file concepts. Directory services are obtained through this layer.

Example of Layer Operations

Figure 2-9 shows how the layers operate. In this simple example, each layer performs one specific function (although each layer can perform many

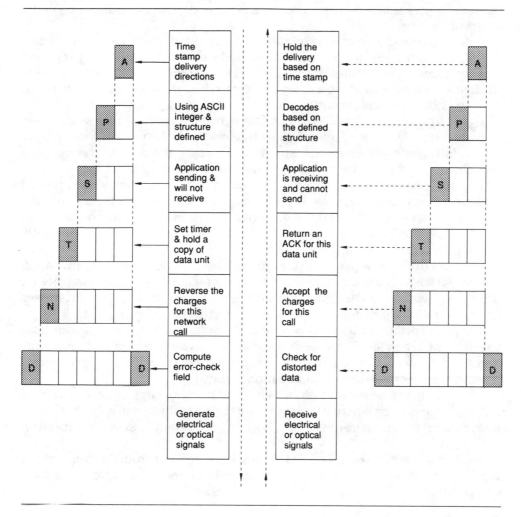

Figure 2-9. Example of Layer Interactions

functions). The functions here are examples of actual functions in the OSI layers.

We begin at the top layer (application layer). A message-handling system (for example, the X.400 Recommendation) creates a header with directions for the remote application layer, pertaining to the time the "letter" is to be delivered. This header and the data (letter) are then passed to the next lower layer (presentation layer). The header is used only by the peer application layer (on the right side of the figure) to invoke the electronic mail time-delivery function.

The presentation layer is tasked with coding this information into ASCII for text and integer values for numeric fields. It is also responsible for creating a header describing the format and structure of the data. This header is used by the remote presentation layer to determine the code, values, and format of the protocol data unit.

Note that the transmitting computer on the left side of Figure 2-9 adds a header at each layer as the data are passed down through the layers. This activity is known as *encapsulation*. The receiving computer on the right side of the figure strips the headers as they are passed into the appropriate layers, an activity known as *decapsulation*.

To continue the analysis, the data unit is now passed to the session layer. Here directions are placed into a header that instructs the remote session layer that it is not allowed to return any data. In other words, the transmitting machine will not accept any reply to this transmission at this time.

The next layer (transport layer) is instructed to retain a copy of the protocol data unit and activate a timer. If problems occur at the lower layers, and the remote transport layer's acknowledgment is not received within a certain time (see the function of the remote transport layer on the right side of Figure 2-9), this layer can retransmit the data.

The data unit is now passed to the network layer, which (among many tasks) is charged with asking the remote network layer if it will accept the charges for this transmission. As the figure indicates, the remote peer network layer uses the network layer header to derive the information for this request.

The protocol data unit is now passed to the data-link layer, which adds both a trailer and a header. These fields are used for several link-control functions, and to perform checks to determine whether the data were damaged during transmission across the communications channel.

Finally, the protocol data unit (which could be quite large by now) is passed to the physical layer, where it is placed onto the communications medium (wire pair, coaxial cable, microwave, etc.). Some systems add headers at this layer, too.

As we have seen throughout this analysis, the headers from the layers at the local computer are used by the peer layers in the remote computer to perform complementary functions.

The X.25 Layers

The X.25 Recommendation is divided into three layers (see Figure 2-10) that correspond to the lower three layers of the OSI Model. The physical layer provides the physical signaling and connections between the user DTE and the DCE. At this layer, such standards as X.21, X.21 *bis*, EIA-232-D, and V.35 are used. This layer is also called X.25, layer 1.

The data-link layer manages the dataflow between the user DTE and the network. It error checks and retransmits the data, if the data were distorted during the transfer on the link. It is responsible for error-free transmission of the X.25 packet across the link. This layer uses the LAPB protocol (link access procedure, balanced). It is also called the frame level, because it creates and uses the LAPB frame.

The network layer creates the X.25 packet and manages the connection with

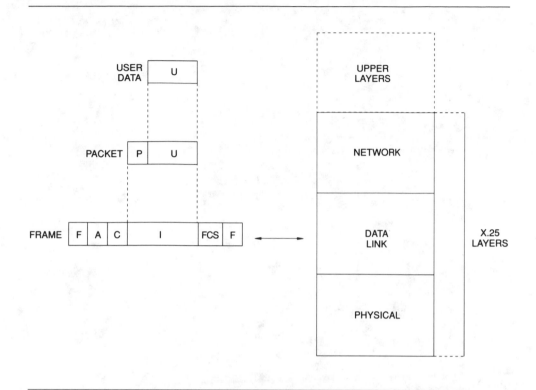

Figure 2-10. The Layers of X.25

the network through the exchange of packets with the network. It relies on the data-link layer to transport the packet safely between the DTE and the network. It is also called the packet level or X.25, layer 3. Notice in Figure 2-10 that the packet is encapsulated into the frame for transmission to and from the DTE and the network.

Conclusions

The X.25 Recommendation uses many concepts of the OSI Model, although it is at variance with some OSI concepts because it was written before the publication of the OSI Model. Examining the X.25 layers in more detail in the next chapters, we take a "building-block" approach. We start with the physical layer, move to the data-link layer, and finally discuss the top layer of X.25, the network layer. After examining the X.25 layers, we discuss other important issues: internetworking X.25 devices, using protocol converters (PADs), and design and implementation issues.

X.25 and the Physical Layer

Goals of Chapter 3

Our goals for Chapter 3 are twofold: (a) to provide a general overview of physical-layer interfaces and protocols, and (b) to explain how X.25 uses the physical layer, identifying the standards and recommendations cited by X.25 for use at this level. We also examine several other physical-layer interfaces that are widely used with X.25 but not included in the X.25 Recommendation.

The next section is a brief tutorial for the uninitiated reader. The more experienced reader can refer directly to the section titled "Relationship of the Physical Layer to X.25."

Introduction

Physical-level protocols (or physical-level interfaces) are so named because machines such as computers, terminals, and modems are physically connected by wires or cables, or by electromagnetic signals through the atmosphere. Physical-level interfaces provide the following:

- Data transfer across the interface between machines

- Control signals between devices

- Clocking signals to synchronize data flow and regulate the bit rate

- Electrical ground

- Mechanical connectors (such as pins, sockets, and plugs)

Most physical-level interfaces describe four attributes of the interface: electrical, functional, mechanical, and procedural. The electrical attribute describes the voltage (or current) levels, the timing of the electrical signals, and other electrical characteristics of the connection.

The functional attribute describes the functions to be performed by the physical interface. For example, the functions of the physical connectors are described by such terms as "request to send" and "ring signal" (for a dial-up connection).

The mechanical attribute describes the dimensions of the connectors and the number of wires on the interface. Usually, the data, signaling, and control wires are enclosed in one cover.

The procedural attribute describes what the connectors must do, and the sequence of events required to effect actual data transfer across the connection between the machines.

Relationship of the Physical Layer to X.25

The relationship of the physical layer to X.25 is shown in Figure 3-1. If the packet exchange (DCE) is connected directly to the user device (DTE), the physical level is the direct connection between the packet switch and the DTE (see Figure 3-1(a)). However, most users do not have a direct connection to the

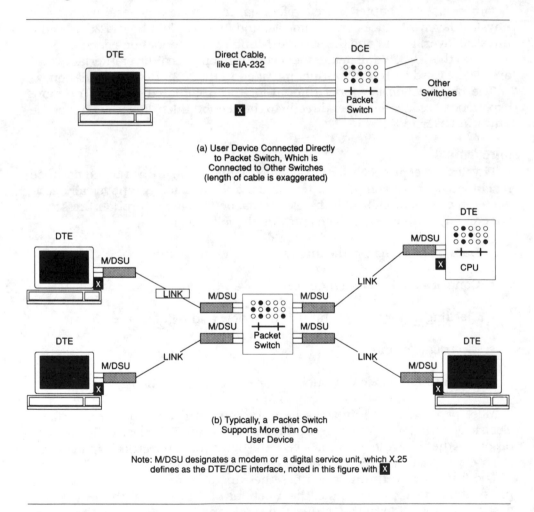

(a) User Device Connected Directly
to Packet Switch, Which is
Connected to Other Switches
(length of cable is exaggerated)

(b) Typically, a Packet Switch
Supports More than One
User Device

Note: M/DSU designates a modem or a digital service unit, which X.25
defines as the DTE/DCE interface, noted in this figure with X

Figure 3-1. The X.25 Physical Configurations

DCE. In this situation, the user station connects first to its local modem or digital service unit (DSU) through physical-level interchange circuits; second, through a communications link; and third, to the remote modem/DSU (see Figure 3-1(b)), again through interchange circuits. The interchange circuit is often simply called a "pin." Also, note that the shadowed X in the figure establishes X.25's delineation at the DTE/DCE interface.

Typically, the communications link is a leased line provided by the local telephone company. Indeed, X.25 specifies only dedicated circuits. Notwithstanding, many vendors now offer dial-up features for their X.25 products, and CCITT has published X.32 to describe how a switched line is to be used on the X.25 interface. This recommendation is examined in Chapter 7.

Several prominent physical-level standards do not specify the complete physical-level interface shown in Figure 3-1(b). Specifically, the span between the modems/DSUs may not be defined. One prominent example is the EIA-232-D standard. Fortunately, this part of the physical-level interface is standardized through the CCITT V Series modem specifications, the "Bell specifications," and others. Figure 3-2 shows the relationship of these specifications to the physical-layer interface.

The Communications Port

Many computers are equipped with more than one communications line. The connection of the user device to the modem, multiplexer, or digital service unit and the communications link is provided through a combination of hardware and firmware functions called the communications *port*. A port represents only one communications interface to a link, so a computer may have many ports (see Figure 3-3).

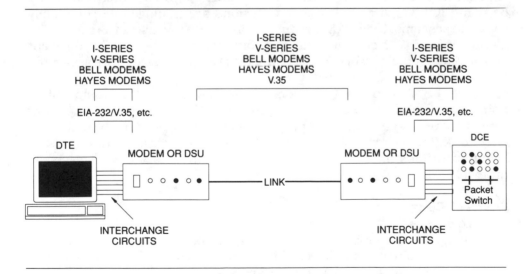

Figure 3-2. X.25 Physical Level Standards

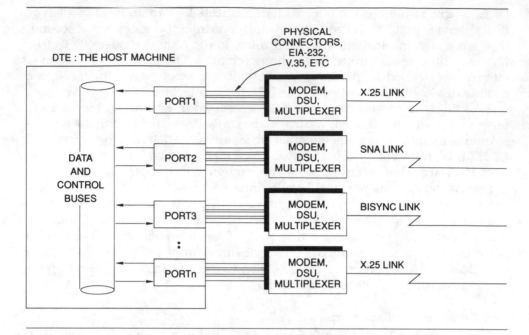

Figure 3-3. X.25 Physical Level Standards

X.25 considers the computer illustrated in Figure 3-3 to have two X.25 links. Each typically has a separate address, and the X.25 sessions on the links are not related to each other. For example, one X.25 user could be transmitting and receiving data on link 1 (port 1), and another user could be using link n (port n). These two sessions are managed as completely separate sessions. Indeed, X.25 could assign these two users the same X.25 identifier (a logical channel number), but because they are on different physical links, the network must ensure that the two sessions are separated and unambiguously identified.

Figure 3-3 also shows that a computer can support other communications protocols as well. Port 2 is configured for SNA, and port 3 for a binary synchronous (bisync) link-level protocol. A computer need not be dedicated only to X.25. As examples, front-end processors manage hundreds of communications lines, and each line is configured to support a specific protocol.

Physical Connectors

The cables and wires between the ports and the modems/DSUs, etc., are actually joined to connectors that take the shape of small metal pins. The pins serve as "plugs" into the computers and modems/DSUs. The connectors are called *interchange circuits*. Figure 3-4 shows several choices for the physical interchange circuits, as well as the ISO mechanical connectors. The

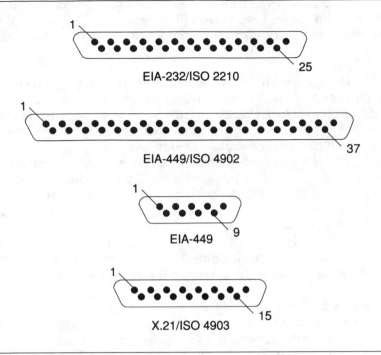

Figure 3-4. Physical Connectors

connectors' interchange circuits are identified by numbers, by alphabetic identifiers (AB, AC, etc.), or by functional descriptions (transmit-data circuit, request-to-send circuit, etc.).

X.25 Physical-Layer Protocols and Interfaces

Those who read the X.25 Recommendation will be surprised to find that the physical-layer description takes up less than two pages of the 155-page specification. The brevity is possible because X.25 states rather tersely that X.21, X.21 *bis*, or the V Series Recommendations are to be used at the physical layer. These documents are rather lengthy, so an interested reader is still faced with reviewing several hundred pages of technical specifications. (My book *Physical Level Interfaces and Protocols*, published by IEEE Computer Society, provides a tutorial on physical-level interfaces.)

X.25-based networks can also operate with other physical-layer standards, although X.25 stipulates only X.21, X.21 *bis*, or the V Series Recommendations. For example, X.25 can be transmitted on T1 circuits, interfaces using the RS-422 standard, proprietary satellite interfaces, and ISDN channels.

The physical level plays a very small role in the *control* of an X.25 network. In essence, it is an electrical or optical path through which the packets are transported. Of course, even though it exercises very few control functions, it must be present; otherwise, nothing happens.

Now we examine the prevalent physical-layer standards used with X.25.

X.21

The X.21 Recommendation is used in several European countries and Japan; it has seen limited implementation in North America. X.21 is based on the X.24 description of interchange circuits. X.24 is analogous to V.24 for the V Series in that it describes the interchange circuits used by the other X Series interfaces. These circuits are summarized in Table 3-1.

X.25 assumes the physical-layer X.21 keeps circuits T (transmit) and R (receive) active for packet exchange across the X.21 interface. It assumes that X.21 is in one of the following data-transfer states: 13S (send data), 13R (receive data) or 13 (data transfer). X.25 further assumes that the X.21 channels C (control) and I (indication) are active.

Given that C and I are active, X.25 uses the X.21 physical interface between the DTE and the DCE as a "packet pipeline" by transmitting and receiving the packets across the transmit T and receive R pins respectively.

The V.24 and V.28 Recommendations

V.24 is used on most low- to medium-speed modems to describe the functions of the interchange circuits (the "pins") on the interface. Many X.25 products use this standard, principally in modems, line drivers, multiplexers, and digital service units. The V.24 100 series interchange circuits are listed in Table 3-2.

Table 3-1. X.24 Interchange Circuits

Interchange Circuit Designation	Interchange Circuit Name	Data From DCE	Data To DCE	Control From DCE	Control To DCE	Timing From DCE	Timing To DCE
G	Signal ground or common return						
Ga	DTE common return				X		
Gb	DCE common return			X			
T	Transmit		X		X		
R	Receive	X	X				
C	Control				X		
I	Indication			X			
S	Signal element timing					X	
B	Byte timing					X	
F	Frame start identification					X	
X	DTE signal element timing						X

Table 3-2. V.24 Interchange Circuits

Interchange Circuit Number	Interchange Circuit Name
102	Signal ground or common return
102a	DTE common return
102b	DCE common return
102c	Common return
103	Transmitted data
104	Received data
105	Request to send
106	Ready for sending
107	Data set ready
108/1	Connect data set to line
108/2	Data terminal ready
109	Data channel received line signal detector
110	Data signal quality detector
111	Data signal rate selector (DTE)
112	Data signal rate selector (DCE)
113	Transmitter signal element timing (DTE)
114	Transmitter signal element timing (DCE)
115	Receiver signal element timing (DCE)
116	Select standby
117	Standby indicator
118	Transmitted backward channel data
119	Received backward channel data
120	Transmit backward channel line signal
121	Backward channel ready
122	Backward channel received line signal detector
123	Backward channel signal quality detector
124	Select frequency groups
125	Calling indicator
126	Select transmit frequency
127	Select receive frequency
128	Receiver signal element timing (DTE)
129	Request to receive
130	Transmit backward tone
131	Received character timing
132	Return to nondata mode
133	Ready for receiving
134	Received data present
136	New signal
140	Loopback/maintenance test
141	Local loopback
142	Test indicator
191	Transmitted voice answer
192	Received voice answer

V.28 is an electrical specification applied to almost all interchange circuits operating below 20,000 bits/s. EIA-232-D uses this specification with some minor editorial variations.

EIA-232-D or RS-232-C

Since many countries have not implemented X.21 extensively, X.25 allows the use of other physical-layer interfaces. The RS-232-C and EIA-232-D standards are widely used throughout the world, and EIA-232-D is functionally aligned with the CCITT V.24 and V.28 Recommendations.

During its last revision, RS-232-C was redesignated as EIA-232-D. The revision includes the definition of three testing circuits, a redefinition of ground, and some other minor changes.

Table 3-3 summarizes the EIA-232-D standard, and its relationship to the CCITT V.24 circuits.

Table 3-3. EIA-232-D Interchange Circuits

Interchange Circuit	CCITT Equivalent	Description	End	Data From DCE	Data To DCE	Control From DCE	Control To DCE	Timing From DCE	Timing To DCE
AB	102	Signal ground/common return	X						
BA	103	Transmitted data			X				
BB	104	Received data		X					
CA	105	Request to send					X		
CB	106	Clear to send				X			
CC	107	DCE ready				X			
CD	108.2	DTE ready					X		
CE	125	Ring indicator				X			
CF	109	Received line signal detector				X			
CG	110	Signal quality detector				X			
CH	111	Data signal rate selector (DTE)					X		
CI	112	Data signal rate selector (DCE)				X			
DA	113	Transmitter signal element timing (DTE)							X
DB	114	Transmitter signal element timing (DCE)						X	
DD	115	Receiver signal element timing (DCE)						X	
SBA	118	Secondary transmitted data			X				
SBB	119	Secondary received data		X					
SCA	120	Secondary request to send					X		
SCB	121	Secondary clear to send				X			
SCF	122	Secondary received line signal detector				X			
RL	140	Remote loopback					X		
LL	141	Local loopback					X		
TM	142	Test mode				X			

X.21*bis*

X.25 also permits the use of X.21*bis*, a standard that define the physical-layer interface for modems using dedicated circuits and packet-switching services. Since X.21*bis* and the EIA-232 interface use the same electrical interface (V.28) and the same definitions for the interchange circuits (V.24), they can be made compatible with each other if the modem and interface vendors so choose. In some parts of the world, X.21*bis* and RS-232-C/EIA-232-D are considered to be functionally aligned with each other.

To use X.21*bis*, X.25 requires that the V.24 circuits 105, 106, 107, 108, and 109 be in the ON condition. Data are exchanged on circuits 103 and 104. If these circuits are off, X.25 assumes the physical layer is inactive, and any upper layers—such as the data-link layer (LAPB) and the network layer (X.25)—will not function.

The principal EIA-232 and V.24 circuits required for X.25 are shown in Table 3-4.

Use of the V Series Recommendations

In the last few years, the CCITT V Series Recommendations have become the prevalent standards for modems designed for telephone-type circuits. X.25 also permits the use of these specifications at the physical layer. Table 3-5 summarizes the V Series interfaces. The column labeled Modulation Technique describes the physical signaling between the modems. A legend in Box 3.1 assists in interpreting the summary.

Bell Modems at the X.25 Physical Level

Many organizations use the Bell modem standards for the X.25 physical interface. Several Bell modems are similar to some of the CCITT V Series modems, but in many instances they vary slightly, and will not communicate properly with a V Series port at the X.25 switch, without some reconfigura-

Table 3-4. X.25 Requirements for EIA-232 or V.24/X.21*bis* Interchange Circuits

	EIA-232	V.24
Signal Ground	AB	102
Send Data	BA	103
Receive Data	BB	104
Request to Send	CA	105
Clear to Send	CB	106
Data Set Ready	CC	107
Data Terminal Ready	CD	108.2
Carrier Detect	CF	109
Timing	DB	114*
Timing	DD	115*

* If Possible

Table 3-5. CCITT V-Series Interfaces

Series Number	Line Speed	Channel Separation	Modulation Rate	FDX or HDX	Modulation Technique	Bits Encoded	Switched Lines	Leased Lines	Use of X.25
V.21	300	FD	300	FDX	FS	1:1	Yes	O	Yes
V.22	1200	FD	600	FDX	PS	2:1	Yes	PP 2W	Yes
V.22	600	FD	600	FDX	PS	1:1	Yes	PP 2W	Yes
V.22 *bis*	2400	FD	600	FDX	QAM	4:1	Yes	PP 2W	Yes
V.22 *bis*	1200	FD	600	FDX	QAM	2:1	Yes	PP 2W	Yes
V.23	600	NA	600	HDX	FM	NA	Yes	O	ND
V.23	1200	NA	1200	HDX	FM	NA	Yes	O	ND
V.26	2400	4-wire	1200	FDX	PS	2:1	No	PP MP 4W	ND
V.26 *bis*	2400	NA	1200	HDX	PS	2:1	Yes	No	Yes
V.26 *bis*	1200	NA	1200	HDX	PS	1:1	Yes	No	Yes
V.26 *ter*	2400	EC	1200	Either	PS	2:1	Yes	PP 2W	Yes
V.26 *ter*	1200	EC	1200	Either	PS	1:1	Yes	PP 2W	Yes
V.27	4800	ND	1600	Either	PS	3:1	No	Yes	ND
V.27 *bis*	4800	4-wire	1600	Either	PS	3:1	No	2W 4W	ND
V.27 *bis*	2400	4-wire	1200	Either	PS	2:1	No	2W 4W	ND
V.27 *ter*	4800	None	1600	HDX	PS	3:1	Yes	No	Yes
V.27 *ter*	2400	None	1200	HDX	PS	2:1	Yes	No	Yes
V.29	9600	4-wire	2400	Either	QAM	4:1	No	PP 4W	ND
V.29	7200	4-wire	2400	Either	PS	3:1	No	PP 4W	ND
V.29	4800	4-wire	2400	Either	PS	2:1	No	PP 4W	ND
V.32	9600	EC	2400	FDX	QAM	4:1	Yes	PP 2W	Yes
V.32	9600	EC	2400	FDX	TCM	5:1(1)	Yes	PP 2W	Yes
V.32	4800	EC	2400	FDX	QAM	2:1	Yes	PP 2W	Yes
V.33(2)	14400	4-wire	2400	FDX	TCM	7:1(1)	FS	PP 4W	ND
V.35	48000	4-wire	NA	FDX	M-FM	NA	No	Yes	ND

Note (1): Coding ratio allows for 2400 redundant bits per second for TCM error correction. Bits are not part of the user data stream.

Note (2): Added to the 1988 Blue Book Recommendations.

Note (3): All interfaces use ISO 2110 connector (ND for V.35).

Note (4): All interfaces use V.28.

ND= Not Defined

NA= Not Applicable

FS= For Further Study

(Note: see explanatory Box 3.1 on the following page).

tions. Also, some Bell modems use the EIA-232 interface in a manner slightly different from what is specified in the EIA-232 standard. Vendors should be consulted for further information.

Table 3-6 briefly summarizes the Bell modems and compares them with the CCITT V modems. The column labeled "Contrast with V Series" lists the major differences between the Bell and V Series modems, but not all the differences. It may be helpful to refer to Table 3-5 while studying Table 3-6.

Box 3.1. Explanation of Table 3-5.

A V Series number may be entered into the table more than once. This means the recommended standard permits more than one option. The initials ND mean not defined in the specification. The initials NA mean not applicable.

Entries	Explanation
Line Speed	Speed in bits per second (bit/s).

Channel Separation	If the recommended standard permits multiple channels, the method of deriving the channels is noted as:
	    FD: Frequency Division
	  4-Wire: Each set of wires carries a channel
	    EC: Echo Cancellation
	Note that the standard may also use a backward channel.

Modulation Rate	The rate of the signal change of the carrier on the channel, in baud.
Full Duplex or Half Duplex	FDX: Full Duplex HDX: Half Duplex

Modulation Technique	The description of the modulation technique where:
	    FS: Frequency Shift
	    PS: Phase Shift
	  QAM: Quadrature Amplitude Modulation
	    AM: Amplitude Modulation
	  TCM: Trellis Coded Modulation

Bits Encoded	Describes the number of bits encoded per signal change (baud). For example, 2:1 means two bits encoded per baud.
Switched Lines	Describes the use of conventional dial-up circuits.
Leased Lines	O: Optional 2W: Two-wire PP: Point-to-point 4W: Four-wire MP: Multipoint
V.25	A CCITT specification which describes the procedures for automatic dial-and-answer. May also offer features on call and answer beyond that of V.25.

The Hayes Modems

Widely used on X.25 links, the Hayes modems have become a de facto standard in the PC-based, dial-and-answer-modem industry. The earlier Hayes modems conformed to the Bell specifications, but the newer versions have adapted the V Series specifications from CCITT. Table 3-7 summarizes the Hayes modems.

X.25 and Digital Interfaces

Many X.25 physical-level connections are achieved with digital (nonanalog) interfaces. A common approach is to use a channel service unit (CSU) and/or a data service unit, or DSU (also called a digital service unit). The DSU converts the DTE signals into bipolar digital signals, and performs clocking and signal regeneration on the channel. The CSU performs such functions as line

Table 3-6. The Bell Modems and DSUs

ID	Reference Manual	Interface	Use of V-Series	Contrast with V-Series
Voiceband Modems				
103/113	41106	EIA-232	V.21	Different Frequencies
108	41215	EIA-232		103F Successor
201	41216	EIA-232	V.26	V.26 Alternative B
202	41212	EIA-232	V.23	Different Frequencies & Modulation Method
208	41211	EIA-232	V.27	V.27 Encoding Method
212	41214	EIA-232	V.22	For 1200 Bit/s & 103/113 for 300 bit/s
209	41213	EIA-232		
V.29		EIA-232		
407	41409	EIA-232		
2024-2096	41910	EIA-449		
Broadband Modems				
303				Proprietary system
306				Proprietary system

Table 3-7. The Hayes Modems

Smartmodem 300	Smartmodem 1200	Smartmodem 2400	Smartmodem 9600
300 bit/s (Bell 103)	1200 bit/s (Bell 212A and Bell 103 300 Bit/s	300, 1200, 2400 bit/s	300, 1200, 2400, 4800
Frequency Shift Keying (PSK)		300 bit/s: Bell 103	300 bit/s: Bell 103
	Phase Shift Keying (PSK)		
1070-1270 Hz and 2025-2225 Hz	1200 and 2400 Hz	1200 bit/s: Bell 212A, CCITT V.22	1200 bit/s: Bell 212A, CCITT V.22
		2400 bit/s: CCITT V.22 *bis*	1200 bit/s: CCITT V.22 *bis*
			4800 bit/s: V.32 HDX
			9600 bit/s: V.32 FDX

conditioning (also known as equalization, which keeps the signal's performance consistent across the channel bandwidth); signal reshaping, which reconstitutes the binary pulse stream; and loop-back testing. In North America, the most common digital physical-level interface is the AT&T/Bell DSU using the 500B device. Most local area networks are based on digital systems that use special encoding and transmission techniques.

Increasingly, the X.25 packet is transferred between user devices within digital transmission systems. For example, the T1 technology is used by a number of manufacturers to support X.25. Moreover, the emerging integrated services digital network (ISDN) contains many provisions for an interface with X.25. Later chapters examine the relationship of X.25 with these systems.

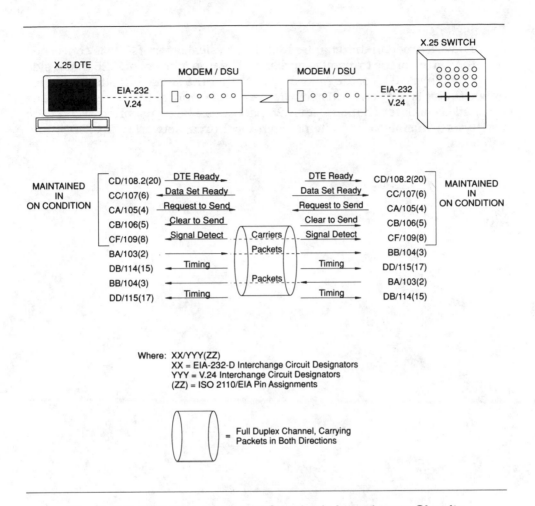

Figure 3-5. X.25 Physical Level Standards Interchange Circuits and X.25 Packets

Example of Packet Transfer across an EIA-232/V.24 Interface

Figure 3-5 summarizes several key points about the X.25 physical layer and provides an example of how the EIA-232/V.24 interchange circuits are used for the transfer of X.25 packets across the interface between the DTE and the modem/DSU. The packets noted in this figure may occupy the full-duplex channel at the same time.

The legend at the bottom of the figure provides a guide to the notations in the figure. Tables 3-2 through 3-4 give additional information on the functions of the interchange circuits used in the exchange of X.25 packets in this figure.

Conclusions

We have learned in this chapter that the physical layer of X.25 is concerned with the nature of the transmission signal. The upper layers of X.25 that reside above the physical layer are unaware of whether the signal is digital or analog, or whether it is sent on a twisted wire-pair cable, optical fiber, etc. Indeed, as we shall see in later chapters, an X.25 packet can be transported over a wide variety of transmissions systems such local area networks, an ISDN, and satellites.

Chapter 4

X.25 and the Data-Link Layer

Goals of Chapter 4

This chapter examines how X.25 packets are transported on the communications link between the user DTE and the network through the use of data-link protocols. Our goals are to understand how these protocols ensure that the packets are received error-free at the receiving machine and how the user device and the packet exchange use link protocols for the sequencing and flow control of the traffic on the link.

This chapter assumes that the reader has read about or used data-link protocols. (If this is not the case, please study Appendix B before reading this material.) The seasoned reader should be able to delve directly into this chapter.

Introduction

The primary purpose of the X.25 data-link layer is to transport the packet free of errors across the communications link between the user device and the packet exchange. The link layer is also responsible for controlling the traffic flow on the link and informing the X.25 network layer about unusual link problems such as excessive errors or a link failure. While these services are limited, they are quite important, and X.25 cannot function without them. The X.25 data-link control layer typically consists of a combination of software and hardware. Several offerings are now available on a chip set.

Most offerings today support the X.25 data-link layer with LAPB (link access procedure, balanced). Earlier versions use LAP (link access procedure). Some organizations still use the older binary synchronous (bisync) protocols for the data-link layer. Increasingly, X.25 packets are now sent across digital ISDN links with the link layer protocol LAPD (link access procedure for the D channel), or in the B channel. Some systems pass X.25 packets through local area networks with the link layer protocol LLC (Logical Link Control).

Most of these link protocols have something in common: They are all derived from the High-Level Data-Link Control (HDLC) standard published by ISO. Consequently, this chapter examines HDLC and analyzes LAPB, LAP, LAPD, and LLC, with emphasis on LAPB. We also take a look at IBM's SDLC to see why it is seldom used on an X.25 link.

The data-link layer provides the following functions for an X.25 interface:

- Synchronizing (logically, not physically) the sender and receiver through flags.

- Controlling dataflow to prevent the sender from sending too fast.

- Detecting and recovering from errors on the link.

- Maintaining awareness of link conditions such as distinguishing between data and control signals, and determining the identity of the communicating stations.

The data-link layer rests above the physical layer in X.25. It is medium independent, and relies on the physical layer to deal with the specific media (wire, radio, etc.) and the physical signals (electrical current, laser, infrared, etc.). Moreover, the X.25 data-link layer is not aware of the specific physical-level interface standard being used on the link, such as CCITT V.32 or Bell V.29. This separation allows the link-control protocols at the data-link layer (and the packet-level procedures at the network layer) to be applied to different transmission media.

Strictly speaking, the X.25 Recommendation allows either LAP or LAPB at the data-link layer. LAP is seldom used today; therefore, the emphasis in this chapter is on LAPB.

The X.25 *packet* is carried within the LAPB *frame* as the I (information) field (see Figure 4-1). LAPB ensures that the X.25 packets are transmitted across the link from/to the DTE/DCE, after which the frame fields are removed and the packet is presented to the network layer. Packets are distinguished from frames by creating a packet header (the packet's control fields) at the network level and then inserting it into a frame whose control fields are created at the data-link level.

High-Level Data-Link Control (HDLC)

HDLC is a bit-oriented line protocol specification published by the International Standards Organization (ISO) and used throughout the world. The standard provides for many functions and covers a wide range of applications. It is frequently used as a foundation for other protocols such as LAPB. Figure 4-2 lists some of these protocols. The names in parentheses identify the system or upper layer protocol supported by the HDLC implementation option.

The reader is encouraged to check with specific vendors for their actual implementation of HDLC. Most vendors have a version available, although the protocol is often renamed or designated by different initials.

The following list summarizes the HDLC specifications published by ISO. The titles have been shortened; the actual title of each document is not listed here.

3309 (two documents):	HDLC frame structure and addendum
4335 (three documents):	HDLC elements of procedures
7448 (one document):	Multilink procedures (MLP)
7776 (one document):	HDLC-LAPB-compatible link-control procedures
7809 (five documents):	HDLC consolidation of classes of procedures; list of standard HDLC protocols that use HDLC procedures
8471 (one document):	HDLC-balanced, link-address information 8885 (one document): HDLC-additional specifications describing use of an XID frame and multilink operations

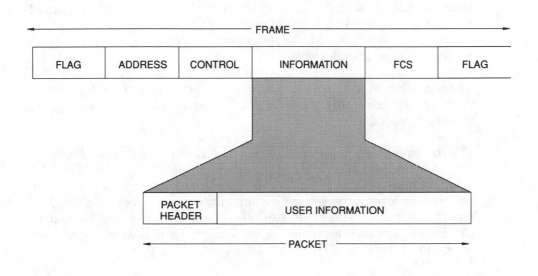

Figure 4-1. X.25 Frame and Packet

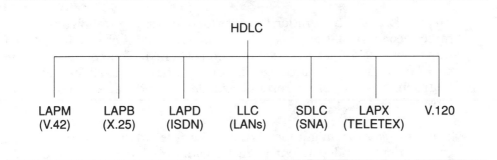

Figure 4-2. THE HDLC "Family"

HDLC and LAPB Characteristics

HDLC provides many options to satisfy a wide variety of user requirements. It supports both half-duplex and full-duplex transmission, and point-to-point and multipoint configuration, as well as switched or nonswitched channels.

However, LAPB is used only on a full-duplex, point-to-point, nonswitched channel, because an X.25 link has only the user DTE and the packet switch attached. Later, we will see how X.32 can be used to obtain an X.25 dial-up (switched) link.

An HDLC station is classified as one of three types, and LAPB uses the combined station approach (see Figure 4-3):

- The *primary* station controls the data link. This station acts as a master and transmits command frames to the secondary stations on the channel. In turn, it receives response frames from those stations. If the link is multipoint, the primary station maintains a separate session with each station connected to the link.

- The *secondary* station acts as a slave to the primary station. It responds to the commands from the primary station in the form of responses. LAP uses this approach.

- The *combined*-station approach is used by LAPB. The DTE and network can transmit and receive commands and responses to and from each other without waiting for a data solicitation. This approach is clearly better than a primary/secondary link configuration, because the X.25 channel is point-to-point, full duplex. It makes no sense to wait for permission to send data when a full-duplex path is available in each direction between the DTE and the network.

HDLC provides three methods to configure the channel for primary, secondary, and combined station use. LAP uses the symmetrical method, and LAPB uses the balanced configuration.

- An *unbalanced* configuration provides for one primary station and one or more secondary stations to operate as point-to-point or multipoint, half duplex or full duplex, switched or nonswitched. The configuration is called unbalanced, because the primary station is responsible for controlling each secondary station and for establishing and maintaining the link. Most SDLC configurations use this approach.

- The *symmetrical* configuration is used very little today. The configuration provides for two independent, point-to-point unbalanced station configurations. Each station has a primary and secondary status. Therefore, each station is considered (logically) to consist of two stations: a primary

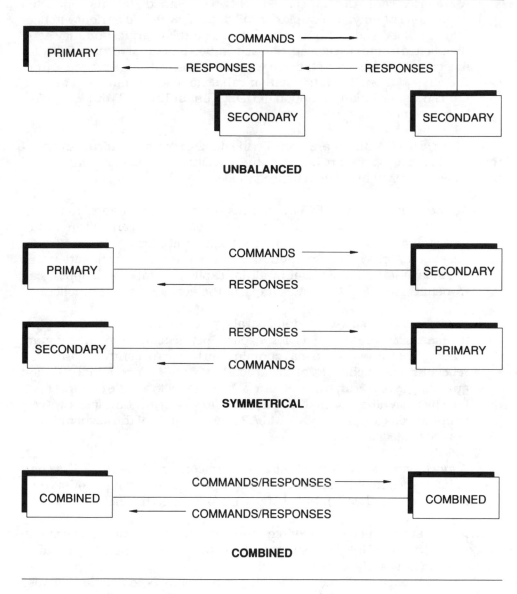

Figure 4-3. Link Configurations

and a secondary station. The primary station transmits commands to the secondary station at the other end of the link and vice versa. Even though the stations have both primary and secondary capabilities, the actual commands and responses are multiplexed onto the one physical link. LAP uses this method.

- A *balanced* configuration consists of two combined stations connected point-to-point only, half duplex or full duplex, switched or nonswitched. The combined stations have equal status on the channel and may send unsolicited frames to each other. Each station has equal responsibility for link control. Typically, a station uses a command to solicit a response from the other station. The other station can send its own command as well. LAPB uses the balanced option of HDLC, but only on full-duplex, point-to-point links.

While the HDLC stations are transferring data, they communicate in one of the three modes of operation. LAP uses the asynchronous response mode, and LAPB uses the asynchronous balanced mode.

- *Normal response mode* (NRM) requires the secondary station to receive explicit permission from the primary station before transmitting. After receiving permission, the secondary station initiates a response transmission that may contain data. After the last frame is transmitted, the secondary station must again wait for explicit permission before it can transmit again. SDLC is an example of the normal response mode.

- *Asynchronous response mode* (ARM) allows a secondary station to initiate transmission without receiving explicit permission from the primary station. The transmission may contain data frames or control information reflecting status changes at the secondary station. A secondary station operating in ARM can transmit only when it detects an idle channel state for a two-way alternate (half-duplex) dataflow, or at any time for a two-way simultaneous (duplex) dataflow. LAP is an example of the asynchronous response mode.

- *Asynchronous balanced mode* (ABM) uses combined stations. The combined station may initiate transmissions without receiving prior permission from the other combined station. LAPB uses this method.

Normal response mode is used frequently on multipoint lines. The primary station controls the link by issuing polls to the attached stations (usually terminals, PCs, and cluster controllers).

The asynchronous balanced mode is better for point-to-point links, because it incurs no overhead and delay in polling. As stated earlier, it is specified for the LAPB protocol.

The LAPB protocol is a "smart" yet simple protocol. It allows the DTE or network node to send traffic at any time, yet it also allows either station to assume a primary or secondary role at any time by issuing commands or responses, respectively. We shall see these concepts in action shortly.

The term *asynchronous* has nothing to do with the data format and the physical interface of the stations. It indicates that the stations need not receive a preliminary signal from another station before sending traffic. In other words, they can transmit without waiting for any other prior link-level signal. X.25 expects the link to operate with synchronous procedures. If asynchronous procedures are needed, they are usually connected to an X.25-based network through a packet assembler-disassembler (PAD). This subject is covered in Chapter 9.

Frame Format

HDLC uses the term *frame* to indicate the independent unit of data (protocol data unit) transmitted across the link from one station to another. Figure 4-4 shows the frame format. The frame consists of four or five fields. The fields and the LAPB field sizes are as follows:

- Flag fields (F): 8 bits

- Address field (A): 8 or 16 bits

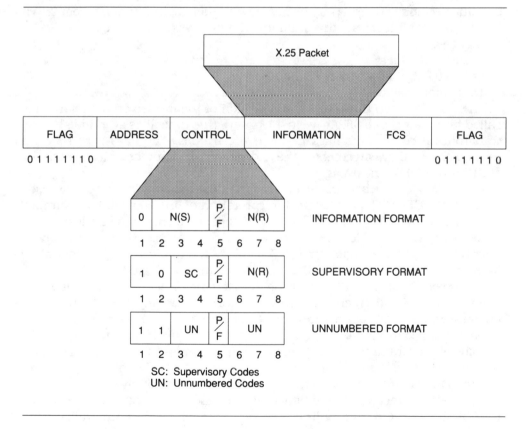

Figure 4-4. X.25 Frame Control Field

- Control field (C): 8 or 16 bits

- Information field (I): variable length; not used in some frames

- Frame check sequence field (FCS): 16 bits (or 32 in some systems)

Flags. All frames must start and end with the flag (F) field. The stations attached to the data link are required to monitor continuously the link for the flag sequence. The flag sequence consists of 01111110. Flags are transmitted on the link between HDLC frames to keep the link active. As such, they are known as *interframe* signals.

Other bit sequences are also used. At least seven, but fewer than 15 continuous 1s is an *abort* signal and indicates a problem on the link. Fifteen or more 1s keep the channel *idle*. One use of the idle state is to support a half-duplex session (not allowed in LAPB). A station can detect the idle pattern and reverse the transmission direction.

Once the receiving station detects a nonflag sequence, it is aware it has encountered the beginning of the frame, an abort condition, or an idle-channel condition. Upon encountering the next flag sequence, the station recognizes it has found the full frame. In summary, the link recognizes the following bit sequences:

01111110: Flags

At least 7, but fewer than 15 1s: Abort

15 or more 1s: Idle

The time between the actual transmission of the frames on the channel is called interframe time fill. As we just learned, this time fill is accomplished by transmitting continuous flags between the frames. The flags may be 8-bit multiples, and they can combine the ending zero of the preceding flag with the starting zero of the next flag.

HDLC is a code-transparent protocol. It does not rely on a specific code (ASCII/IA5, EBCDIC, etc.) for the interpretation of line control. For example, bit position *n* within a control field has a specific meaning, regardless of the other bits in the field. However, on occasion a flaglike field, 01111110, may be inserted into the user-data stream (I field) by the application process. More frequently, the bit patterns in the other fields appear flaglike.

To prevent "phony" flags from being inserted into the frame, the transmitter inserts a zero bit after it encounters five continuous 1s anywhere between the opening and closing flags of the frame. Consequently, zero insertion applies to the address, control, information, and FCS fields. This technique is called *bit stuffing*. As the frame is stuffed, it is transmitted across the link to the receiver.

Recovering the frame of the receiver is more involved. The "framing" receiver logic can be summarized as follows: The receiver continuously monitors the bit stream. After it receives a zero bit with five consecutive 1 bits, it inspects the next bit. If it is a zero bit, it pulls this bit out; in other words, it unstuffs the bit. However, if the seventh bit is a 1, the receiver inspects the eighth bit. If it is a zero, it recognizes that a flag sequence of 01111110 has been received. If it is a 1, then it knows an abort or idle signal has been received and counts the number of succeeding 1 bits to take appropriate action. Figure 4-5 illustrates the operations at the receiver.

In this manner, HDLC and its "subsets" such as LAPB achieve code and data transparency. The protocol is not concerned about any particular bit code inside the data stream. Its main concern is to keep the flags unique and unambiguous.

Address Field. The address field (A field) identifies the primary or secondary station involved in the frame transmission or reception. In LAPB, the address field is used only to identify a station on a data link and does not contain any higher layer address (such as a network address).

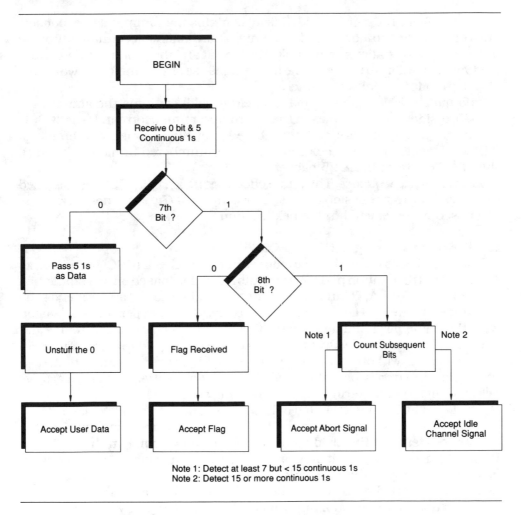

Note 1: Detect at least 7 but < 15 continuous 1s
Note 2: Detect 15 or more continuous 1s

Figure 4-5. Framing the Frame

A unique address is associated with each station. In an unbalanced configuration, the address field in both commands and responses contains the address of the secondary station. In balanced configurations, such as LAPB, a command frame contains the destination station address, and the response frame contains the sending station address.

A summary of the LAPB addressing rules follows:

- A station places its own address in the address field when it transmits a response.

- A station places the address of the receiving station in the address field when it transmits a command.

Control Field. The control field (C field) contains the commands, responses, and the sequence numbers used to maintain the dataflow accountability of the link between the stations on the link. The format and the content of the control field vary according to the use of the frame. Because of its complexity, we devote a section to it later in this chapter.

Information Field. The information field (I field) contains the actual user data. It resides only in frames in the information frame format. Usually, it is not found in supervisory or unnumbered frames, although one option of HDLC allows the I field to be used with an unnumbered frame. With LAPB, the I field contains the X.25 packet.

Frame Check Sequence. The frame check sequence field (FCS field) is used to check for transmission errors between the DTE and network. It is discussed in more detail in the next section.

LAPB Error Checking with the FCS Field

The FCS field is created by a cyclic redundancy check (CRC) of the frame. The transmitting station performs modulo 2 division (based on an established polynomial) on the A, C, and I fields plus 16 leading zeros, and appends the remainder as the FCS field. In turn, the receiving station performs a division with the same polynomial on the A, C, I, and FCS fields. If the remainder equals a predetermined value, the chances are quite good that the transmission occurred without any errors. If the comparisons do not match, a transmission error is probable, and the receiving station sends a negative acknowledgment, requiring frame retransmission.

The LAPB FCS is implemented in hardware with a shift register (see Figure 4-6). The transmitter initializes the register to all 1s, and then changes the register contents by the dividing the generator polynomial on the A, C, and I fields. The 1s complement of the remainder is then transmitted as the FCS field. At the receiver, the register is also set to all 1s, and the A, C, I, and FCS fields are subjected to the calculation and checked for errors.

LAPB uses a convention in which the calculation by the generator polynomial $x^{16} * x^{12} * x^5 * 1$ always is 0001110100001111 (7439 decimal) if no

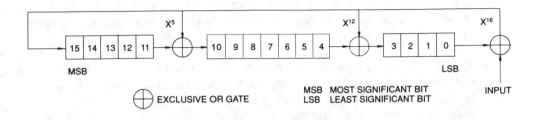

Figure 4-6. CRC Operations

bits have been damaged during the period between the two calculations at the transmitter and receiver.

Table 4-1 shows the probability of a pattern of errors not being detected by a 16-bit frame check sequence (FCS). For a typical frame containing an X.25 packet of 1122 bits (128 octets * 8 bits of user data + 3 octets * 8 bits of packet header + 5 octets * 8 bits of internal network header + 4 octets * 8 bits of frame header and trailer = 1122 bits, rounded to 1000). The probabilities of an undetected error are approximately $5 * 10^{-10}$ for a link operating at a relatively poor 10^{-4} bit error rate.

The Control Field in More Detail

The control field should be discussed in more detail because it determines how the link protocol controls the communications process (see Figure 4-4). The control field defines the frame functions and therefore invokes the logic to control traffic between the receiving and sending stations. The field can be in one of three formats:

- The *information* format frame is used to transmit end-user data between the two devices. The information frame may also acknowledge the receipt of data from a transmitting station. It also can perform such functions as a poll command.

- The *supervisory* format frame performs such control functions as acknowledgment of frames, request for retransmission of frames, and request for

Table 4-1. Undetected Bit Error Rate from Errors within Frames

Bits in frame	Bit error rate				
	10^{-3}	10^{-4}	10^{-5}	10^{-6}	10^{-7}
100	1×10^{-8}	1×10^{-9}	1×10^{-10}	1×10^{-11}	1×10^{-12}
300	9×10^{-8}	9×10^{-9}	9×10^{-10}	9×10^{-11}	9×10^{-12}
1000	7×10^{-9}	5×10^{-10}	4×10^{-11}	4×10^{-12}	4×10^{-13}
3000		2×10^{-11}	1×10^{-12}	1×10^{-13}	1×10^{-13}
10000		1×10^{-10}	2×10^{-11}	2×10^{-12}	2×10^{-13}
30000		$\sim10^{-5}$	$\sim10^{-6}$	$\sim10^{-7}$	$\sim10^{-8}$

the temporary suspension of frame transmission. The actual usage of the supervisory frame depends on the operational mode of the link (normal response mode, asynchronous balanced mode, asynchronous response mode).

- The *unnumbered* format is also used for control purposes. The frame performs link initialization, link disconnection, and other link-control functions. The frame uses five bit positions for up to 32 commands and 32 responses. The type of command and response depends on the HDLC class of procedure.

The actual format of the HDLC and LAPB frame determines how the control field is coded and used. The simplest format is the information-transfer format. The N(S) (send sequence) number indicates the sequence number associated with a transmitted frame. The N(R) (receive sequence) number indicates the sequence number expected at the receiving site. The value of N(R) also acknowledges all frames that were transmitted previously.

Piggybacking, Flow Control, and Accounting for Traffic

The X.25 link layer accounts for the traffic and controls the flow of frames by state variables and sequence numbers. Briefly, the traffic at both the transmitting and receiving sites is controlled by counters called state variables. The transmitting site maintains a send state variable V(S), set to the value of the sequence number of the next frame to be transmitted. The receiving site maintains a receive state variable V(R), which contains the number expected to be in the sequence number of the next frame. The V(S) is incremented with each frame transmitted and placed in the send sequence field in the frame. In full-duplex operations, both stations have V(R) and V(S).

When it receives the frame, the receiving station checks the send sequence number with its V(R). If the CRC passes and if V(R) = N(S), it increments V(R) by one, places the value in the receive sequence number field in a frame, and sends it to the original transmitting site to acknowledge the transmission.

If the V(R) does not match the sending sequence number N(S) in the frame (or the CRC does not pass), an error has occurred. Therefore, the V(R) value at this machine is *not* incremented. When the next frame is checked, its N(S) will not equal the V(R). This means that LAPB has found a sequencing error. As a consequence, the V(R) value is placed in the N(R) in the control field, which is coded as a negative acknowledgment frame. This frame is sent to the transmitting site. The V(R) value informs the transmitting machine of the next frame that it is expected to send, i.e., the number of the frame to be retransmitted.

The Poll/Final Bit

The fifth bit position in the control field is called the P/F or poll/final bit. It is recognized only when set to 1 and is used by the primary and secondary stations for a dialogue:

- The primary station uses the P bit = 1 to solicit a response frame from a secondary station. The P bit signifies a poll. The P bit = 1 is used with LAPB to request a status frame, and not an I frame.

- The secondary station responds to a P bit with a status frame, and with the F bit = 1. LAPB only sends back a status frame with an unnumbered or supervisory format. It does not permit an information frame to be returned in the response. The F bit can also signify the end of transmission from the secondary station under normal response mode (NRM). With LAPB, this means the polled station has fulfilled its responsibility to respond, and the station can continue to transmit frames.

The P/F bit is called the P bit when used by the primary station, the F bit when used by the secondary station. LAPB permits one P bit (awaiting an F-bit response) to be outstanding at any time on the link. Consequently, a P set to 1 can be used as a checkpoint. That is, the P = 1 means, "Respond to me, because I want to know your status."

How does a station know whether a received frame with the fifth bit = 1 is an F or a P bit? After all, it is in the same bit position in all frames. HDLC uses the address field. The fifth bit is a P bit and the frame is a command if the address field contains the address of the *receiving* station; it is an F bit and the frame is a response if the address is that of the *transmitting* station. This distinction is quite important because a station may react quite differently to the two types of frames. For example, a command (address of receiver, P = 1) requires the station to send back specific types of frames.

HDLC Commands and Responses

Table 4-2 shows the HDLC commands and responses, which are briefly summarized in this section. A later section explains how LAPB uses the HDLC commands and responses. Figure 4-7 shows the HDLC commands and responses.

The primary or secondary station uses *receive ready* (RR) to indicate that it is ready to receive an information frame and/or acknowledge previously received frames. This is done in the N(R) field. The primary station may also use the receive ready command to poll a secondary station by setting the P bit to 1.

The *receive not ready* (RNR) frame is used by a station to inform the transmitting station that it cannot accept additional incoming data. The RNR frame may acknowledge previously transmitted frames by using the N(R) field. The busy condition can be cleared by sending the RR frame.

The *selective reject* (SREJ) is used by a station to request the retransmission of a single frame identified in the N(R) field. As with inclusive acknowledgment, all information frames numbered up to N(R) - 1 are acknowledged. Once the SREJ has been transmitted, subsequent frames are accepted and held for the retransmitted frame. The SREJ condition is cleared upon receipt of an I frame with an N(S) equal to V(R).

Table 4-2. HDLC Control Field Format

Format	Control Field Bit Encoding								Commands	Responses
	1	2	3	4	5	6	7	8	C	R
Information	1	—	N(S)	—	•	—	N(R)	—	I	I
Supervisory	1	0	0	0	•	—	N(R)	—	RR	RR
	1	0	0	1	•	—	N(R)	—	REJ	REJ
	1	0	1	0	•	—	N(R)	—	RNR	RNR
	1	0	1	1	•	—	N(R)	—	SREJ	SREJ
Unnumbered	1	1	0	0	•	0	0	0	UI	UI
	1	1	0	0	•	0	0	1	SNRM	
	1	1	0	0	•	0	1	0	DISC	RD
	1	1	0	0	•	1	0	0	UP	
	1	1	0	0	•	1	1	0		UA
	1	1	0	1	•	0	0	0	NR0	NR0
	1	1	0	1	•	0	0	1	NR1	NR1
	1	1	0	1	•	0	1	0	NR2	NR2
	1	1	0	1	•	0	1	1	NR3	NR3
	1	1	1	0	•	0	0	0	SIM	RIM
	1	1	1	0	•	0	0	1		FRMR
	1	1	1	1	•	0	0	0	SARM	DM
	1	1	1	1	•	0	0	1	RSET	
	1	1	1	1	•	0	1	0	SARME	
	1	1	1	1	•	0	1	1	SNRME	
	1	1	1	1	•	1	0	0	SABM	
	1	1	1	1	•	1	0	1	XID	XID
	1	1	1	1	•	1	1	0	SABME	
	1	1	1	0	•	1	1	1	TEST	TEST

Legend:

I	Information	NR0	Non-Reserved 0
RR	Receive Ready	NR1	Non-Reserved 1
REJ	Reject	NR2	Non-Reserved 2
RNR	Receive Not Ready	NR3	Non-Reserved 3
SREJ	Selective Reject	SIM	Set Initialization Mode
UI	Unnumbered Information	RIM	Request Initialization Mode
SNRM	Set Normal Response Mode	FRMR	Frame Reject
DISC	Disconnect	SARM	Set Async Response Mode
RD	Request Disconnect	SARME	Set ARM Extended Mode
UP	Unnumbered Poll	SNRM	Set Normal Response Mode
RSET	Reset	SNRME	Set NRM Extended Mode
XID	Exchange Identification	SABM	Set Async Balance Mode
DM	Disconnect Mode	SABME	Set AMB Extended Mode
•	The P/F Bit	TEST	Test
C	Command	R	Response

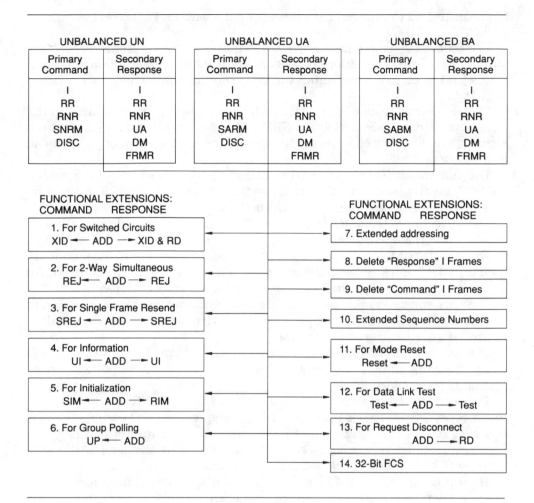

Figure 4-7. HDLC Schema

A *SREJ* frame must be transmitted for each frame in error; each frame is treated as a separate error. Only one SREJ frame can be outstanding at a time, since the N(R) field in the frame inclusively acknowledges all preceding frames. To send a second SREJ would contradict the first SREJ because all I frames with N(S) lower than N(R) of the second SREJ would be acknowledged.

The *reject* (REJ) is used to request retransmission of frames starting with the frame numbered in the N(R) field. Frames numbered N(R) - 1 are all acknowledged. The REJ frame can be used to implement the go-back-N technique.

The *unnumbered information* (UI) format allows for transmission of user data in an unnumbered (i.e., unsequenced) frame. The UI frame is actually a form of connectionless-mode link protocol; the absence of the N(S) and N(R) fields precludes flow-controlling and acknowledging frames. The IEEE 802.2 Logical

Link Control (LLC) protocol uses this approach with its LLC type 1 version of HDLC.

The *request initialization mode* (RIM) format is a request from a secondary station to a primary station for initialization. Once the secondary station sends RIM, it can monitor frames but can respond only to SIM, DISC, TEST, or XID.

The *set normal response mode* (SNRM) places the secondary station in the normal response mode (NRM). The NRM precludes the secondary station from sending any unsolicited frames. This means the primary station controls all frame flow on the line.

The *disconnect* (DISC) places the secondary station in the disconnected mode. This command is valuable for switched lines; it provides a function similar to hanging up a telephone. UA is the expected response.

The *disconnect mode* (DM) is transmitted from a secondary station to indicate it is not operational.

The *test* (TEST) frame is used to solicit testing responses from the secondary station. HDLC does not stipulate how the TEST frames are to be used. An implementation can use the I field for diagnostic purposes, for example.

The *set asynchronous response mode* (SARM) allows a secondary station to transmit without a poll from the primary station. It places the secondary station in the information-transfer state (IS) of ARM.

The *set asynchronous balanced mode* (SABM) sets mode to ABM, in which communicating stations are peers. No polls are required to transmit, since each station is a combined station.

The *set normal response mode extended* (SNRME) sets SNRM with two octets in the control field. This is used for extended sequencing and permits the N(S) and N(R) to be 7 bits long, increasing the window to a range of 1 to 127.

The *set asynchronous balanced mode extended* (SABME) sets SABM with two octets in the control field for extended sequencing.

The *unnumbered poll* (UP) polls a station without regard to sequencing or acknowledgment. Response is optional if the poll bit is set to zero. There is one opportunity to respond.

The *reset* (RESET) is used as follows: The transmitting station resets its N(S), and the receiving station resets its N(R). The command is used for recovery. Previously unacknowledged frames remain unacknowledged.

Timers and Parameters

HDLC defines two timers T1 and T2. Most implementations use T1 in some fashion. T2 is used, but not as frequently as T1. LAPB also defines a third timer, called T3. The timers are used as follows:

T1: A primary station sends a frame and checks to see if a response to the P bit is received within a defined time. This function is controlled by the timer T1 and is called the "wait for F" time-out.

T2: T2 is set to the amount of time available at the DTE or network before an acknowledging frame must be sent.

T3: In LAPB, T3 is used to signify to the network layer that an excessively long idle time is occurring on the link. LAPB requires that T3 > T1.

N2: HDLC also defines N2. It is set to the number of times a frame will be retransmitted. If this parameter is exceeded, the link is considered out of order.

K: Maximum number of frames that the transmitting station may have outstanding at any given time.

Example of the HDLC Frame Process

Figure 4-8 shows the operations of several of the major HDLC entities' operations within the data-link layer. Using the concepts of encapsulation and decapsulation discussed in Chapter 2, the fields of the HDLC frame are constructed at the transmitting side and used at the receiving side to invoke the desired operations.

The order of operations is important. For example, it makes no sense to perform the bit-stuffing operations at the transmitting side until all bits in the frame have been constructed. Also, the last event at the transmitting side is the placement of the flags in front of and behind the frame. This operation occurs after the bit stuffing, since it makes no sense to bit-stuff the flags.

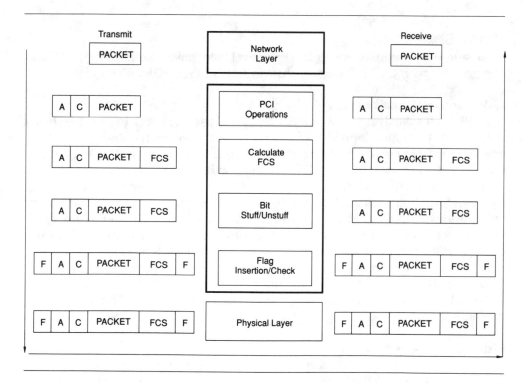

Figure 4-8. Creation of the Data-Link Frame

HDLC Subsets

Many other link protocols are derived from HDLC. While they are referred to as implementation options or subsets, they sometimes include other capabilities not found in HDLC. The major subsets are summarized in this section. The overall HDLC schema is shown in Figure 4-7.

The three boxes at the top of the figure show the basic options for link configuration. Two options are provided for unbalanced links: normal response mode (UN) and asynchronous response mode (UA). One is provided for balanced links: asynchronous balanced mode (BA). The boxes numbered 1 through 14 describe the functional extensions to the standard. Some extensions allow the feature to be added only as a command frame; others, only as a response frame. Some extensions allow the feature to be added as either a command or a response frame. Several of the functional extensions do not relate to commands or responses. For example, functional extension 14 stipulates that a 32-bit frame check sequence field is to be used for error checking instead of the HDLC default of 16 bits.

To classify a protocol, the terms UN, UA, and BA conveniently denote which subset of HDLC is used. In addition, most subsets use the functional extensions. For example, a protocol classified as UN 3,7 uses the unbalanced normal response mode and the selective reject and extended address functional extensions.

LAPB: A Closer Look

In our discussion of the X.25 link level, we have examined HDLC and compared it with LAPB. We now focus on LAPB in more detail.

LAPB Subset Classification

LAPB is classified as a BA 2, 8 or BA 2, 8, 10 subset of HDLC. Figure 4-9 shows these subsets. Option 2 provides for simultaneous rejection of frames in a two-way transmission mode. Option 8 does not permit the transmitting of information in the response frames. This restriction presents no problem. In the asynchronous balanced mode, the information can be transferred in command frames, and both stations are combined stations, so both can transmit commands at any time. Moreover, with LAPB, the sending of a command frame with the P bit = 1 occurs when the station wants a "status" frame (unnumbered or supervisory), and not an information frame. Consequently, the responding station is not expected to return an I field.

Option 10 provides for extended sequencing, which permits the N(S) and N(R) fields to be extended from the default length of 3 bits to 7 bits. The next section explains the use of extending sequencing as well as its associated format.

Link Setup Conventions

Table 4-3 shows the commands and responses in the LAPB Recommendation. LAPB uses the HDLC commands and responses. The table lists the two LAPB sequencing options established with SABM and SABME frames. Figure

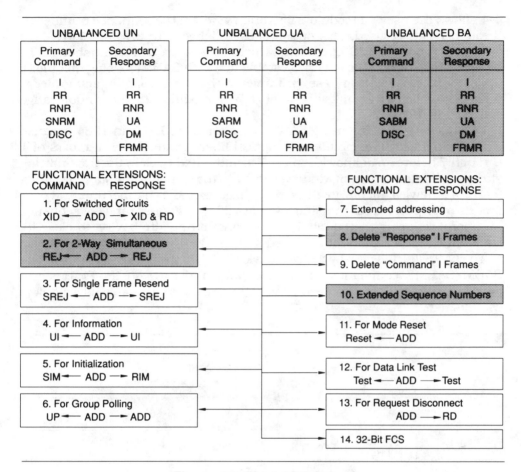

Figure 4-9. The LAPB Subset

Table 4-3. LAPB and the Control Field

Format	Control Field Bit Encoding									
	1	2	3	4	5	6	7	8	C	R
Information	0	—	N(S)	—	P	—	N(R)	—	I	I
Supervisory	1	0	0	0	P/F	—	N(R)	—	RR	RR
	1	0	0	1	P/F	—	N(R)	—	REJ	REJ
	1	0	1	0	P/F	—	N(R)	—	RNR	RNR
Unnumbered	1	1	0	0	P	0	1	0	DISC	
	1	1	0	0	F	1	1	0		UA
	1	1	1	0	F	0	0	1		FRMR
	1	1	1	1	F	0	0	0		DM
	1	1	1	1	P	1	0	0	SABM	
	1	1	1	1	P	1	1	0	SABME	

4-4 shows the use of a modulo 8 operation wherein the sequence numbers 1 through 7 can be used. This option is established with SABM. Figure 4-10 shows the modulo 128 operation, which uses a sequence number range between 1 and 127. This option is established with SABME. Using modulo 8, the stations can send up to seven frames without receiving an acknowledgment (also called a transmit window of 7). With modulo 128, the window range is from 1 to 127.

Extended sequencing using SABME was added to LAPB in 1984 because such links as satellite circuits and optical fibers exhaust the numbers of 1 through 7 before an acknowledgment is transmitted back to the transmitting station. A limited "transmit window" results in the transmitting station waiting for the acknowledgments; in other words, it causes idle channel time and poor link throughput. Larger transmit windows allow a greater range of sequence numbers, reducing the possibility of a transmitting site having to close its transmit window because it has used all its send sequence number values.

The LAPB link is set up by the user device (DTE) or the packet-exchange. The SABM/SABME commands set up the link, and turn on its T1 timer to determine when it should expect a reply. Figure 4-11 illustrates how a link is established.

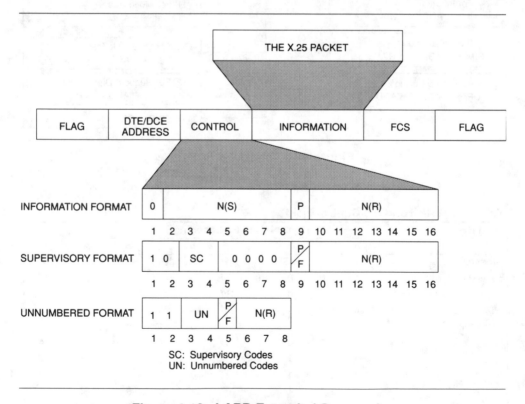

Figure 4-10. LAPB Extended Sequencing

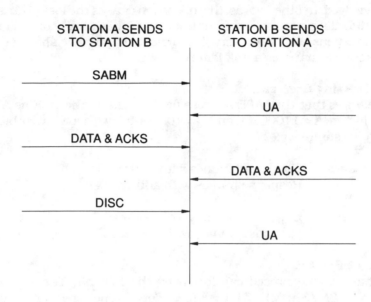

Figure 4-11. Link Set up and Disconnect

Either station can establish the link. A station indicates it is able to set up the link by transmitting continuous flags. Before link setup, either station can send DISC to make certain all traffic and modes are cleared. If the link cannot be set up, DM must be returned.

If the receiving station accepts the SABM/SABME, it sends back a UA frame. Upon receipt of the UA, the station resets its send and receive state variables to zero, and stops the T1 timer. The link is then ready for traffic. The link will not accept any other frames after issuing the link-setup commands except another SABM/SABME, UA, or DM.

A station can disconnect the link at any time by issuing the DISC command. UA is the expected response. After entering the disconnect phase, a station may initiate link setup again. If the initiation is successful, the UA is returned.

The two stations may receive logically inconsistent frames. For example, both stations could simultaneously issue a SABM command. This problem is called a *frame collision*. If a collision of the same unnumbered commands occurs, LAPB requires both stations to send a UA response as soon as possible. If the commands are different, both stations must enter the disconnected phase and issue a DM response as soon as possible. The purpose of these rules is to return the link to a state permitting reinitialization for link setup.

Even though the SABM/SABME frames are link-setup commands, they can also be used to clear any busy signal established by an earlier RNR frame. Upon acceptance of the SABM/SABME frame, the state variables must be set to zero, and any previously transmitted I frames that are unacknowledged will remain unacknowledged. In other words, this operation causes the loss of outstanding frames. LAPB does not recover from the loss of these frames; a higher level protocol is responsible for recovery. In the next chapter, we shall see how the X.25 packet layer handles a link failure.

LAPB Addressing Conventions

X.25 requires that the LAPB address field designate the DTE as A and the DCE as B (where A = 11000000 and B = 10000000, with low-order bits shown to the left). In summary:

- DTE issues: Command frames with address B
                    Response frames with address A

- DCE issues: Command frames with address A
                    Response frames with address B

LAPB Use of P/F Bit

LAPB has specific procedures for using the P/F bit. The station, upon receiving a SABM/SABME, DISC, Supervisory frame, or Information frame with P = 1, must set the F to 1 in the next response it transmits. The following conventions apply:

Frame Sent with P bit set to 1	Response Required with F bit set to 1
SABM/SABME, DISC,	UA, DM
I (Information Transfer)	RR, REJ, RNR, FRMR
I (Disconnected Mode),	DM
Supervisory (RR, RNR, REJ)	RR, REJ, RNR, FRMR

LAPB Actions with Commands and Responses

LAPB requires exact actions with the command and response frames. These rules are essential to the operation of an unambiguous protocol between the DTE and the DCE. If a station issues a frame unacceptable to the receiving station, the frame is usually rejected with the reject frame. Table 4-4 summarizes these rules.

LAPB Exception Conditions

LAPB provides several procedures for recovering from the following exception conditions: busy, N(S) sequence error, invalid frame, frame rejection, and excessive idle channel time.

A *busy* condition occurs when a station is unable to receive I because of internal problems. The RNR frame must be transmitted from the busy station. When a busy condition is to be cleared, a transmission of UA, SABM, SABME, RR, or REJ is permitted.

Table 4-4. LAPB Required Actions for Commands and Responses

RR	(1)	Clears a busy condition set with RNR.
	(2)	With P=1, asks station for its status.
RNR	(1)	With P=1, asks station for its status.
	(2)	A busy station is allowed to transmit I frames.
REJ	(1)	Requests a retransmission of frames beginning with N(R).
	(2)	Only one REJ can be outstanding at a time.
	(3)	Condition is cleared when an I frame is received with its N(S) equal to the N(R) in the initial REJ frame.
	(4)	With P=1, asks station for its status.
	(5)	Can clear a busy that was set by RNR.
SABM	(1)	Clears any busy condition.
	(2)	Clears values in V(S) and V(R).
	(3)	Previously unacknowledged frames remain unacknowledged.
	(4)	Expects a UA in response.
DISC	(1)	Terminates previous mode.
	(2)	Notifies receiver that transmitting station is suspending operation.
	(3)	Expects a UA in response.
	(4)	Previously unacknowledged frames remain unacknowledged.
UA	(1)	Clears a busy condition.
	(2)	Received mode setting commands are not acted upon until UA is transmitted.
DM	(1)	Used to report status.
	(2)	Can be sent with or without a preceding DISC command.
	(3)	Monitors received commands; if it receives an SABM and it cannot act, then it sends DM.
FRMR	(1)	Received a command or response field that is not used by LAPB.
	(2)	I field is too long.
	(3)	Invalid N(R) received.
	(4)	I field is in a frame other than an I frame.
	(5)	Supervisory or unnumbered frame received with incorrect length.
	(6)	An error condition noted that is not recoverable by retransmission of the identical frame.

If LAPB encounters the *N(S) sequence error* condition, it discards the out-of-sequence frames. This condition occurs when an I frame is received in which the value of N(S) does not equal the receive state variable V(R). LAPB is very clever here. When any problem with a frame is detected by the receiver, it does not increment its receive state variable. As a consequence, when it returns the value of an acknowledgment back to the transmitter in the N(R) field, this value is different from the transmitter's send state variable. This condition alerts the transmitter that it must go back to the value contained in the N(R) field and retransmit frames from that point forward.

LAPB does not allow the N(R) field in itself to be any type of negative acknowledgment. Some link protocols, such as SDLC, do allow implicit rejection of frames. LAPB requires that a negative acknowledgment use the N(R) field with the reject frame.

The *invalid frame* condition occurs because of the conditions listed in the FRMR. The *frame rejection* condition occurs because of the conditions discussed earlier.

Finally, the *excessive idle time* condition occurs because the station waits for a specified period within the value of T3 without taking any action. It must wait to detect a return-to-active channel state. However, if T3 expires, a higher level of protocol is notified of the excessive idle channel state condition. LAPB does not attempt any remedial actions.

LAPB handles the frame check sequence error with the series of actions described in Table 4-5.

Information-Transfer States

Like many communications protocols, LAPB is state driven. While executing a specific state, it accepts certain types of frames for action, rejects other frames that are logically inconsistent with the state, and ignores frames that have no bearing on the state and the activities on the link. Table 4-6 shows the actions pertaining to one state (the information-transfer state).

A few more words are in order for the disconnect commands and responses.

Table 4-5. LAPB Conventions for an FCS Error

1. A frame with an FCS error is discarded and no action is taken as a result of that frame.

2. This means V(R) is not incremented.

3. Therefore, the next valid frame will have a N(S) that does not equal the receiver's V(R).

4. The REJ frame will be used to initiate a recovery. (The REJ is a command. If an acknowledged transfer of the retransmission request is required, P=1; otherwise, it can be a response.)

5. The received REJ will require the station to set its V(S) to equal the N(R) in the REJ and:

   (a) In all cases, if other unacknowledged I frames had already been transmitted following the one indicated in the REJ, then those frames will be retransmitted by the station following the requested I frame. The "rejecting" station will then discard the I field of all I frames until the expected I frame is correctly received.

   (b) If the REJ frame is a P=1, the station will first transmit RR, RNR or REJ with F=1, before sending the corresponding I frame.

6. X.25 further requires the packet exchange DCE to handle the received REJ in the following manner:

   (a) If the DCE is transmitting a supervisory command or response when it receives the REJ frame, it will complete that transmission before commencing transmission of the requested I frame.

   (b) If the DCE is transmitting an unnumbered command or response when it receives the REJ frame, it will ignore the request for retransmission.

   (c) If the DCE is transmitting an I frame when the REJ frame is received, it may abort the I frame and commence transmission of the requested I frame immediately after abortion.

   (d) If the DCE is not transmitting any frame when the REJ frame is received, it will commence transmission to the requested I frame immediately.

Table 4-6. LAPB Actions in the Information Transfer State

Frame Received or an Event Occurs	Frame Sent	Change State To:
I, P=1	RR, F=1	—
RR, P=1	RR, F=1	—
REJ, P=1	RR, F=1	—
RNR, P=1	RR, F=1	Remote Station Busy
RNR, P=0	RR, F=0	Remote Station Busy
SABM, P=0 or 1	UA, F=P	—
DISC, P=0 or 1	UA, F=P	Disconnected
RR, F=1	SABM, P=1	Link Setup
REJ, F=1	SABM, P=1	Link Setup
RNR, F=1	SABM, P=1	Link Setup
RNR, F=0	—	Remote Station Busy
UA, F=0 or 1	SABM, P=1	Link Setup
DM, F=1 or 0	SABM, P=1	Link Setup
FRMR, F=1 or 0	SABM, P=1	Link Setup
Local Start	SABM, P=1	Link Setup
Local Stop	DISC, P=1 or 0	Disconnect Request
Station Becomes Busy	RNR, F=P	Station Busy
T1 Expires	RR, P=1	Waiting Acknowledgment
N2 Exceeded	SABM, P=1	Link Setup
Invalid N(S) Received	REJ, F=P	REJ Frame Sent
Invalid N(R) Received	FRMR, P=1	Frame Reject
Unrecognized Frame Rec'd	FRMR, P=1	Frame Reject

LAPB uses the disconnect command to terminate previous mode settings. This action is used infrequently because modes are usually static with either SABM or SABME. The disconnect can also be used to inform the other station that a station is suspending operations. The UA is the expected response to the disconnect command. Disconnect commands will cause unacknowledged I frames to be discarded and lost. As stated before, higher level protocols are responsible for any lost frames.

The disconnect mode response can be used by either station to indicate that it has entered a disconnect phase, even though it may not have received the disconnect command. It can also be a response to a mode setting command to inform the station that it is disconnected and cannot accept the command.

Relationship of the OSI Model and LAPB

Until 1988, CCITT did not publish an OSI-based service definition for a data-link layer that implemented LAPB. In the 1988 Blue Books, CCITT added an appendix to the X.212 service definition recommendation (Appendix III). The purpose of X.212 Appendix III is to define how to provide connection-mode data-link services with LAPB.

X.212 is a service definition recommendation. As such, it describes the primitives transferred between the network layer and the data-link layer to define the services the data-link layer is to perform for the network layer. The X.212 primitives are mapped into LAPB frames as shown in Table 4-7.

Other HDLC Subsets Supporting the X.25 Packet Layer

As we have seen, LAPB is intended to be the link layer for the X.25 interface. However, this rule does not mean that other link protocols cannot be used. This section describes some of the more prominent HDLC subsets that can be and are used to transport the X.25 packet across a channel.

LAP: Link Access Procedure

LAP (link access procedure) is an earlier subset of HDLC. LAP is based on the HDLC set asynchronous response mode (SARM) command on an unbalanced configuration. It is classified UA 2, 8 except it does not use the DM response. LAP is still used to support some X.25 network links.

To establish a LAP data link, the sending end (primary function) transmits a SARM in the control field to the receiving end (secondary function). While transmitting the SARM, the primary function will start a no-response timer (T1). When the secondary function receives the SARM correctly, it transmits an acknowledgment response (UA: unnumbered acknowledgment). Receipt of the UA by the primary function initiates one direction of the link and resets the T1

Table 4-7. X.212 and LAPB Mapping

X.212 Primitives	LAPB Frames
DL-CONNECT request	SABM or SABME
DL-CONNECT indication	SABM or SABME
DL-CONNECT response	UA
DL-CONNECT confirm	UA
DL-DISCONNECT request	DISC or DM
DL-DISCONNECT indication	DISC or DM
DL-DATA request	I Frame
DL-DATA indication	I Frame
DL-RESET request	SABM or SABME
DL-RESET indication	SABM or SABME
DL-RESET response	UA
DL-RESET confirm	UA
Primitive Parameters	**Fields in the LAPB Frame**
Called Address	Address Field (note 1)
Calling Address	Address Field (note 1)
Responding Address	Address Field (note 1)
QOS Parameters	None (note 2)
Originator & Reason	None (note 2)
User Data	Information (I) field
Note (1): Contents mapped according to LAPB's rules on identifying a command or a response	
Note (2): Only one option available to LAPB, so OSI options not used in LAPB	

timer. The receipt of the SARM in a given direction will be interpreted by the secondary function as a request to initiate the other direction of transmission, so the procedure can be repeated in the other direction, at the discretion of the secondary function.

LLC: Logical Link Control (IEEE 802.2)

LLC (Logical Link Control) is a standard sponsored by the IEEE 802 standards committee for local area networks. The standard permits the interfacing of a LAN to other local networks, as well as to a wide area network. LLC uses a subclass of the HDLC "superset" and is classified as BA, with several options on how to use the functional extensions.

LLC permits three types of HDLC implementations: type 1, using the UI frame (unacknowledged connectionless service); type 2, using the conventional I frame (acknowledged connection-oriented service); and type 3, using AC frames (acknowledged connectionless service). Table 4-8 summarizes the LLC commands and responses (compare with Table 4-2).

LLC is designed for IEEE LANs, and several standards now published describe how to use LLC to transport X.25 packets across a LAN channel (Chapter 8).

LAPD: Link Access Procedure, D Channel

LAPD (link access procedure, D channel) is another subset of the HDLC structure, although it has extensions beyond HDLC. It is derived from LAPB. LAPD is used as a data-link control protocol for the D channel on an integrated services digital network (ISDN).

ISDN uses LAPD to allow DTEs to communicate with each other across the ISDN D channel. It is specifically designed for the link across the ISDN user-network interface.

LAPD has a frame format very similar to HDLC and LAPB. Moreover, it

Table 4-8. LLC Commands and Responses

Type of Frame	Format	Command or Response	
		Commands	Responses
Type 1		UI	—
		XID	— XID
		TEST	— TEST
Type 2	(I Format)	I	— I
	(S Format)	RR	— RR
		RNR	— RNR
		REJ	— REJ
	(U Format)	SABME	—
		DISC	— UA
		—	DM
		—	FRMR
Type 3		AC	AC

provides for unnumbered, supervisory, and information-transfer frames. LAPD also allows a modulo 128 operation. The control octet to distinguish between the information format, supervisory format, or unnumbered formats is identical to HDLC.

LAPD allows two octets for the address field. This is used to identify the multidropped ISDN stations that are attached to the D channel. Each ISDN basic access can support up to eight stations. The address field is used to identify the specific terminal and service access point identifier (SAPI). The SAPI is used to identify the nature of the contents in the I field and is now used to identify signaling information with SAPI = 0 or packet data with SAPI = 16. The address field contains the address field extension bits, a command/response indication bit, a service access point identifier (SAPI), and a terminal end-point identifier (TEI).

LAPD differs from LAPB in a number of ways. The most fundamental difference is that LAPB is intended for point-to-point operation (user DTE-to-packet exchange [DCE]). LAPD is designed for multi-point access on the ISDN link. Other major differences are

- LAPB and LAPD use different timers.

- As explained earlier, the addressing structure differs, because LAPD must deal with multipoint station configurations.

- LAPD implements the HDLC unnumbered information frame (UI).

- LAPB uses only the sequenced information frames.

LAPD is capable of replacing LAPB on an ISDN D channel. It could be used to transport the X.25 packet from the DTE to a packet handler in an ISDN node. However, most implementations use LAPD to set up an ISDN B channel, then transport LAPB and the I field (containing the X.25 packet) through the B channel to the packet handler in the ISDN node.

Chapter 8 provides more information on the use of LAPD to transport X.25 packets across an ISDN interface, with a discussion of X.25 and ISDN internetworking.

SDLC: Synchronous Data Link Control

SDLC (Synchronous Data Link Control) is IBM's widely used version of HDLC. SDLC uses unbalanced normal response mode, which means the link is managed by one primary station and can support a multipoint configuration. Of course, a multipoint configuration is not supported in the X.25 Recommendation, making SDLC unsuitable for an X.25 interface.

In addition, SDLC uses several options of HDLC. SDLC has a number of implementations, and one of its classifications is UN-1, 2, 4, 5, 6, 12—but it does use other options of HDLC.

SDLC uses the same frame format as HDLC (see Figure 4-4). The information field contains SDLC control data or the basic transmission unit (BTU) that is passed down from the path-control layer.

SDLC allows the single-byte address field to be extended by setting the last bit of the address byte to 1. This setting indicates that another address byte follows. The last address byte sets the last bit in its byte to zero.

As we just learned, SDLC does not operate well on an X.25 interface, because the NRM is intended as a primary/secondary operation. LAPB uses the ABM peer-to-peer operation, since the X.25 link is a full-duplex, point-to-point configuration. Therefore, IBM uses LAPB in most of its products that interface with X.25.

Examples of Data-Link Operations

Figures 4-12 through 4-14 are examples of LAPB link operations. Each figure shows the transmission of frames from station A to station B or from

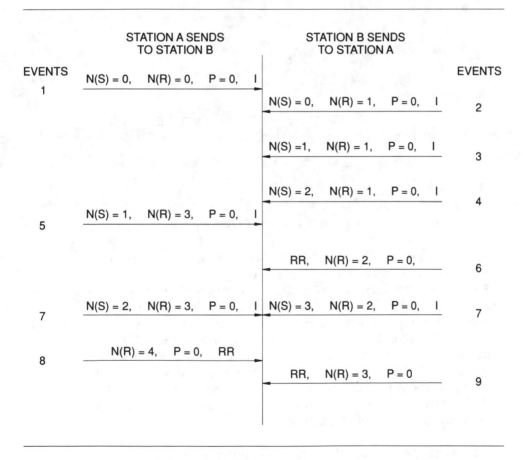

Figure 4-12. Normal Data Transfer

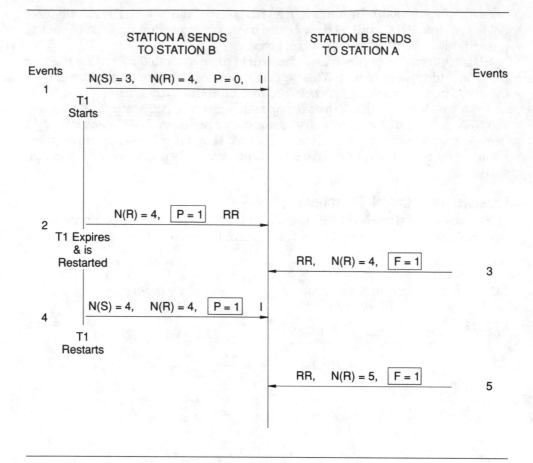

Figure 4-13. Timer Operations

station B to station A. The term "station" refers to any type of machine that uses HDLC, such as a computer or a terminal.

Each figure has an explanation of the activities on the link. The arrows depict the time sequences of the frame transmissions. The notation "I" means the frame is carrying the information field, which contains user data and/or control information from the upper layers (typically, the X.25 packet created in the network layer). The P/F indicator shows whether the poll (P)/final (F) bit is set to 0 or 1. The N(S) and N(R) notations show the values of the send and receive sequence numbers, respectively. Field positions in these figures do not show the order of field or bit transmission on the LAPB link. They are drawn to show the sequence of operations.

The figures depict the following link configurations:
Figure 4-12: Normal frame transfer

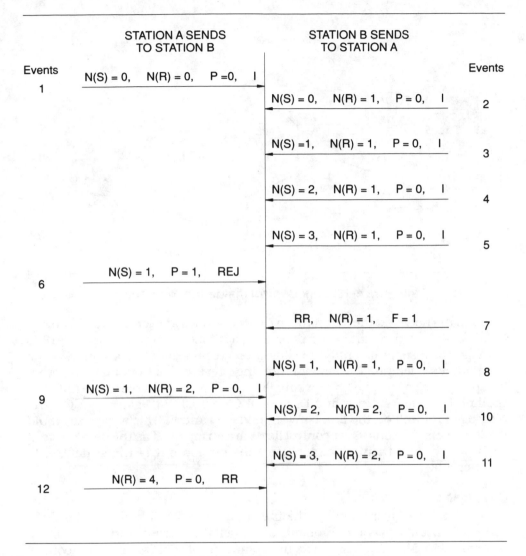

Figure 4-14. Error Recovery with Reject

Figure 4-13: Timer operations
Figure 4-14: An error recovery with reject

Data-Link Control within the Network

Before leaving data-link controls, we should examine Figure 4-1 again with a view inside the network cloud (see Figure 4-15). Remember that X.25 is a network interface standard. As such, it does not dictate the actions of the network. Nonetheless, if multiple switches are involved in transporting the data

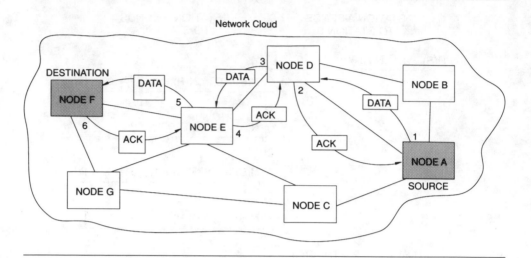

Figure 4-15. Link Control inside the Network

through the network, the data-link layer may be used at each switch to provide link-level flow control and error detection. If it is, each link in Figure 4-15 is managed as a separate entity; the link protocols on each link are unaware of each other's operations. Therefore, nothing prevents us from using different link protocols on each link. For example, it is certainly possible to use LAPB on the link between nodes A and D, and DEC's DDCMP (Digital Data Control Message Protocol) on the link between nodes D and E. This approach would work, because the link-layer control fields are stripped off as the data arrive at each switch, and then added for the transmission out of the switch on to another link.

Conclusions

The data-link layer manages the traffic on the X.25 link. It provides flow-control mechanisms and retransmits the data if they were distorted during the transmission. Most X.25 products use some type of HDLC-based link-control technique, and most manufacturers have adapted the LAPB standard. However, in the past few years, a number of X.25 systems have been implemented with other data-link controls, such as LAPD (and a B channel set up by LAPD) and LLC. This trend will continue as users acquire more ISDN circuits and local area networks.

Chapter 5

The X.25 Network Layer

Goals of Chapter 5

Our goals for Chapter 5 are to examine and understand the operations of the third layer of the X.25 Recommendation, the network layer. These operations entail the key functions of switched virtual calls, permanent virtual circuits, logical channel assignments, session management, and packet flow control and sequencing.

The contents and functions of the X.25 packet header are examined in relation to the various X.25 packet types. At the end of the chapter, we tie together the concepts that are elucidated in Chapters 3, 4, and 5 by examining the operating relationships of the three layers of X.25.

Introduction

The top layer of the X.25 protocol suite is the network layer, also called layer 3 or simply the packet layer. Its main functions are

- Managing virtual circuits between the network DCE and the user

- Creating and using headers for the control and data packets

- Exchanging packets between the local DTE and DCE

- Exchanging packets between the remote DTE and DCE

- Negotiating and providing certain network services between the communicating DTEs and the intervening DCEs

This chapter is devoted to the layer 3 functions. Chapters 6 and 7 also cover this topic, with emphasis on facilities and other supporting standards. The subject is divided into three chapters to simplify its examination.

This chapter uses time-sequence diagrams and state-transition diagrams. The techniques were introduced in Chapter 2.

Virtual Circuits and Logical Channels

As an interface protocol that defines the operations between the user DTE and the packet network DCE, X.25 does not define any actions that take place within the network "cloud." These points were introduced in Chapter 1 and are emphasized again by contrasting a *virtual circuit* with a *logical channel.* The principal differences between the two are:

- A logical channel has local significance between the DTE and the DCE.

- A virtual circuit has end-to-end significance between the DTEs.

These differences are illustrated in Figure 5-1. X.25 stipulates that any two communicating DTEs must have a virtual circuit association between them before they can exchange data. The term "virtual" means that the DTEs are logically associated with each other by the X.25 software, but are not physically connected. As the figure shows, the packets transferred between the DTEs might actually take different paths through the network. The network chooses the best routes for the packets, and "remembers" the proper destinations of the packets associated with each virtual circuit connection. After the packets have arrived at the destination DCE, the DCE presents them in the proper order to the DTE.

X.25 also operates with logical channel services. With a logical channel, a user perceives a dedicated physical circuit between the DTE and the DCE.

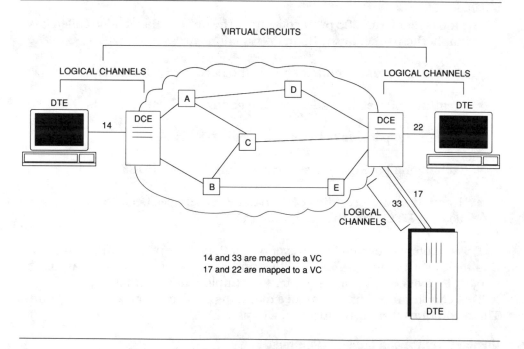

Figure 5-1. X.25 Relationship to the Packet Network

However, the physical circuit is usually allocated to multiple users. Through statistical multiplexing techniques, different users' packets are interleaved onto one physical channel. Ideally, channel performance is good enough to ensure that each user does not notice degraded service from other traffic on the channel.

X.25 uses *logical channel numbers* (LCN) to identify each DTE X.25 session with its local DCE. As many as 4095 logical channels and user sessions can be assigned to a physical channel, although not all numbers are actually assigned at one time, because of performance considerations. For example, the Western Electric 1 Packet Switching System (1PSS) supports 2047 logical channels on each of its 56-Kbits/s lines.

The value of 4095 is determined simply by the length of the LCN field inside the X.25 packet. Since it is 12 bits long, it can range from 0 to 4096 ($2^{12} = 4096$). The limit of 4095 is established because LCN 0 is reserved for DCE use.

Even though the LCNs have local significance between the DTE and the DCE, the network must map these LCNs through the network to provide an end-to-end logical association between the two DTEs. That is to say, the network administration must map the local logical channels into an end-to-end virtual circuit. X.25 does not define how virtual circuits are to be created and managed between the DCEs. It is considered an internal network matter. Nonetheless, later in this chapter, we will see an example of how X.25 logical channels can be mapped into virtual circuits.

In summary, the logical channel serves as an identifier for each user's packets transmitted between the local DTE and DCE. The virtual circuit is an end-to-end association between the DTEs.

Relationship between Layers 2 and 3 of X.25

What happened to the layer 2 link-control protocol LAPB? Remember that the layer 3 packets are placed into the I field of a layer 2 LAPB frame and sent to the packet exchange. At the packet exchange, LAPB checks the frame for any damage. If the contents are error free, the LAPB fields are stripped away, and the packet in the I field is used by the packet exchange to manage the X.25 session and to route the packet to the next node inside the network and/or to the remote DCE.

When the packet arrives at the remote packet exchange, it is placed into an I field of LAPB and delivered to the DTE. The DTE's LAPB checks for any errors, and passes the I field (i.e., the packet) to the DTE's level 3 packet logic. Of course, this process usually takes place in both directions. This discussion focuses on the packet flow in one direction.

LAPB transports different user packets inside each I field. In other words, it supports all the logical channel sessions between the DTE and the network. Indeed, a level 2 protocol such as LAPB is not aware of what is inside the I field. Its job is to transmit the data between the DTE and the network.

One final point about level 2 support: Is it needed within the network between the packet nodes? For example, is it necessary to have LAPB between nodes A and C in Figure 5-1? While it is not necessary to use LAPB, it certainly is a good idea to have some type of link control to convey the packets between the switching nodes. Some network administrations use LAPB only at the boundaries of the network cloud (at the DTE/network interface), and place the packet inside their proprietary link-control protocol for transport through the network. If the cloud is a very reliable network like a LAN, it is certainly conceivable that the supporting level 2 protocol could be a very simple procedure, and invoke only a few functions such as flag delineation and link flow control. Therefore, as long as LAPB is used at the DTE/DCE interface, level 2 conforms with the X.25 specification.

X.25 Interface Options

X.25 provides a variety of interface options to the end user. We begin a more detailed discussion of X.25 with its options for establishing and maintaining sessions between the DTE and the DCE (see Figures 5-2 through 5-4):

- Permanent virtual circuit (PVC)

- Switched virtual call (SVC)

- Fast select call

Note that these figures are labeled at the top as follows:

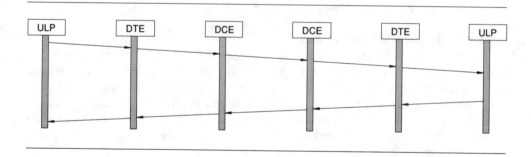

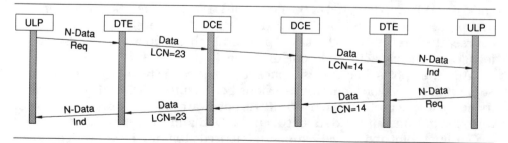

Figure 5-2. Permanent Virtual Circuit

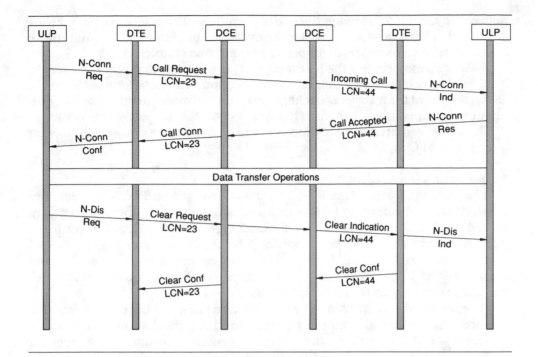

Figure 5-3. Switched Virtual Call

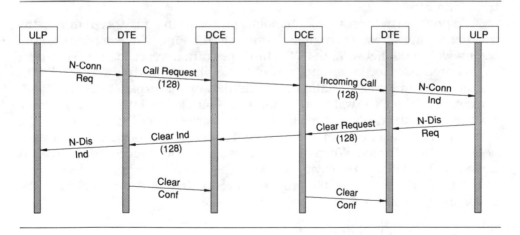

Figure 5-4. Fast Select with Immediate Clear

The notations of ULP, DTE, and DCE in the boxes on the left sides of the figures represent the local X.25 operations. The ULP, DTE, and DCE notations on the right sides represent the remote X.25 operations. The upper layer protocol (ULP) resides in the local or remote DTE. As we learned in Chapter 2, it invokes the network layer of X.25 through the use of primitives. The primitives for X.25 are described in X.213 and X.223, which are explained in Chapter 7. The uninitiated reader may wish to review them before reading this chapter.

The notations between the DTE and DCE are abbreviated notations for the X.25 packet, which are examined in this chapter. The notations between the DCEs represent the transfer of packets within the network; therefore, we say little about those operations, because they are beyond the subject of this book.

The arrows represent the time sequence diagram operations that were introduced in Chapter 2.

Permanent Virtual Circuit (PVC)

A permanent virtual circuit is analogous to a leased line in a telephone network. The transmitting DTE is assured of a session (connection) with the receiving DTE through the packet network (see Figure 5-2). X.25 requires a permanent virtual circuit be established before the session begins. Consequently, the two users and the packet network carrier must negotiate before a permanent virtual connection will be allocated. Among other things, this includes reserving an LCN for the PVC user.

Thereafter, when a transmitting DTE sends a packet to the packet network, the identifying logical channel number in the packet indicates that the requesting DTE has a permanent virtual circuit connection to the receiving DTE. Consequently, services will be provided by the network and the receiving DTE without further session negotiation. PVC requires no call setup or clearing procedures, and the logical channel is continuously in a data-transfer state.

X.25 provides two methods for handling problems that may occur during the transfer of data across a permanent virtual circuit. First, if a *momentary* failure occurs within the network, the DCE must perform a "reset" of the permanent virtual circuit (see section on supervisory packets below), and notify the DTE with a special control packet stating that the network is experiencing "network congestion." The DCE will then continue to handle the DTE's data packets. Second, if a *temporary* failure occurs within the network, the DCE must reset the permanent virtual circuit and notify the DTE with a control packet saying the network is "out of order." When the network is again ready to accept data, it sends a control packet to the DTE saying "network operational." During all this activity, the DTE need only wait for the proper control packet, and simply resume the sending of packets.

Switched Virtual Call Service (SVC)

A switched virtual call resembles some of the procedures associated with telephone dial-up lines, because call setup and breakdown procedures are used (see Figure 5-3). The *calling* DTE issues a special X.25 packet called a call request packet to the network, with a logical channel number and the address of the *called* DTE. The network uses the address to route the call request packet to the DCE that is to support the call at the remote end. This DCE then sends an incoming call packet to the proper DTE. (Remember that routing is not specified in the X.25 Recommendation.)

Logical channel numbering is done on each side of the network, and the logical channel number at the local DTE/DCE is most likely a value different from the logical channel number at the remote DTE/DCE. The critical requirement is to keep the specific DTE-to-DTE session identified at all times with the same pair of LCNs. Inside the network, the intermediate packet-switching nodes may also perform their own LCN numbering, but X.25 does not require LCN identification within a network. The activities within the network are beyond the scope of the X.25 Recommendation.

If the receiving DTE chooses to acknowledge and accept the call request, it transmits a call accepted packet to the network. The network then transports this packet to the requesting DTE in the form of a call connected packet. The channel enters a data-transfer state after call establishment. This action has created an end-to-end virtual circuit.

To terminate the session, a clear request packet is sent by either the DTE or DCE. It is received as a clear indication packet, and confirmed with the clear confirm packet. After the call is cleared, the logical channel numbers are made available for another session. If the DTEs establish another virtual call session with each other, they must repeat the procedures we just discussed.

To summarize virtual call connection establishment:

Packet	LCN Selected By
Call request	Originating DTE
Incoming call	Destination packet network node (DCE)
Call accepted	Same LCN as in incoming call
Call connected	Same LCN as in call request

Fast Select Call

Eliminating the overhead and time delay of the session establishment and disestablishment packets makes good sense for certain applications, such as those with very few transactions or short sessions on the network. Consequently, the fast select facility was incorporated into X.25. The 1984 release of X.25 provides the fast select as an essential facility, which usually means that vendors or manufacturers implementing X.25 should implement fast select to pass an X.25 conformance test. Most vendors have implemented fast select.

Fast select provides two options. The first is *fast select call*. A DTE can request this facility on a per-call basis to the DCE with an appropriate request in a packet header. The fast select facility allows the call request packet to contain user data of up to 128 octets. The called DTE is allowed to respond with a call accepted packet, which can also contain user data. The call request/incoming call packet indicates whether the remote DTE is to respond with clear request or call accepted. If a call accepted is transmitted, the X.25 session continues with the normal data-transferring and clearing procedures of a switched virtual call. This procedure is the same as the switched virtual call (see Figure 5-3), except that the fast select procedure allows the packets to contain a user-data field as large as 128 octets.

Fast select also provides another feature for the X.25 interface, the *fast select with immediate clear* (see Figure 5-4). As with the other fast select option, a call request contains user data. This packet is transmitted through the network to the receiving DTE, which upon acceptance transmits a clear request (which also contains user data). The clear request is received at the origination site as a clear indication packet. This site returns a clear confirmation packet, which cannot contain user data. Thus, the forward packet sets up the network connection, and the reverse packet brings the connection down.

When to Use the PVC, VC, and Fast Select Options

The permanent virtual circuit is typically used for applications that need absolute assurance that a connection is always available to the network and the remote DTE. Moreover, since no call-establishment packets need be exchanged, the PVC option should give good response time. PVCs are commonly used for computer-to-computer links, wherein the logical channel "stays up" continuously. Another clever use is its connection to a printer, which does not have the intelligence to return call accepted packets to its DCE.

A PVC entails a reserved logical channel number, and this theoretically means that the network must be able to support all PVC allocations, just in case their users all decide to send data at the same time. While such an event is highly unlikely, the network administration must carefully monitor the assignment and use of permanent virtual circuits.

The virtual call option is used for applications that do not need permanent logical connectivity to the network, do not need complete assurance of a successful connection attempt, or do not need immediate data transfer.

The fast selects support user applications that have only one or two transactions, such as inquiry/response applications (point of sale, credit checks, funds transfers). These applications cannot effectively use a switched virtual call because of the overhead and delay required in session establishment and disestablishment. Moreover, they cannot benefit from a permanent virtual circuit, because their occasional use would not warrant the permanent assignment of resources at the sites and the extra costs involved. Consequently, the fast selects have been incorporated into X.25 for specialized uses of a network, and for more connection-oriented support than a connectionless service offers. Both DTEs must subscribe to fast select or the network will block the call and return a clear indication packet to the DTE with the clear cause of "fast select acceptance not subscribed."

Demise of the X.25 Datagram

The datagram facility is a connectionless service (Chapter 2). Call setup and clear are not required, nor is (network) error recovery stipulated. Datagram service (see Figure 5-5) was supported in the 1980 release of the recommendation. However, it received little support from the commercial industry, because it lacked end-to-end data integrity and security. Consequently, the later releases of X.25 do not contain the option.

Mapping the Logical Channels into a Virtual Circuit

Figure 5-6 shows how an X.25 virtual call (VC) is created and mapped into a virtual circuit. This is a generic example. The exact method is vendor-specific, and X.25 does not define how this important task is accomplished. To begin the process, the local DTE sends a call request packet to its DCE (see Figure 5-6(a)). The packet header contains the following information for the DCE to use to begin the mapping process (other fields may be also used and are discussed later):

- Called (and perhaps calling DTE) addresses

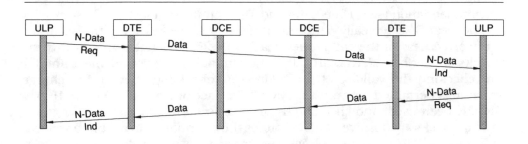

Figure 5-5. Datagram Connectionless Service

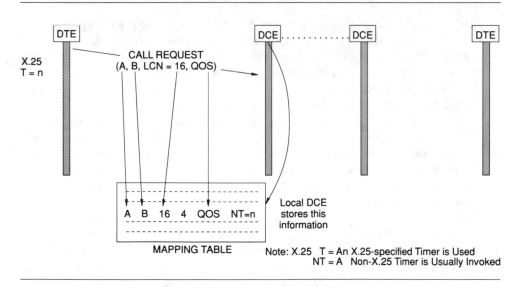

Figure 5-6(a). Call Setup: The Request

- A logical channel number

- Facilities that identify a certain quality of service for the connection

For this example we assume that the calling address is A and the called address is B. The logical channel number selected by the DTE is 16. A request to "reverse charges" for the connection has been placed into the facilities field (QOS) of the packet.

The local DCE detects the call request packet on its link number 4. Therefore, it knows it has received a reverse charge call request using LCN 16 on link 4 from address A, destined for address B.

The local DTE activates an X.25 timer upon the transmission of this packet to the DCE to ensure a response within a certain time. If the timer expires before a response is received, the DTE must initiate recovery action defined in the X.25 Recommendation (see "Time-Outs and Time Limits" below).

The local DCE typically performs numerous checks to verify the accuracy and correctness of the call request packet. X.25 does not define how these checks are performed; they are left to the vendor's discretion. Some examples are checking the validity of the addresses, checking whether the charge reversal is permitted between the two DTEs, checking whether LCN = 16 has already been used, and checking the packet for correct format and length.

If all checks are positive, the DCE stores the information in a table, as shown in Figure 5-6(a). (A similar table with fewer entries is also used at the DTE, but for simplicity is not shown here.)

The called address is now used to determine where to route the packet. X.25 suggests several formats and address types (see "X.25 Addressing Conventions" below).

The next step is transmitting the packet to the receiving user. Typically, the X.25 packet is encapsulated into the vendor's proprietary network protocol for transport through the network cloud. The network may also turn on an internal network timer (NT=n), which is not defined by X.25.

If all goes well inside the network, the packet arrives at the remote DCE (see Figure 5-6(b)). The DCE also performs numerous checks on the packet, including an examination of the called DTE address. This address is used by the DCE to determine the specific link to which the called DTE is attached. Assuming the link is number 9, the DCE stores information about the call in the table shown in Figure 5-6(b), identifies it as an incoming call packet, selects an available LCN (in this example LCN = 24), turns on an X.25 timer, and sends the packet to the DTE.

X.25 and the vendor's network have now completed one half of the call establishment. Let us pause and reflect on what has happened at the DTEs and DCEs. Each DCE and DTE has stored information about the call. The local DTE has selected an LCN and started a timer for the local connection. The packet was received by the local DCE and sent through the network in a vendor-specific protocol not defined by X.25. The remote DCE has selected an LCN and started a timer on the remote connection. To complete the call establishment, the following takes place.

The remote DTE verifies the incoming call packet, and if it accepts the call, it returns a call accepted packet to the remote DCE. It must place the same LCN (24) that was in the incoming call packet in its call accepted packet. It must also place the address and facility fields into this packet (see Figure 5-6(c)).

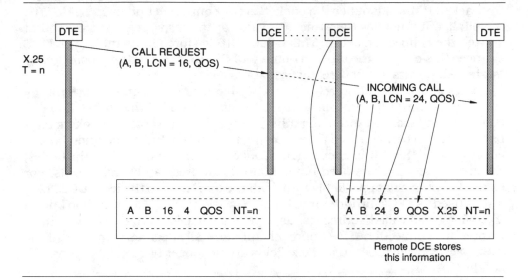

Figure 5-6(b). Call Setup: The Incoming Call

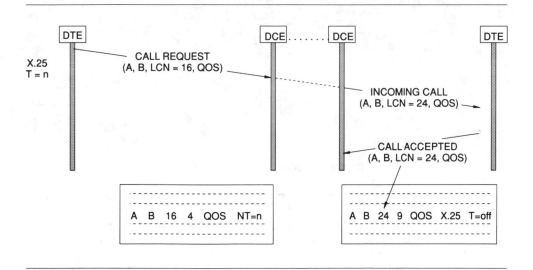

Figure 5-6(c). Call Setup: The Call is Accepted

After the remote DCE verifies the incoming call packet, it turns off its timer, and places an entry into the table that logical channel number 24 is ready to transfer data packets. It then determines where to route the packet, and the network transports it to the originating DCE.

In Figure 5-6(d), the local DCE receives and verifies the packet, and turns off the internal network timer (if one was turned on). It examines the address fields to determine which session connection and data link are associated with the packet. It then identifies the packet as call connected and passes it to DTE A on link 4. It must use the same LCN value as in the call request packet that started the connection setup. This value of 16 is stored in its table. The DCE changes this entry in the table to note that LCN 16 is in a data-transfer-ready "state." All parties are now ready for data exchange.

Let us pause again and reflect on what has been accomplished. First, by creating the entries in the tables, the LCNs at each end of the connection can be logically associated with each other, as the data and control packets pass back and forth between the DTEs. Second, this end-to-end association has, in effect, created the virtual circuit. Third, once the call is mapped into the tables, the subsequent packets need not contain the address and facility fields. For example, when a data packet is sent from the local DTE to the local DCE, LCN = 16 is used as a look-up index into the LCN session table. The DCE then knows the calling and called addresses, as well as the facilities that are to be used during this connection. This approach substantially decreases the size of the X.25 packet header, because these fields are no longer needed to support the session.

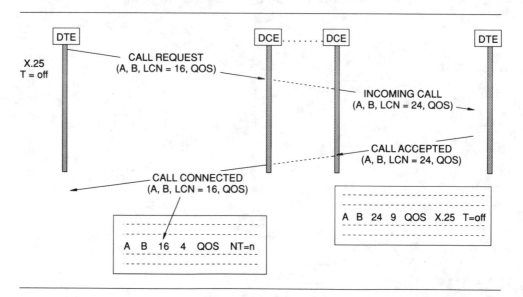

Figure 5-6(d). Call Setup: The Call is Confirmed

To conclude, two more points should be emphasized:

- A permanent virtual circuit (PVC) need not go through all this activity because it is "premapped" through the network. In other words, its table entries are prestored. It need only send the data packet with the reserved LCN, and the DCE performs the session table lookup to extract the addresses and facility information for the session.

- A connection-mode protocol such as X.25 carries very little overhead in the data packets. In contrast, a connectionless protocol like a datagram or the Internet Protocol (IP), must carry the addresses and facilities fields in each and every packet, because a virtual circuit is not created with connectionless protocols.

X.25 Packet Structure

This section introduces the packet structure and the fields within the packet. Later sections will explain them in more detail. Figure 5-7 shows the convention in the X.25 document. Octets (bytes) in the packet are on a vertical plane, with the first octet stacked on top of the second octet, etc. The 8 bits of

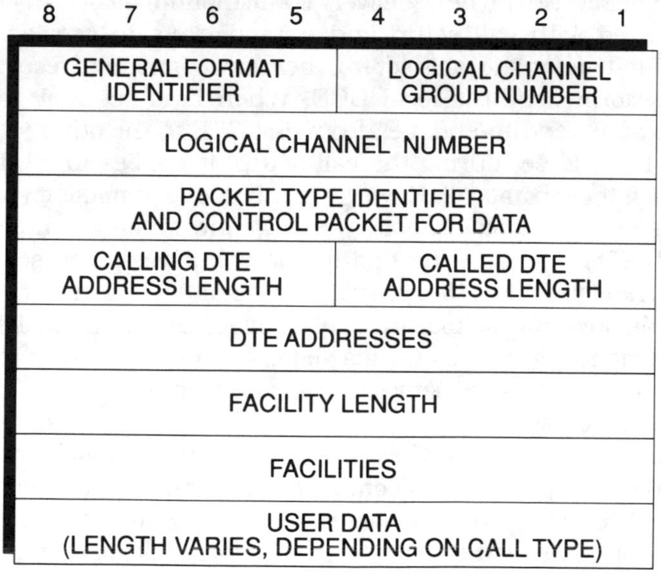

8 7 6 5	4 3 2 1
GENERAL FORMAT IDENTIFIER	LOGICAL CHANNEL GROUP NUMBER
LOGICAL CHANNEL NUMBER	
PACKET TYPE IDENTIFIER AND CONTROL PACKET FOR DATA	
CALLING DTE ADDRESS LENGTH	CALLED DTE ADDRESS LENGTH
DTE ADDRESSES	
FACILITY LENGTH	
FACILITIES	
USER DATA (LENGTH VARIES, DEPENDING ON CALL TYPE)	

**Figure 5-7. The X.25 Packet Format
(For Connection Management Packets)**

each octet are aligned on a horizontal plane, with the low-order bits placed to the right side of the page.

Every X.25 packet must contain a three-octet header. The header consists of the general format identifier (GFI), logical channel fields, and packet-type identifier.

General Format Identifier (GFI)

Bits 5 through 8 of the first octet contain the general format identifier (GFI), which serves a number of functions. Figure 5-7 shows placement of the GFI.

Sequence Numbering Information. Bits 5 and 6 of the general format identifier indicate the sequencing for the packet sessions. Two sequencing options are allowed in X.25. The first is modulo 8, which permits packet sequence numbers from 0 through 7. Modulo 128 is also available and permits sequence numbers ranging from 0 through 127.

These two bits can be coded in four possible combinations. X.25 uses the combinations as follows:

Bits 5 6	Use
0 1	Modulo 8 sequencing
1 0	Modulo 128 sequencing
1 1	Extension to an expanded format (under study)
0 0	Reserved for other applications

The D Bit. The seventh bit or D (delivery confirmation) bit of the general format identifier is used with call setup and data packets to provide one of two capabilities. First, when the bit is set to 0, acknowledgment of receipt of the data packets is performed by the local DCE. When D is set to 1 the packet is acknowledged from end-to-end, i.e., from one DTE to the other.

Since the D bit is set during the call setup, it applies to all data packets associated with the virtual call. However, X.25 does not make it mandatory for all data packets. In a later section, we will show some examples of how to manipulate the D bit for selective end-to-end acknowledgments.

The Q Bit. The eighth bit of the general format identifier is the Q bit (or qualifier bit). It is relevant for data packets and is used by X.25 to distinguish between two types of information in the user-data field. For example, it is used in X.29 (Chapter 9) to differentiate between user and control data. The Q bit is operational if set to 1.

The local DTE sets the Q bit if it is to be used, and it must remain the same value for all the data packets in a complete sequence. At the remote side of the network, the DCE will deliver the packets to the DTE as a complete sequence.

X.25 does not care how the Q bit is used. For example, some vendors set it to 1 to inform the remote DCE or DTE that the packet contains control information for a protocol conversion process. X.25 is unaware of this type of activity.

The A Bit. The A bit feature was added to the 1988 X.25 document. The A bit is the same bit as the Q bit, but is relevant only for call setup and clearing packets (the Q bit is relevant only for data packets). The A bit used to identify two possible formats for the address fields:

- A = 0: The non-TOA/NPI address format is used.

- A = 1: The TOA/NPI address format is used.

The acronyms TOA and NPI stand for type of address and numbering plan identification, respectively. (The address fields are rather involved and are discussed below in "X.25 Addressing Conventions.")

Logical Channel Fields

The two logical channel fields are the logical channel group number in bits 1 through 4 of the first octet and the logical channel number in the second octet. These fields must be present in all packets, except the restart, diagnostic, and registration packets. The logical channel number (LCN) combined with the logical channel group number (LCGN) provides the complete logical channel identification of 12 bits, giving a total possibility of 4095 logical channels (256×16 less the zero channel). The zero LCN is reserved for DCE control use. Networks use these two fields in various ways. Some networks use the two together; other networks treat them as separate fields. Later sections cover logical channels in more detail.

Packet Type Identifier

The third octet of the packet header is the packet-type identifier field, used to identify the type of packet and provide other control functions for a data packet. The field is coded according to the scheme shown in Table 5-1.

Other Fields in the Packet

Some of the packets also contain other fields. They are briefly summarized here and described in more detail later.

- *Cause and diagnostic codes fields.* Several control packets contain fields to describe the reason the DTE, DCE, or the network invoked certain actions, such as resets and restarts.

- *DTE address fields.* The call setup and clearing packets contain an address block, which contains the called and calling DTE addresses.

- *User data.* Obviously, the data packet carries this field. Several other control packets are also allowed to contain data, within certain restrictions described later.

- *Facility fields.* The call setup and clearing packets must contain the facility fields.

Table 5-1. Packet Type Identifiers (Third Octet) (Modulo 8 Format is Shown)

Packet Type		Octet 8 Bits							
From DCE to DTE	From DTE to DCE	8	7	6	5	4	3	2	1
Incoming Call	Call Request	0	0	0	0	1	0	1	1
Call Connected	Call Accepted	0	0	0	0	1	1	1	1
Clear Indication	Clear Request	0	0	0	1	0	0	1	1
Clear Confirmation	Clear Confirmation	0	0	0	1	0	1	1	1
Data	Data		P(R)		M		P(S)		0
Interrupt	Interrupt	0	0	1	0	0	0	1	1
Interrupt Confirmation	Interrupt Confirmation	0	0	1	0	0	1	1	1
Receive Ready (RR)	Receive Ready (RR)		P(R)		0	0	0	0	1
Receive Not Ready (RNR)	Receive Not Ready (RNR)		P(R)		0	0	1	0	1
	Reject (REJ)		P(R)		0	1	0	0	1
Reset Indication	Reset Request	0	0	0	0	1	1	0	1
Reset Confirmation	Reset Confirmation	0	0	0	1	1	1	1	1
Restart Indication	Restart Request	1	1	1	1	1	0	1	1
Restart Confirmation	Restart Confirmation	1	1	1	1	1	1	1	1
Diagnostic		1	1	1	1	0	0	0	1
	Registration Request	1	1	1	1	0	0	1	1
Registration Confirmation		1	1	1	1	0	1	1	1

Conventions for User Data in the Packet

X.25 provides several options for transporting user data. The default user-data field length in a data packet is 128 octets, but X.25 provides other options: 16, 32, 64, 256, 512, 1024, 2048, and 4096 octets. The last two sizes were added in the 1984 revision. Each logical channel can have a different packet size.

If the user-data field in the packet exceeds the maximum field permitted by the network, the receiving DTE will reset the virtual call by issuing a reset packet.

User data may exist in the setup and clearing packets. The maximum size is 16 octets. This field is useful for such entries as passwords and accounting information for the receiving DTE. It may also be used to convey additional protocol identification. For instance, a PAD uses this field to identify itself as a PAD when it is calling a host DTE. In this context, this field is not an ordinary user-data field.

Finally, for the fast select option, 128 octets of user data are allowed in the data field.

Use of the Third Octet for the Data Packet. The packet header is modified to facilitate the movement of user data through the network. The third octet of the header, normally reserved for the packet-type identifier (see Table 5-1), is broken into four separate fields for user-data packets:

Bits	Description or Value
1	0
2-4	Packet send sequence P(S)
5	More data bit (the M bit)
6-8	Packet receive sequence P(R)

These fields function as follows: The first bit of zero identifies the packet as a data packet. Three bits are assigned to a send sequence number P(S). One bit is assigned to an M-bit function (more about this later). The three remaining bits are assigned to a receiving sequence number P(R). Note that sequence numbers exist at both this level (network) and the data-link level (LAPB).

Why Sequence at the Packet and Frame Levels? The sending and receiving numbers coordinate and acknowledge packet transmission between the DTE and DCE. The receiving DTE or DCE must know which packet receiving-sequence number to send back to the transmitting device to acknowledge the specific packet properly. X.25 has features similar to those found in LAPB; the use of P(R) and P(S) at the network level requires the P(R) to be one greater than the P(S) in the data packet.

Remember that LAPB and X.25 provide for independent (R) and (S) sequencing. However, the difference between the link and network sequencing is significant. The link-level sequence numbers are used to account for *all* the logical channels' traffic on the communications link, and to manage the flow control on the link. The network-level sequence numbers can be used to manage the traffic of *each* logical channel session.

The M Bit. The M (more data) bit in the third octet identifies a sequence of related packets passing through the network. This capability aids the network and DTEs in preserving the identification of data blocks when the user device or the network divides these blocks into smaller packets. For example, a series of packets relating to a database needs to be presented to the receiving DTE as a logical whole. The capability is quite important when networks are internetworking with each other, a topic discussed later.

The M bit is frequently used when a block of user data created in a layer above the network layer is larger than the permissible packet size on the X.25 link or within the network. In this situation, the data are segmented. In most instances, this practice diminishes the number of input/output calls made at the upper levels, in turn reducing host computer use. In a similar manner, incoming data can be assembled into the larger user blocks from the smaller packets. Segmentation and reassembly can be controlled with the M bit.

Some vendors use the M bit to buffer incoming packets before presenting a larger block of data to an output device. For example, data may be withheld from a CRT workstation until a full screen has arrived and is available for display.

A and B Packets. The combination of M and D bits provides for the two categories in X.25. These categories are designated *A packets* and *B packets*. This feature allows a DTE or DCE to indicate a sequence of more than one packet and the network to combine packets.

X.25 defines a complete packet sequence as a single category-B packet and all contiguous category-A packets, if any. The A packet has the exact maximum user-data field length, with the M bit set to 1, and the D bit set to zero.

The B packet ends a related sequence of packets. Only B packets can have a D bit set to 1 for an end-to-end acknowledgment. Category-A packets and the immediately following B packet can be combined into one packet by the network. B packets themselves must maintain separate entities as separate packets. Combining packets can be useful when different packet sizes are supported along the route through a network, or at the receiving end. If this is the case, the M bit can be used to indicate to the receiving DTE that there is a related sequence in the packet flow.

X.25 treats the D and M bits when sent by the source DTE as shown in Table 5-2.

An Examination of Each Packet Type

Now that we understand their general structure, we examine and compare X.25 packets in more detail. To simplify matters, this section groups the packets according to similarities in their formats.

Call Setup Packets

As discussed previously, call setup packets consist of call request, incoming call, call accepted, and call connected. Used only for a virtual call connection, they are not used on a permanent virtual circuit, because call setups are not required. Figure 5-7 shows the format for these packets.

Call Clear Packets

Figure 5-8 show the format for call clear packets. The clear request and clear indication packets must contain all the information in the call setup packets, plus the clearing cause field (mandatory) and the diagnostic code (optional). The clear confirmation packet uses the same format as the call setup packet, except no user data are allowed.

An X.25 network uses the clear packet for a number of functions, but primarily to clear a DTE-DTE session. Another use is to indicate that a call request cannot be completed. If the remote DTE refuses the call (because of the lack of resources, for example), it issues a clear request packet to its network node. The packet is sent through the network to the originating network node, and a clear indication packet is sent to the originating DTE. If the network cannot complete the call (for example, the remote network DCE node has no free logical channel, or the network is congested), it must send a clear indication packet to the originating DTE. X.25 provides several codes to indicate the reason for the clear packet. A clear packet cannot be used on a permanent virtual circuit.

Supervisory Packets

Supervisory packets include the restart and reset packets (see Figure 5-9). Notice that octet 4 contains a cause field to provide additional information on the

Table 5-2. A and B Categories

Category	M	D	Full?	Network will Combine with Subsequent Packets
B	0 or 1	0	no	no
B	0	1	no	no
B	1	1	no	no
B	0	0	yes	no
B	0	1	yes	no
B	1	1	yes	no
A	1	0	yes	yes

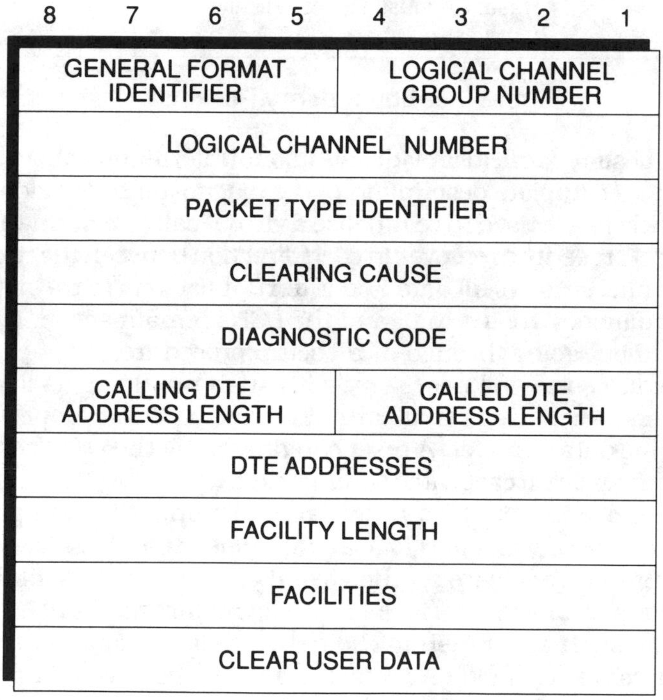

8	7	6	5	4	3	2	1
GENERAL FORMAT IDENTIFIER				LOGICAL CHANNEL GROUP NUMBER			
LOGICAL CHANNEL NUMBER							
PACKET TYPE IDENTIFIER							
CLEARING CAUSE							
DIAGNOSTIC CODE							
CALLING DTE ADDRESS LENGTH				CALLED DTE ADDRESS LENGTH			
DTE ADDRESSES							
FACILITY LENGTH							
FACILITIES							
CLEAR USER DATA							

Packet Type Identifier:
Clear Request, Clear Identification, Clear Confirmation
Note: Confirmation does not contain the Cause,
Diagnostic, and User Fields

Figure 5-8. The Clear Packets

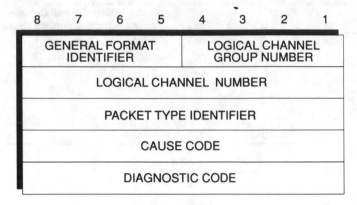

8	7	6	5	4	3	2	1

GENERAL FORMAT IDENTIFIER	LOGICAL CHANNEL GROUP NUMBER
LOGICAL CHANNEL NUMBER	
PACKET TYPE IDENTIFIER	
CAUSE CODE	
DIAGNOSTIC CODE	

Packet Type Identifiers
Restart Request, Restart Indication,
Reset Request, Reset Indication

Figure 5-9. Supervisory Packets

event. The diagnostic code field provides additional information about a problem. Appendix D has a complete description of the diagnostic code fields in X.25.

The reset packets are used to reinitialize a virtual call or a permanent virtual circuit. The reset procedure removes in each direction between the two DTEs (for one logical channel session) all data and interrupt packets in the network. The P(S) and P(R) numbers are set to 0, and the LCNs remain active. Data can be transmitted without going through a call setup procedure.

Reset procedures may be necessary with such problems as lost packets, duplicate packets, or packets that cannot be resequenced properly. Reset is used only during data transfer. A reset can be sent by the DTE (reset request packet) or the network (reset indication packet).

The restart procedure is used to initialize or reinitialize the packet-level DTE/DCE interface. Up to 4095 logical channels on a physical port can be affected. The procedure clears all the virtual calls and resets all the permanent virtual circuits at the interface level. The restart might be needed for a severe problem, such as a crash in the network. (For example, the network control center computer fails.) A restart is a convenient way to place all the connections at the DTE/DCE interface to a known state.

When a restart is issued, all outstanding packets may be lost and must be recovered by a higher level protocol. Because of its wide-scale effect, this packet must be used judiciously.

The network may use a restart when reinitializing or starting up the system, to ensure that all sessions are reestablished. When a DTE sends a restart, the network must send a clear to every DTE that has a switched virtual call connection with the "restarting" DTE. The network must also send a reset to all affected permanent virtual circuit connections.

Possible Loss of Packets with Resets, Restarts, and Clears

Packet loss is not unusual in a network that uses the X.25 interface. The clear, reset, and restart packets can cause undelivered packets to be discarded. A user may exercise these choices for such reasons as restarting a session or breaking a dialogue. These control packets often arrive at the destination node before user-data packets, because control packets may not be subject to the delay inherent in the flow-control procedures used with user-data packets. Consequently, higher level protocols at the transport layer are required for recovering lost packets. Appendix D provides more information on what happens to data when resets, restarts, or clears are issued.

Confirmation Packets of Interrupt, Reset, and Restart

The confirmation packets are restart confirmation, reset confirmation, and interrupt confirmation (see Figure 5-10). They acknowledge that a previously received packet (request) has been accepted and implemented. The clear confirmation is not included here, because it uses a different format.

Data Packets

Figure 5-11 shows the format for the data packet. Two formats are permitted, one for modulo 8 and one for modulo 128. Remember that the Q, M, and D bits can be used with data packets to obtain special services from the network.

Flow-Control Packets

The flow-control packets are receive ready (RR), receive not ready (RNR), and reject (REJ) (see Figure 5-12).

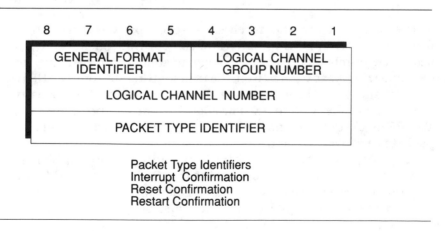

Figure 5-10. The Confirmation Packets

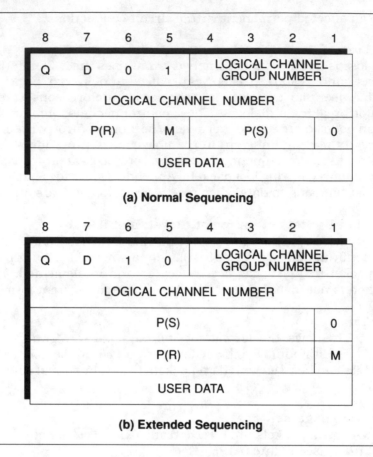

(a) Normal Sequencing

(b) Extended Sequencing

Figure 5-11. Data Packets

The receive ready and receive not ready packets serve the important function of DTE- or DCE-initiated flow control. Both packets provide a receive sequence number P(R) in the packet header to indicate the next packet sequence number expected from the transmitting station. The RR packet tells the transmitter to begin sending data packets and also uses the receive sequence number P(R) to acknowledge any packets previously transmitted. The RR packet can acknowledge packets received when there are no data packets to convey to the transmitting site.

The RNR packet is used to ask the transmitting site to stop sending packets. It also uses the receive sequence field P(R) to acknowledge any packets previously received. The RNR is often issued when a computer or terminal is temporarily unable to receive traffic. Thus, both packet types provide flow control.

Note that an RNR issued for a specific DTE will likely cause the network to

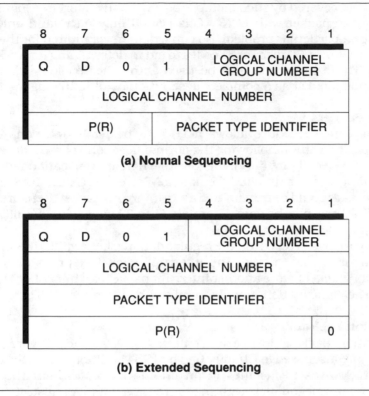

(a) Normal Sequencing

(b) Extended Sequencing

Figure 5-12. Flow Control Packets

issue RNR to the other associated DTE to prevent excess traffic from entering the network. Since the network packet-switching nodes have finite buffering and queuing capabilities, an RNR often requires "choking" the packet flow at both sides of the DTE/DTE session.

As stated earlier, these two packet types provide X.25 with an additional form of data flow control beyond the data-link level support of the HDLC subset LAPB. The data-link level does not perform flow-control measures on individual user sessions (channels). X.25 at the network layer uses RR and RNR with specific logical channel numbers to accomplish individual flow control. Thus, X.25 achieves a finer level of control than LAPB. We return to this point shortly.

The Reject (REJ) packet specifically rejects the received packet. The DTE requests retransmission of packets beginning with the count in the receive sequence field P(R). The DCE is not allowed to use the Reject packet. Most implementations of X.25 do not use this packet.

Diagnostic Packets
The diagnostic packet is used by X.25 networks to indicate certain error

conditions not covered by such methods as reset and restart (see Figure 5-13). The diagnostic packet with LCN = 0 is issued only once (and only by the network) for a particular problem. No confirmation is required for the packet.

X.25 defines over 60 diagnostic codes to aid in determining network or DTE problems. These codes can also be used with other packets (clear, reset, restart). Appendix D has a complete description of all X.25 diagnostic codes.

Interrupt Packets

The interrupt procedure allows a DTE to transmit one nonsequenced interrupt packet without following the normal flow-control procedures established in X.25 (see Figure 5-14). It is useful when an application requires the transmittal of data for unusual conditions. For example, an extremely high priority message could be transmitted as an interrupt packet to ensure that the receiving DTE accepts the data. User data (1 to 32 octets) are permitted in an interrupt packet.

An interrupt has no effect on the regular data packets within the virtual call or permanent virtual circuit. The interrupt packet requires an interrupt confirmation packet before another interrupt packet can be sent on the logical channel. The confirmation must be returned by the remote DTE.

Registration Packets

Registration packets invoke or confirm the X.25 facilities (registration operations are discussed in Chapter 6). The 1984 addition allows the end user to request changes to facilities in an on-line mode, without the manual intervention and negotiation with the network vendor. A registration confirmation packet is returned to give the status of the request. Figures 5-15(a) and 5-15(b) depict the formats for the registration packets.

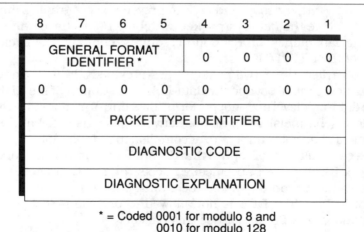

Figure 5-13. Diagnostic Packets

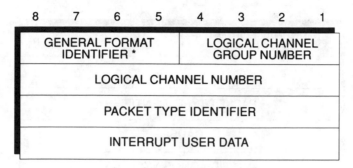

8	7	6	5	4	3	2	1
GENERAL FORMAT IDENTIFIER *				LOGICAL CHANNEL GROUP NUMBER			
LOGICAL CHANNEL NUMBER							
PACKET TYPE IDENTIFIER							
INTERRUPT USER DATA							

* = Coded 0001 for modulo 8 and
     0010 for modulo 128

Figure 5-14. Interrupt Packets

8	7	6	5	4	3	2	1
GENERAL FORMAT IDENTIFIER *				0	0	0	0
0	0	0	0	0	0	0	0
PACKET TYPE IDENTIFIER							
CALLING DTE ADDRESS LENGTH				CALLED DTE ADDRESS LENGTH			
DTE ADDRESSES							
REGISTRATION LENGTH							
REGISTRATION							

* = Coded 0001 for modulo 8 and
     0010 for modulo 128

Figure 5-15(a). Registration Request Packets

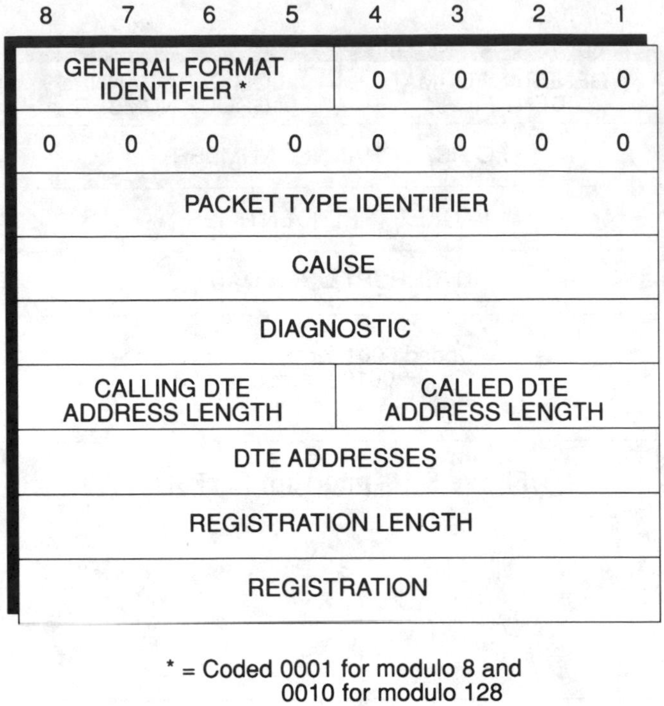

8	7	6	5	4	3	2	1
GENERAL FORMAT IDENTIFIER *				0	0	0	0
0	0	0	0	0	0	0	0
PACKET TYPE IDENTIFIER							
CAUSE							
DIAGNOSTIC							
CALLING DTE ADDRESS LENGTH				CALLED DTE ADDRESS LENGTH			
DTE ADDRESSES							
REGISTRATION LENGTH							
REGISTRATION							

* = Coded 0001 for modulo 8 and
0010 for modulo 128

Figure 5-15(b). Registration Confirm Packets

Logical Channel Assignments

We have learned that logical channel numbers (LCNs) are used to identify the user session to the packet node (DCE) and vice versa. As shown in Figure 5-16, the numbers may be assigned to permanent virtual circuits, one-way incoming calls, two-way calls, and one-way outgoing calls. The term "one way" refers to the direction in which the call establishment occurs. After the call is established, the DTE and DCE can transmit and receive packets in a full-duplex mode.

The switched logical channels are usually assigned as

- *One-way incoming:* DTEs can receive but not initiate calls

- *One-way outgoing:* DTEs can initiate calls but cannot receive them

- *Two-way:* DTEs can receive and send calls

The LCNs are split into four groups, with the lowest group assigned to permanent virtual circuits. The size of a group is not defined by X.25, and is

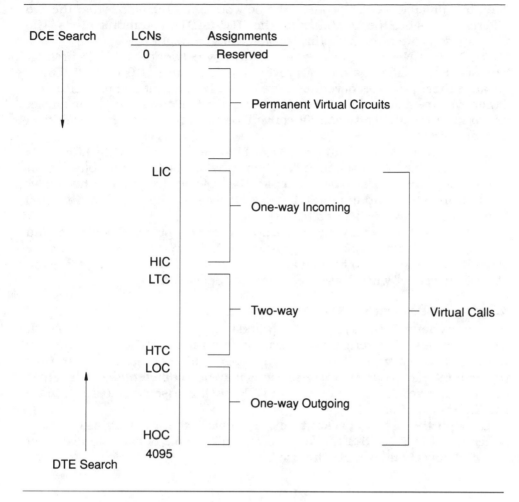

Figure 5-16. Logical Channel Assignments

left to the discretion of the user and the network. However, X.25 does recommend that the LCN assignment within a group be contiguous.

The DTE and DCE may use the same LCN when beginning communication. For example, an outgoing DTE call request packet could possibly use the same LCN as an incoming DCE incoming call packet. To minimize this possibility, the network (DCE) searches for a number starting at the low-number end and the DTE starts at the high-number end. If the outgoing call (call request packet) from a DTE has the same LCN as an incoming call (incoming call packet) from the network DCE, X.25 stipulates that the incoming call be cleared and the call request processed.

The assignment of LCNs is pertinent only to the DTE and its packet-exchange DCE. At the other end of the network, the very same packet may contain a different LCN. Of course, the network must remember that the two different LCNs are the identifiers for the DTE-to-DTE communications. The vendor's software must keep this "bookkeeping" straight.

The X.25 LCN scheme is used many ways by networks and X.25 product vendors. Some offerings do not provide the full range of 0 to 4095 LCNs, because these products never use more than a few channels simultaneously. Other systems place rules on how the LCNs are allocated. The public packet networks often establish a specific convention (within the X.25 framework) on LCN allocations.

In retrospect, one could argue that CCITT should have made the LCN fields either of variable length or optional. In many instances, the full 12 bits are not needed. However, the fixed fields simplify the logic needed to build the header at the transmitter and interpret it at the receiver. In the long run, the fixed format is probably the better alternative.

As discussed previously, the zero LCN is reserved for network control and is used with the diagnostic packet type. Each X.25 product vendor should be consulted for the availability of diagnostic messages. They usually are available, if the vendor will release them to your application.

X.25 Logical Channel States

Logical channel states provide the foundation for managing the DTE/DCE connection. A state describes the logical condition of the DTE/DCE connection for each LCN. Remember that X.25 can manage 4095 separate sessions on one physical interface. Each of these sessions may be in different states, such as data transfer, reset, or call request. The DTE and DCE use the states to manage the X.25 connection.

Through the various packet types, the logical channel may assume the states listed in Table 5-3. Table 5-4 gives an example of call establishment showing how channel states are used.

Table 5-3. X.25 States

State Number	State Description
p1 or d1 or r1	Packet level ready
p2	DTE waiting
p3	DCE waiting
p5	Call collision
p4	Data transfer
p6	DTE Clear Request
p7	DCE Clear Indication
d2	DTE Reset Request
d3	DCE Reset Indication
r2	DTE Restart Request
r3	DCE Restart Indication

Time-Outs and Time Limits

Most data communications protocols have timers and X.25 is no exception. Timers establish limits on how long it takes to obtain connections, clear channels, reset a session, etc. Without such timers, a user might wait indefinitely for an event if that event did not go to completion. X.25 timers simply force the system to make decisions in the event of problems; they facilitate error recovery. For example, when a DTE issues a call request packet, the T21 time-limit parameter is started, and the logical channel state moves from p1 to p2. If there is a delay or no response from the network or the remote DTE, the timer expires. The DTE may then attempt another call request or ask for assistance from other support sources, such as a network operator.

X.25 provides five DTE *time limits* and four DCE *time-outs* (see Tables 5-5 and 5-6). In all cases, if problems persist and the timers are reset and retried, the channel must be considered out of order, and network diagnostics and troubleshooting measures should be performed. These measures depend on the vendor's specific implementations of X.25. The next section explains these timers further.

DTE/DCE State Diagrams

X.25 provides several state diagrams to define the operations at the DTE/DCE interface. The figures in this section are arranged in order of priority, with

Table 5-4. State Changes Resulting from a Call Setup

Sequence of Events	Packet	From	To	Channel State From	To Current Channel State
1	Call Request	Local DTE	Local DCE	p1	p2
2	Incoming Call	Remote DCE	Remote DTE	p1	p3
3	Call Accepted	Remote DTE	Remote DCE	p3	p4
4	Call Connected	Local DCE	Local DTE	p2	p4

Table 5-5. DTE Time-limits

Time-Limit Number	Time-Limit Value	Started When	State of the Logical Channel	Normally Terminated When
T20	180s	DTE issues a restart request	r2	DTE leaves the r2 state
T21	200s	DTE issues a call request	p2	DTE leaves the p2 state
T22	180s	DTE issues a reset request	d2	DTE leaves the d2 state
T23	180s	DTE issues a clear request	p6	DTE leaves the p6 state
T28	300s	DTE issues a registration request	Any	DTE receives the registration confirmation or a diagnostic packet

Table 5-6. DTE Time-outs

Time-Limit Number	Time-Limit Value	Started When	State of the Logical Channel	Normally Terminated When
T10	60s	DCE issues a restart indication	r3	DCE leaves the r3 state
T11	180s	DCE issues an incoming call	p3	DCE leaves the p3 state
T12	60s	DCE issues a reset indication	d3	DCE leaves the d3 state
T13	60s	DCE issues a clear indication	p7	DCE leaves the p7 state

the first figure having the highest priority and the subsequent figures having a lower priority. That is to say, a transferred packet that belongs to a higher order diagram has precedence over a transferred packet that belongs to a lower order diagram.

Restart Procedure

Figures 5-17 and 5-18 show how the restart procedure is performed: Figure 5-18 shows the X.25 state diagram; Figure 5-17, the effect of the restart at each end of the virtual circuit. All SVCs are returned to the p1 state, and all PVCs are returned to the d1 state.

In Figure 5-17, notice how the remote DCE uses the restart. It sends a clear indication packet to all SVCs and a reset indication packet to all PVCs. Why not issue the restart at the remote end? To do so might remove some calls at the remote end not associated with the user that initiated the restart. Therefore,

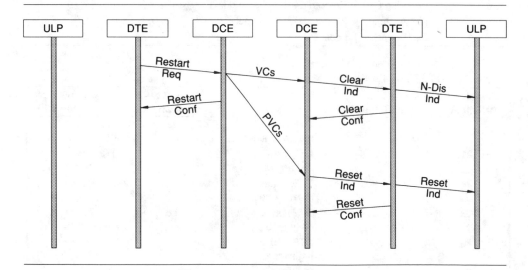

Figure 5-17. Restart Procedure

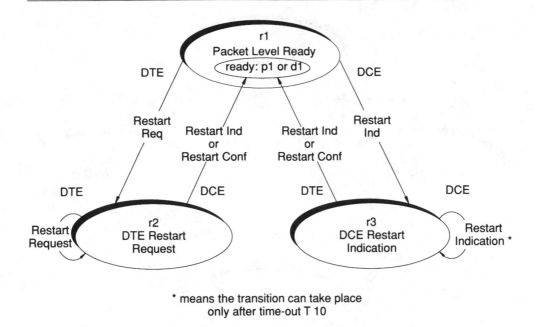

Figure 5-18. Restart State Diagram

the remote DCE must examine its virtual call (mapping) tables to determine which of its local channels are communicating with the restart requester, and clear or reset only these virtual circuits.

Call Setup Procedure

The call setup procedure follows the state diagram in Figure 5-19. The diagram has been annotated with the four events described in Table 5-4 to make it easier to follow.

Earlier in this chapter we saw that it is possible for an LCN value selected by the DTE in a call request packet to be the same as the LCN value selected by the DCE in an incoming call packet. This problem is called a call collision. When it occurs, the local DTE call is processed, and the remote DTE's incoming call is cleared.

Clear Procedure

Either the DTE or the DCE can clear a call (see Figure 5-20). The DTE issues a clear request packet and the DCE issues a clear indication packet to begin the clear procedure. The station that receives the request or indication will return a clear confirmation packet. The released channel is then placed in the ready state (d1).

The clear procedure is also used if a call cannot be established. The DCE

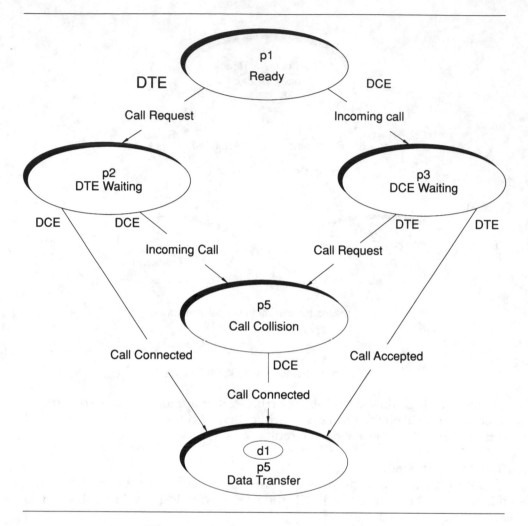

Figure 5-19. Call Setup State Diagram

must send back to the DTE a clear indication packet containing the same LCN that was in the call request packet.

A clear collision can occur when the DTE and DCE send a clear request and clear indication packet at the same time with the same LCN. Under these conditions, the logical channel is considered to be in the ready state (p1).

Reset Procedure

The reset procedure reinitializes the virtual call or permanent virtual circuit (see Figure 5-21). After the reset procedure is complete, the logical channel is in the ready state (p1). The reset can apply only to the data-transfer state (p4)

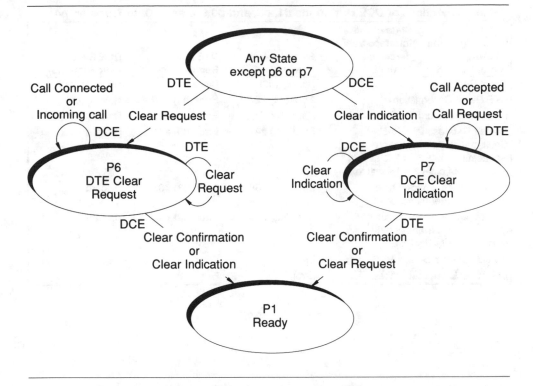

Figure 5-20. Call Clear State Diagram

of the DTE/DCE interface. Any other state causes the reset packets to be ignored and unconfirmed.

However, the data-transfer state actually has three states within it (d1, d2, d3). Therefore, X.25 specifies a variety of actions taken by the DCE on the receipt of packets from the DTE with the d1, d2, and d3 states (see Table 5-7).

The reset procedure forces the channel into a ready state, so data sequencing can begin from zero, and the flow-control packets RR and RNR can be used. Unlike the restart procedure, the reset affects only the LCN identified in the reset packets.

The reject procedure can also start a data transfer on a PVC, which has been set to out of order. The reset request packet specifies the LCN that is to be reset.

Effects of Clear, Reset, and Restart on the X.25 Interface

X.25 specifies three rules for the use of clear, reset, and restart packets. Before we examine the rules, note once again that their use may result in the loss of data and interrupt packets, and X.25 provides no convention for their recovery. Ordinarily, this recovery is done by the network administration or the transport-layer protocol at the user site. A synopsis of the rules follows. Appendix D explains them in more detail.

Table 5-7. Actions of DCE During the d1, d2, and d3 States of Data Transfer p4

Packet from the DTE with assigned LCN	State of the Interface as perceived by the DCE:	Flow Control Ready (d1)	DTE Reset Request (d2)	DCE Reset Indication (d3)
Reset Request		Normal (d2)	Discard	Normal (d1)
DTE Reset Confirmation		Error (d3) #27	Error (d3) #28	Normal (d1)
Data, Interrupt, or Flow Control		Normal (d1)	Error (d3) #28	Discard
Restart Request, DTE Restart Confirmation or Registration Request with bits 1-4 of octet 1 or bits 1-8 of octet 2 not equal to 0		Error (d3) #41	Error (d3) #41	Discard
Packet having a packet type identifier shorter than 1 octet		Error (d3) #38	Error (d3) #38	Discard
Packet having a packet type identifier which is undefined or not supported by DCE		Error (d3) #33	Error (d3) #33	Discard
Invalid packet type on a PVC		Error	Error	Discard
Reject packet not subscribed		Error	Error	Discard

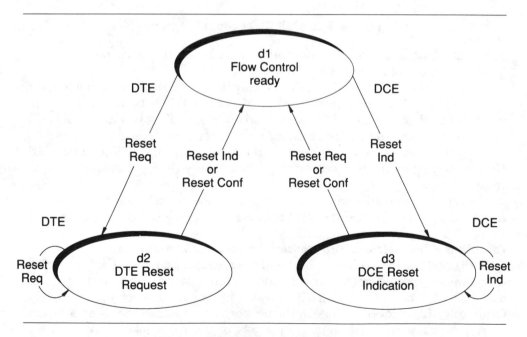

Figure 5-21. Reset State Diagram

- Data and interrupt packets generated by the local DTE (or the DCE) before its generation of a clear, reset, or restart packet will be delivered to the remote DTE before the remote DCE transmits the corresponding indication to the remote DTE, or they will be discarded by the network.

- Once the local DTE/DCE has issued a reset (or a restart for a PVC), any subsequent data or interrupt packets will not be delivered to the remote DTE until the corresponding reset procedure is complete at the remote DTE or the network discards the packets.

- Any outstanding data or interrupt packets from the remote DTE will either be delivered to the initiating DTE by the DCE before it issues a confirm, or they will be discarded by the network.

X.25 does not state how many packets can be discarded. The number is a function of individual network throughput and delay characteristics. However, if the packets are transferred with the D bit set to 1, the maximum number of packets that can be discarded is not larger than the window size in the direction of transmission.

Data-Transfer Procedures

As stated earlier, the data-transfer state (p4) includes the flow-control ready state (d1), DTE reset request state (d2), and the DCE reset indication state (d3). Table 5-7 shows the DCE's actions on receipt of specific packets while in these three states. The rules for the DTE are not as clearly defined in X.25. Also, be aware that X.25 has several tables that define the rules for other procedures as well, such as restarts, resets, call setups, and clears. X.25, Annex C, provides more information.

Flow-Control Principles

X.25 allows the DTE or DCE to limit the rate at which it accepts packets. This feature is very useful in preventing excessive traffic from arriving at the DTE or DCE. A limited-capacity user terminal or a workstation may need to use flow-control procedures.

Flow control can be established separately for each direction of transmission and is governed by the receiving DTE or DCE. As we learned earlier in this chapter, X.25 uses flow-control techniques and window concepts quite similar to HDLC, LAPB, and SDLC (which are data-link-control protocols).

A data packet combines two sequence numbers—send P(S) and receive P(R)—to coordinate packet flow between the DTE and DCE. The extended numbering scheme allows the sequence fields to contain a maximum number of 127, using modulo 128. At the DTE/DCE interface, the data packets are controlled separately for each direction based on the authorizations coming from the DTE/DCE in the form of the receive sequence P(R) numbers in the data packets, the reject packet, the receive ready packet, and the receive not ready packets.

The numbering of the packets at the packet level (third layer) proceeds the same as it does with the second-layer HDLC/LAPB standard. The packet sequence number cycles through the entire range of 0 and 7 and returns to 0 again. If modulo 128 is used, the sequence number cycles goes through the entire range of 0 to 127.

With X.25, a standard window size of 2 is recommended for each direction of flow, although other window sizes can be made available by networks. Obviously, the value of 2 limits the flow of packets outstanding at any one time. This limitation also necessitates faster acknowledgment of the packets from the receiving DTE/DCE.

When the P(R) is transmitted across the DTE/DCE interface, its value sets the lower window edge. For example, if a window of 2 exists, and a P(R) = 5 is received, the receive window becomes 6 and 7. Remember, the P(R) value indicates the *next* packet expected. Also, do not confuse the default window of 2 with the sequence number ranges of 7 or 127. Even though a DTE may have a window of 2, it still "cycles" through 1 to 7 or 1 to 127 during its packet transfer.

If the sequence number P(S) of a data packet is out of sequence, outside the prescribed receive window or not equal to zero for the first packet transmitted after entering the flow-control ready state (d1), the DTE/DCE resets the virtual call or the permanent virtual circuit.

Figure 5-22 illustrates several of the X.25 flow-control procedures (the D bit is ignored in this example for simplicity). The left-side DTE (local) has a window of 2 and the right-side DTE (remote) has a window of 3. The local DTE begins data transfer by sending two packets to its DCE. It sequences the packets with the P(S) field being set to 0 and 1 respectively in the first and second packets. X.25 requires that sequencing begin with the value 0. The P(R) fields are set to 0 to convey that the local DTE is expecting a packet with P(S) = 0 from the DCE (actually from the remote DTE). Since the window is 2 on the local side, the DTE is now flow controlled.

The remote DTE sends a packet with P(S) = 0 and P(R) = 2. When received at the local side, this opens the local DTE's window by 2, after which it sends two more packets with P(S) = 2, P(R) = 1, and P(S) = 3, P(R) = 1, respectively. The value of 1 in the P(R) field is used to acknowledge the remote DTE's packet.

The remote DTE has no more data to send at this time. Therefore, the local DCE sends the local DTE a receive ready (RR) packet with P(R) = 4. This allows the local DTE to continue sending data, even though it is not receiving any data from the remote DTE.

Networks may issue flow-control packets to ensure that the network does not become congested. In this example, the local DCE issues a receive not ready (RNR), which closes the transmit window of the local DTE, even though the DTE had a window of 1 still available in its original default window size.

Next, the remote DTE sends its second packet with P(S) = 1, P(R) = 5. At the local side, this packet serves to reopen the window of the local DTE.

Finally, the last two packets at the bottom of the figure show that the process is full duplex; both sides can send data at any time within the constraints of their

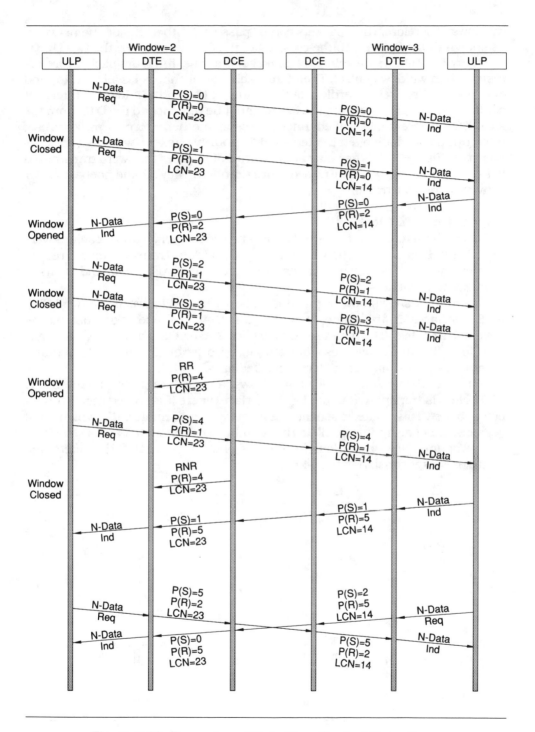

Figure 5-22. Examples of Data Flow Control Operations

windows. Therefore, their packets could "pass each other" inside the network, as shown in the figure with the crossing of the arrows between the two DCEs.

Figure 5-23 shows the interrupt packet operations. Interrupt packets are not restricted to window control. Therefore, each logical channel is allowed to send one interrupt packet, regardless of the status of its send window. An interrupt confirm packet (not shown in the figure) must be returned to the DTE from the local DCE before the logical channel can issue another interrupt packet. Also, interrupt packets are often treated as high-priority packets by the network. As shown in Figure 5-23, they may arrive ahead of packets that were transmitted before them. Since they have no sequence numbers, they should not be used for conveying regular traffic.

Segmenting and Blocking

Earlier in this chapter, the M and D bits and the category A and B packets were examined. This section shows examples of the data-transfer procedures for segmenting and blocking operations. Both procedures use the M and D bits to form A and B packets.

Figure 5-24 shows how segmentation is performed between the two DTE/DCE interfaces. In this example, we assume that local operations use packet sizes of 512 octets. The remote interface uses 256 octets. Various reasons may exist for different packet sizes. For example, because of different buffer requirements, machines may use different packet sizes.

Whatever the reason, as the figure shows, a user-data protocol data unit of 400 octets is transported to the local interface where it is placed inside a 512-octet packet. This packet is sent across a network to a remote DCE, which must segment this packet into packets that can be accommodated across the 256-octet-size interface. In so doing, it creates one full packet of 256 octets and another packet consisting of 144 octets.

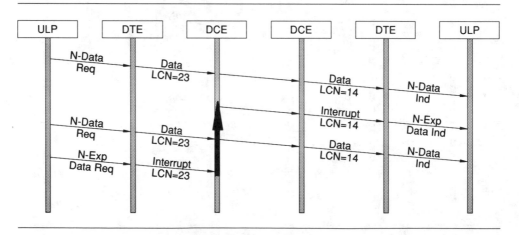

Figure 5-23. The Interrupt Packet Procedures

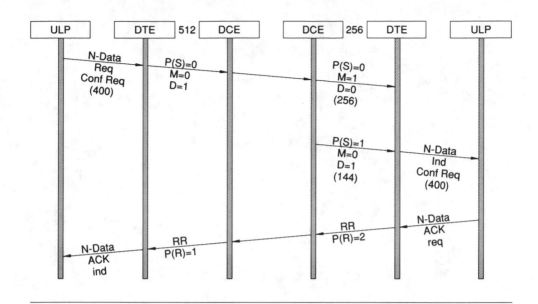

Figure 5-24. The Segmentation Procedures

Notice how the M and D bits are set at the remote interface. For the first packet, M = 1 and D = 0. These values indicate a complete packet is not within this protocol data unit. As we learned earlier in the chapter, this packet is called a category-A packet. The second packet containing 144 octets has M set to 0 and D = 1. This is a category-B packet. The effect of the D bit is to require an end-to-end confirmation. Also notice that the upper layer protocol sends the N-Data request confirmation request primitive to the local side. The effect of this primitive is to ask for an end-to-end confirmation of the traffic.

Figure 5-25 shows a blocking operation. In this situation the packet size requirements are changed. The local interface operates at 256 octets, and the remote interface operates at 512 octets. In effect, operations here are the same as the operations in Figure 5-24, but the blocking is performed at the remote side of the network cloud. As before, the primitives were invoked to request and end-to-end confirmation. These primitives were used to create the proper settings for the D bit.

Relationship of the Frame and Packet Levels

Figure 5-26 shows the relationships (and differences) between the frame level (LAPB) and the packet level. We assume users A, B, and C are in sessions with remote users. User A is assigned to logical channel number (LCN) 26, user B to LCN 33, and user C to LCN 45. The LAPB frames are sequenced with the N(S) field in the frame header, and *each* logical channel is sequenced with the packet-level P(S) field in the packet header. This feature allows users A, B, and

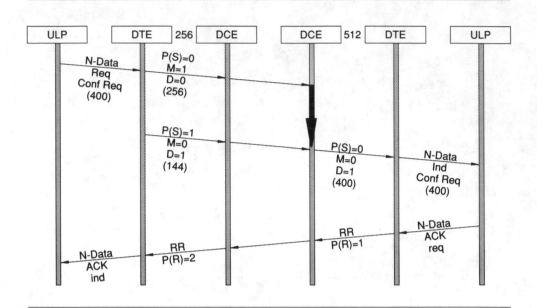

Figure 5-25. The Blocking Procedures

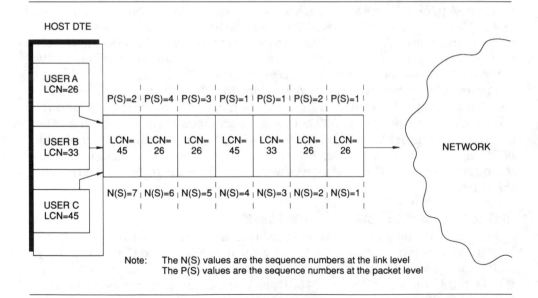

Note: The N(S) values are the sequence numbers at the link level
The P(S) values are the sequence numbers at the packet level

Figure 5-26. Relationship of the Packet and Frame Levels

C to control flow and sequence their traffic into and out of the network. For example, if user B issues a packet-level RNR on logical channel 33, it does not affect the other users on the X.25 interface.

The packet-level activity takes place without LAPB's awareness and vice versa. Of course, LAPB's actions can affect all users on the interface. For example, if LAPB issues a link-level RNR, then all logical channels are in a flow-control state.

A quick study of Figure 5-26 shows that LAPB sequencing and flow control are performed for all users on the link, and the packet-level sequencing and flow control pertain only to a specific logical channel. The relationship is as follows:

Frame Number	LCN	Packet Number
1	26	1
2	26	2
3	33	1
4	45	1
5	26	3
6	26	4
7	45	2

X.25 Addressing Conventions

In the earlier X.25 releases, X.25 did not specify the contents of the calling and called DTE address fields. Consequently, in some implementations of X.25, users have developed their own addressing conventions.

However, the 1984 and 1988 CCITT recommendations are quite specific on how the X.25 address fields are to be coded. The addressing directions say to use the following: 1) the A bit, for which several addressing schemes are stipulated; 2) the X.213 convention, in which the use of the initial domain part (IDP) and the domain-specific part (DSP) are defined; 3) and the main and complementary addresses.

Earlier in this chapter, the A-bit option was introduced. The A bit is used to identify two possible formats for the address fields:

- A = 0: The non-TOA/NPI address format is used. Address conforms to recommendations X.121 and X.301.

- A = 1: The TOA/NPI address format is used. Address conforms to the scheme depicted in Figure 5-27.

The acronym TOA stands for type of address, and NPI stands for numbering plan identification. The non-TOA/NPI format must be supported by all networks. The TOA/NPI format is optional. X.25 also provided for complementary addresses (Chapter 8, "The X.300 Internetworking Recommendations").

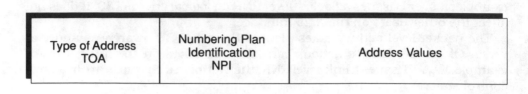

Type of Address TOA	Numbering Plan Identification NPI	Address Values

Figure 5-27. Main Address Format with A=1

Earlier in this chapter we saw that the address fields of the X.25 packet contain the called and calling DTE addresses. X.25 permits a specific network identification plan to be coded in these fields. Its conventions require an address subfield and an identification subfield to be coded at the beginning of the address field.

The address subfield contains the following information: international address, national number, network-dependent number, and reserved. The identification subfield contains the following information: use of E.163/ E.164, use of X.121, use of F.69, network-dependent number, and reserved.

X.25 and OSI Addressing Conventions

The OSI Model permits a network address to take several forms. The prevalent implementations are as follows:

- A value referred to as a subnetwork address can represent the end-user interface to a network. An example is a user-DTE calling or called address to an X.25 packet network.

- The address can be the network service access point (NSAP). Examples are the called address, calling address, and responding address parameters in the network-level N-connect primitive. Other examples are the source address and destination address in the connectionless-mode N-UNITDATA primitives.

- An address can be the address code found in the network protocol control information (N-PCI). Typically, the NSAP address is mapped into the N-PCI address code in the protocol data unit. An example is an addressing convention such as X.121 or E.164

E.163 and E.164

The CCITT E.163 Recommendation describes a numbering plan for the international telephone service, and E.164 describes the plan for ISDN. It contains the familiar dialing digits for world zones and national numbers. The E.164 plan describes a variable-length code consisting of the following fields:

- The *country code* (CC) is a variable-length code stipulated in E.163.

- The *national (significant) number* [N(S)N] is a code consisting of two other codes: the *national destination code* (NDC), a variable-length code that can be used as a network code or a trunk code as defined in E.163, and the *subscriber number* (SN), a variable-length code, coded in accordance with E.164.

X.213 (Annex A) and ISO 8348/DAD 2

ISO 7498/PDAD 3 and X.213 (Annex A) describe a hierarchy for the NSAP address, and ISO 8348/DAD 2 (Draft Addendum 2) specifies the structure for the NSAP address (see Figure 5-28). The NSAP address consists of four parts:

- *Initial domain part* (IDP) contains the authority format identifier (AFI) and the initial domain identifier (IDI).

- *Authority format identifier* (AFI) contains a two-digit value between 0 and 99 used to identify the IDI format and the syntax of the domain-specific part (DSP).

- *Initial domain identifier* (IDI) specifies the addressing domain and the network addressing authority.

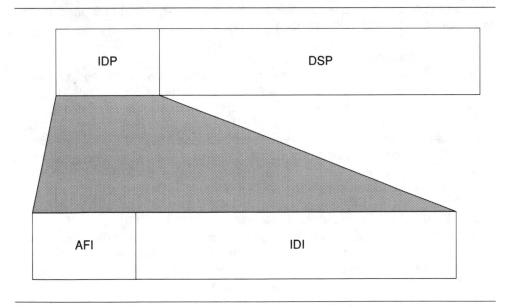

Figure 5-28. NSAP Addressing Structure

- *Domain-specific part* (DSP) contains the address determined by the network authority, an address below the second level of the addressing hierarchy. It can contain addresses of user end systems on an individual subnetwork.

International Numbering Plan for Data Networks (X.121)

CCITT publishes and administers the X.121 Recommendation used in almost all countries to identify the public data networks, and in some instances, private data networks. Many X.25-based networks use the X.121 scheme. The X.121 plan is based on a four-digit data network identification code (DNIC) with the following format:

- DCCN   Where DCC is a three-digit data country code and N is the network digit to identify a specific network within a country

The first digit of the DNIC must not be a 1 (which is reserved). Additionally, the first digit value of 8 indicates the digits that follow are from the F.69 Telex numbering plan; a value of 9 or 0 indicates that the digits that follow are from the E.164 and E.163 ISDN numbering plans, respectively. The 0, 8, and 9 values are called escape codes, and allow the stations to stipulate that additional conventions are to be used.

Some countries have more than 10 networks. In this situation, multiple DCCs are assigned to the country. For example, the United States is assigned the DCC values of 310 through 316.

X.121 also defines a network terminal number (NTN). This value identifies the computer, terminal, etc., within the network. It consists of a 10-digit identifier. Optionally, the NTN can be included as part of the terminal identifier. In this situation, the 11-digit field is called a national number (NN).

X.223 and X.25 Addressing

X.223 (Appendix II) provides further guidance on how NSAP addresses are encoded into the X.25 address fields. As a general rule, X.25 and X.223 rely on the AFI and the IDI for the NSAP value and the subnetwork point of attachment. If this is the case, and if the AFI is agreeable to the network provider, the IDI value can be used directly in the address field, and conveying the AFI is not necessary. If the AFI is not consistent with the network provider's addressing scheme, some type of directory look up is needed for further address resolution. If the DSP is present, it must be coded into the address extension field.

Are X.25 Addresses Sufficient for Internal Network Routing?

Note again that X.25 data packets do not contain the DTE called and calling addresses. Consequently, a network administration must determine how to route the X.25 packets through the network with only the LCNs available as identifiers. This section discusses some solutions.

If the network uses a session-oriented, nonadaptive routing technique, the X.25 call setup packets can be used to "map" the call through the network. The local DCE can receive the packet from an identified line, and use the LCN and line number as a look-up index into the mapping table. The table reveals the called address (that was stored during call setup), and the local DCE makes a routing decision.

However, the local LCN may not be unique within the network, because other DCEs may be using the same values for their LCNs. The network must distinguish these packets as they traverse through the network cloud. One solution is to assign a clearly distinguishable and unambiguous identifier to the packet. The identifier is then used at the packet nodes to determine how to route the packet.

A dynamic routing network has the same problem and similar identifiers are needed. In many instances, the internet protocol (IP) addresses are used to identify uniquely the IP datagrams (and therefore the X.25 packets in the datagram). The IP is a widely used connectionless network protocol designed for adaptive routing through packet switches and gateways. Its header contains unique source and destination addresses to determine the packet route.

If an IP-type approach is not used, the network must either append a destination identifier, or keep the packet session on a fixed path within the network and make certain the logical channel numbers are allocated to identify uniquely each session within the network. The latter choice may not a very good, since the X.25 Recommendation allows each DTE and DCE to choose their logical channels at each DTE/DCE interface.

Examples of X.25 Layers and Protocol Data Units

Figure 5-29 illustrates the relationship of the X.25 layers and the protocol data units. Starting from the bottom of the figure, we assume user data are to be sent from a user computer (DTE) through a packet network to a remote destination. The user data are passed from the upper layer protocols to the X.25 network layer. Here the packet header is created, and several of the operations described in this chapter are performed. The packet and the user data are passed to the data-link layer, which encapsulates the packet into the frame. The frame is then passed to the physical layer, across an interface such as EIA-232-D or V.32, to the modem or digital service unit, and onto the communications link.

If the DTE is near the packet exchange (a few hundred feet away, for example), modems, DSUs, or the communications link would not be necessary. Instead, the DTE could be connected directly to the packet exchange with an EIA-232-D interface, or practically any other physical-level convention chosen by the DTE and DCE manufacturers.

The frame is received at the packet exchange. It passes through the physical, data-link, and network layers of X.25. The network performs its requisite X.25 functions and passes the packet to the vendor's proprietary network management software. which contains the routing logic to relay the packet to the next node in the network.

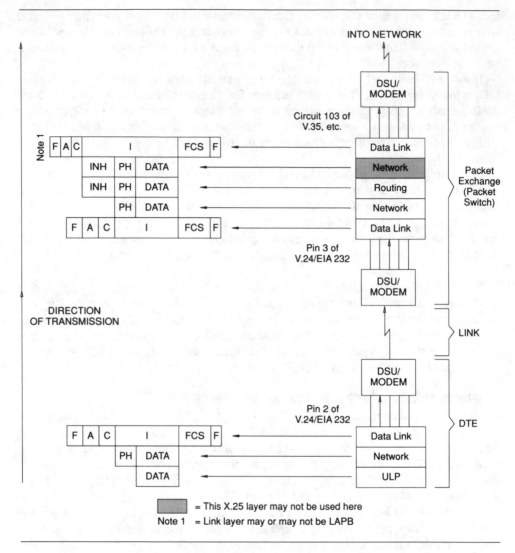

Figure 5-29. X.25 Layers and Protocol Data Units

Typically, the network adds its own internal network header (INH) to the packet. Notice that the X.25 packet header is not disturbed, but is encapsulated with the user data into the internal network protocol data unit. Also notice the shaded X.25 network layer on the outbound side of the DCE. This layer may not be invoked if the internal network does not use X.25. In fact, most networks do not use X.25 internally.

The packet is then routed to the final destination, where it goes through a process the reverse of that depicted in Figure 5-29. To imagine this process, reverse the arrows in the figure.

Figure 5-30 is another view of the process. The internal network has been drawn around the layers and protocol data units not in the X.25 specification. Even though the figure shows the X.25 network and data-link layers inside the network cloud on the outbound side of the packet switch, they need not reside there. Sometimes the LAPB frame is not used inside the network. Some vendors place the X.25 packet and the INH inside other link protocols such as SDLC.

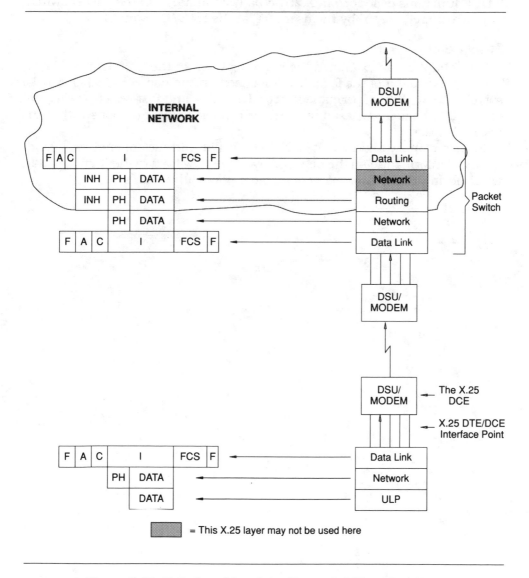

Figure 5-30. Relationship of the Network "Cloud" to X.25

Several offerings multiplex the packets into a T1 carrier frame. As we shall see later, some offerings carry the X.25 packet on an ISDN basic rate interface channel.

Also, the notation in Figure 5-30 "X.25 DTE/DCE Interface Point" shows where X.25 considers the X.25 interface to reside. This view reflects the CCITT idea of providing a complete service to the user DTE, including the modems/ DSUs and communications link. The X.25 DCE functions do not emanate at notations in the figure titled "The X.25 DCE." Almost all the layer 2 and layer 3 DCE functions described in X.25 actually emanate from the packet switch. They are merely "seen" by the user DTE at the DTE/DCE interface.

Conclusions

This chapter has examined the major features of the X.25 network layer, with the exception of the facilities. It focused on the use of logical channels, switched virtual calls, permanent virtual circuits, and fast select. The format of the X.25 packet was examined, as well as the fields' functions within the packet header.

Supplementary information on X.25 is available in the appendixes, including more information on the network layer. We now turn to the X.25 facilities, which form the basis for many of its more powerful features.

X.25 Facilities

Goals of Chapter 6

The X.25 Recommendation is rather terse in its explanation of the X.25 facilities. It provides unambiguous rules on how they are used, but does not provide much information on how they can be used to support the network user. Therefore, our goal in this chapter is to explain how the X.25 facilities operate and provide the reader with ideas on how they may be implemented to enhance a user session.

To meet this goal, we examine each of the facilities and give some examples of how they are used in public and private networks. The first part of the chapter explains each facility, and the last part shows how they are coded in the X.25 packet.

The reader should refer to Table 7-1 (in Chapter 7) for a list of the X.2 facilities that pertain to packet-switched data networks. Readers unfamiliar with the concept of facilities will find reviewing this table useful before delving into this chapter. It might also prove useful for reviewing a vendor's product, because a number of vendors publish this table and indicate whether they are "compliant" with the recommended standard.

Introduction

The 1988 release of X.25 provides many service features called *facilities*. Some are not required for a vendor to pass a conformance test, yet they provide some very useful functions to end users. Some are considered essential to a network. The facilities allow a user to "tailor" somewhat how the network supports the user session. They also provide some very powerful and useful services for the packet network user and supplier.

Some facilities are requested by the facility field in the call request packet; X.25 requires the user to identify others at subscription time. They are then invoked by coding values in the facilities field of a call request packet. Some facilities can be dynamically allocated.

The facilities are classified as follows:
- International facilities (in Recommendation X.2)
- CCITT-specified DTE facilities
- Facilities offered by the originating public data network (PDN)
- Facilities offered by destination PDN

For continuity in our discussions, we must examine some X.25 conventions that do not fit into the category of a facility. For example, use of the D bit may or may not entail the use of one facility, but it is simpler to discuss these issues in one chapter rather than to separate them into different parts of the book.

To supplement our brief description of each facility specified in X.25, the reader should consult Section 7 of the X.25 Recommendation. However, this chapter is a good introduction, and serves as a tutorial and a reference guide.

Call Restriction Facilities

Incoming Calls Barred/Outgoing Calls Barred

The incoming calls barred/outgoing calls barred facilities prevent incoming calls from being presented to the DTE and prevent the DCE from accepting outgoing calls from the DTE. Both facilities apply to all logical channels at the DTE/DCE interface and cannot be changed on a per-call basis. A DTE subscribing to incoming calls barred can initiate calls but cannot accept them. A DTE subscribing to outgoing calls barred can receive calls but cannot initiate them. Once the call is established, the session operates at full duplex.

Some network administrations use the calls barred facility to restrict DTE access to the network on the basis of the permitted protocol-to-protocol agreement between DTEs. This technique, called protocol screening, is enforced by the DCE or the PAD. If the permitted protocols for either user do not include the protocol of the other, the call is cleared by using the calls barred facility.

One-Way Logical Channel Outgoing/
One-Way Logical Channel Incoming

The one-way logical channel outgoing/one-way logical channel incoming facilities restrict a logical channel to originating calls only or receiving calls only. They are set when the user subscribes to the network and cannot be changed on a per-call basis. These facilities provide more specific control than the calls barred facilities, because they operate on a specific channel or channels.

The facilities are useful in reserving a group of logical channels at the DTE/DCE interface. They help place a limit on the number of X.25 calls that can be made. For example, a time-sharing computer might keep some channels designated as incoming only for the customers that call in to use the facility. The idea is similar to a telephone-based PBX (private branch exchange) that restricts certain telephone lines to incoming or outgoing calls only.

Note the following relationships:

- A situation where all virtual calls are one-way outgoing is equivalent to the incoming calls barred facility.

- A situation where all virtual calls are one-way incoming is equivalent to the outgoing calls barred facility.

Closed User Groups (CUG)

The closed user groups facilities allow users to form groups of DTEs to which access is restricted, for security and privacy in an "open" network. Some people call this feature a virtual private network. The CUG facilities are established for a period of time, although a DTE that has subscribed to the facility can call other CUGs on a per-call basis. A DTE can belong to a variable number of CUGs; the limit depends on the network.

The facilities that make up this set are summarized here and then followed with more specific rules and examples:

- *Closed user group:* This facility allows a DTE to belong to one or more closed user groups. It is established for a period of time. When a DTE belongs to more than one CUG, a preferential closed user group must be specified.

- *Incoming calls barred within a CUG:* A DTE may initiate calls to other members of the CUG but cannot receive calls from them. This facility is equivalent to establishing all logical channels as one-way outgoing (originate only).

- *Outgoing calls barred within a CUG:* A DTE may receive calls from other members of the CUG but cannot initiate calls to them. This facility is equivalent to establishing all logical channels as one-way incoming (terminate only).

- *CUG with incoming access:* A DTE will receive calls from DTEs belonging to the open (non-CUG) part of the network, and from DTEs that are members of other CUGs with outgoing access.

- *CUG with outgoing access:* A DTE may initiate calls to all DTEs in the open part of the network, and to DTEs that are members of other CUGs with incoming access. If the DTE has a preferential CUG, then only the facility for closed user group selection can be used at the DTE/DCE interface (this facility is explained next).

- *Closed user group selection:* This facility may be used by the DTE in a call request to specify the closed user group for the call. It can be used if the DTE has subscribed previously to the closed user group facility, the closed user group with outgoing access facility, or the closed user group with incoming access facility. That is to say, it cannot be requested in a call setup, unless one of these facilities has been assigned for a contractual period.

- *Closed user group with outgoing access selection:* This facility allows the DTE to specify in the call request packet the closed user group for the virtual call. Obviously, it also indicates that outgoing access is desired. The called DTE receives the incoming call packet with the identification of the closed user group. The packet also indicates that outgoing access is applied at the calling DTE.

Bilateral Closed User Groups (BCUG)

The bilateral closed user groups facilities are similar to the other CUGs, but they allow access restrictions between pairs of DTEs, and exclude access to or from other DTEs. The idea is to support bilateral relationships between two DTEs, and to allow access between them, while excluding access to and from other DTEs. Three facilities are available:

- The *bilateral closed user group* facility allows a DTE to belong to more than one BCUG.

- The *bilateral closed user group with outgoing access* facility allows the DTE to belong to one or more BCUGs, and to originate calls into the open part of the network.

- The *bilateral closed user group selection* facility is used by the calling DTE in the call request to identify the BCUG for the virtual call.

Permissible Combinations of Closed User Group Facilities

At first glance, the facilities for permissible combinations of closed user groups can be somewhat confusing. In some instances, they cannot be used with each other, because they are logically inconsistent. In other cases, they are redundant. Table 6-1 identifies the inconsistent or redundant facilities. Tables 6-2 and 6-3 show how to interpret the closed user group facilities in the call request and incoming call packets.

Table 6-1. Inconsistent and Redundant Pairings of X.25 Options

X.25 Option	Pairing is Inconsistent (I) or Redundant (R)
Two-Way Logical Channels	Outgoing Calls Barred = I Incoming Calls Barred = I
Closed User Group	Closed User Group with Incoming Access = I Closed User Group with Outgoing Access = I
One-Way Outgoing Logical Channel	Outgoing Calls Barred = I Incoming Calls Barred = R
Incoming Calls Barred	One-Way Incoming Logical Channel = I Reverse Charging Acceptance = I Closed User Group with Incoming Access = I Hunt Group = I Fast Select Acceptance = I Outgoing Calls Barred = I
Outgoing Calls Barred	One-Way Incoming Logical Channel = R Closed User Group with Outgoing Access = I
Reverse Charging Acceptance	Local Charging Prevention = I

Table 6-2. Meaning of Closed User Group Facilities in Call Request Packets

Contents of *call request* packet / Closed user group subscription of the called DTE	*Closed user group selection* facility	*Closed user group with outgoing access selection* facility	Neither *closed user group selection* nor *closed user group with outgoing access selection* facility
CUG with preferential	CUG specified		Preferential or only CUG
CUG/IA with preferential	CUG specified		Preferential or only CUG
CUG/OA with preferential outgoing access	CUG specified + outgoing access	Not allowed (call cleared)	Preferential or only CUG + outgoing access
CUG/IA/OA with preferential	CUG specified + outgoing access	Not allowed (call cleared)	Preferential or only CUG + outgoing access
CUG/IA without preferential	CUG specified	Not allowed (call cleared)	Not allowed (call cleared)
CUG/OA without preferential	CUG specified	CUG specified + outgoing access	Outgoing access
CUG/IA/OA without preferential	CUG specified	CUG specified + outgoing access	Outgoing access
No CUG	Not allowed (call cleared)	Not allowed (call cleared)	

Table 6-3. Meaning of Closed User Group Facilities in Incoming Call Packets

Contents of *call request* packet / Closed user group subscription of the called DTE	*Closed user group selection* facility	*Closed user group with outgoing access selection* facility	Neither *closed user group selection* nor *closed user group with outgoing access selection* facility
CUG with preferential	CUG specified		Preferential or only CUG
CUG/IA with preferential	CUG specified		Preferential or only CUG
CUG/OA with preferential	CUG specified + incoming access	Not applicable	Preferential or only CUG + incoming access
CUG/IA/OA with preferential	CUG specified + incoming access	Not applicable	Preferential or only CUG + incoming access
CUG/OA without preferential	CUG specified	Not applicable	Not applicable
CUG/IA without preferential	CUG specified	CUG specified + incoming access	Incoming access
CUG/IA/OA without preferential	CUG specified	CUG specified + incoming access	Incoming access
No CUG	Not applicable	Not applicable	

Charging-Related Facilities
Reverse Charging and Reverse Charging Acceptance

The facilities for reverse charging and reverse charging acceptance allow the packet network charges to accrue to a receiving DTE. They can be used with virtual calls and fast selects and are like "calling collect" on a telephone. Although these facilities have a close association, they need not be used together.

The reverse charging facility asks the remote DTE to pay for the call. It is requested by the calling DTE on a per-call basis. The reverse charging acceptance facility authorizes the remote DCE to pass to the DTE the incoming calls that request the reverse charging. Otherwise, the DCE will not pass the calls, and the originating DTE will receive a clear indication packet.

Some networks keep records in their accounting/customer database on attempts to use the user-data field in an unsuccessful reverse-charge call. The network then charges the user for this call to discourage the free one-way transmission of data.

The reverse charging facilities are quite useful for organizations that wish to simplify their accounting procedures. For example, the reverse charge can be used to accrue charges to one account. Additionally, some service organizations use this facility to mask their customers' network charges by having the customers' connection and usage charges billed to the service organization.

Local Charging Prevention

This facility for local charging prevention authorizes the DCE to prevent the establishment of calls for which the subscribing DTE would ordinarily pay. The DCE can prevent the calls from taking place by not passing them to the DTE. The DCE may also charge another party (e.g., identify the third party by the NUI facility).

This facility is often implemented to force all calls from public telephone dial-up ports to use reverse charging, since the originators of dial-up connections are very difficult to identify. The approach greatly facilitates charging for the connection.

X.25 requires reverse charging to be enforced if the call request packet has not identified the charged party. The remote DCE will insert the facility code into the incoming call packet.

Network User Identification (NUI)

The network user identification facilities enable the DTE to provide billing, security, or management information to the DCE on a per-call basis. They can also invoke subscribed facilities or a different set of subscribed facilities with each call, so the user can tailor the X.25 facilities to the specific call. If invalid, the call is cleared. The three facilities are grouped under NUI and are described in this section.

Network user identifiers associate a set of facilities with an identifier. Each network user identifier can be associated with a different set of facilities. The identifier is transmitted to the DCE by the DTE; it is never transmitted to the remote DTE. Furthermore, the calling address in the packet is independent of the network user identifier, and its value should not be inferred from this value.

The *NUI subscription* facility is established for a period of time. It allows the DTE to furnish the network information on billing, security, or management. The information is contained in either the call request packet or the call accepted packet by using the NUI selection facility. It may be used regardless of any subscription to the local charging prevention facility.

The *NUI override* facility is established for a period of time and then used on a per-call basis by the NUI selection facility to override the subscription-time facilities. The override pertains only to the specific call. X.25 places restrictions on which subscription-time facilities may be associated with the NUI and the NUI override facilities. The following facilities may be associated with the override (all others are not allowed):

Nonstandard default packet sizes
Nonstandard default window sizes
Default throughput classes assignment
Flow-control parameter negotiation (subscription time)
Throughput class negotiation (subscription time)
Closed user group (CUG)
CUG with outgoing access
Bilateral closed user group (BCUG)
BCUG with outgoing access
Charging information (subscription time)
RPOA selection

The *NUI selection* facility is requested by the DTE for a given call, if it has subscribed to one or both of the other NUI facilities. The facility permits the DTE to identify which network user identifier is to be used with the other two NUI facilities.

Networks have many uses for the NUI facilities. For example, the NUI can identify a network user, independent of the port being used, so a dial-up port can be used without requiring a reverse charge call. Some vendors' products use NUI to prevent calls into specific ports; for example, a particular port may not be made available unless the DTE furnishes a valid NUI. Some networks also use the NUI to check against its accounting/customer database to determine the billing address for the call.

Charging Information

The charging information facility requires the DCE to provide the charged DTE information about the packet session relating to the charges. The facility can be invoked on a per-call basis or as a subscription for a period of time. If the latter option is in effect, the DTE to be charged does not have to ask for the charging information in the call request or call accepted packet.

Quality-of-Service Facilities
Nonstandard Default Packet Sizes

The nonstandard default packet sizes facility provides for the selection of nonstandard default packet sizes for an agreed time. The default size is 128 octets of user data. The size can be different for each direction of dataflow. Some networks that allow different priority levels will also allow different packet sizes for different priority calls.

Some vendors use different packet-size options for the DTE/DCE, DTE/PAD, and STE/STE interfaces (X.75 gateway interfaces). The default sizes for each interface should be checked against the charges for a transmitted packet.

Moreover, the choice of a packet size must be weighed against the requirement for larger buffers at all the machines that process the packet. Larger packet sizes reduce the opportunity for other users to share the channel, and in the event of an error, more data must be retransmitted. On the other hand, a larger packet reduces the ratio of overhead fields to user data. These factors may not matter, since most networks provide either the default size of 128 octets or an optional size of 256 octets.

Another consideration is the use of different packet sizes at each end of the DTE-DTE connection. Figure 6-1(a) shows that the DTE/DCE interface at A supports a packet size of 256 octets, and the DTE/DCE interface at B supports a size of 128 octets. The buffering is probably not a big problem, but what about the sequence numbers? The 256-octet packet is transported from interface A through the network to interface B. Here the packet must be segmented into the smaller 128-octet packets.

Since each packet is sequenced with the $P(S)$ field, the larger packet at interface A with $P(S) = 3$ is "mapped" into $P(S) = 3$ and $P(S) = 4$ in the two smaller packets at interface B. The local DCE and remote DTE have little problem with this procedure. They simply return the corresponding $P(R)$ values of 4 and 5 to acknowledge the two packets (as in Figure 6-1(a)).

However, if the D bit is set to 1, the network is instructed to pass the packet to the remote DTE for an end-to-end acknowledgment. (The D bit is discussed in more detail later in this chapter.) The network must remember that packets at the remote interface numbered 3 and 4 in the $P(S)$ fields must be mapped back to the local interface with a sequence number of 4 to keep the sequencing in order at the local interface (as in Figure 6.1(b)). These tasks can certainly be written into some "bookkeeping" software, but the overhead in providing the service constrains most networks to allow only one different packet size in each direction of transmission. If different-size data units are needed, the transport layer, or an intermediate gateway between networks, can provide the service.

Nonstandard Default Window Sizes

The nonstandard default window sizes facility allows the window sizes to be expanded beyond the default size of 2, for all calls on the interface for an agreed period of time. Window sizes can be different at each end of the connection, and some networks constrain the default window size to be the same for each

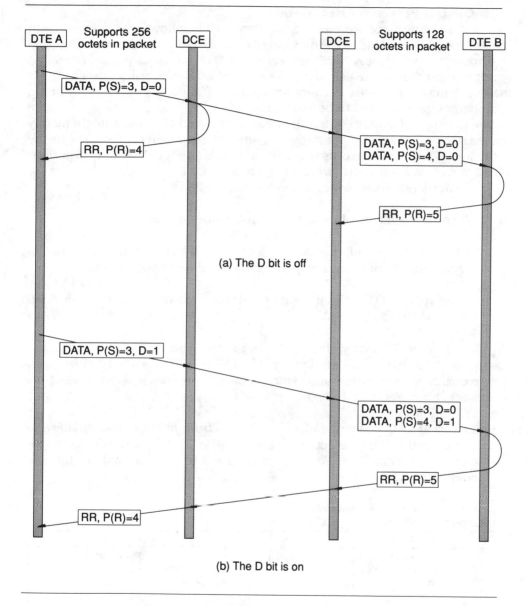

Figure 6-1. Different Packet Sizes

direction of transmission across the DTE/DCE interface.

The DCE may change the DTE/DCE packet window size according to the negotiated packet size and throughput class (discussed shortly). Such an action allows the network to control the buffer requirements in the packet switches.

Flow-Control Parameter Negotiation

The flow-control parameter negotiation facility allows the window and packet sizes P(R) and P(S) to be negotiated on a *per-call* basis for each direction of transmission. In many X.25 networks, the DTE suggests packet sizes and window sizes during the call setup. The called DTE (if it subscribes to these facilities) may reply with a counterproposal. If it does not, the call setup parameters are assumed to be acceptable.

The network DCE may control the window and packet sizes. It might modify the parameters from the sending DTE and present different values to the receiving DTE. Some networks require that the negotiated flow-control parameters be the same for each direction of transmission.

X.25 stipulates the following rules for this facility:

- When the facility is absent, the default values are used.

- The values in the call request packet may be different from the values in the incoming call packet (e.g., the network may change them).

- At the remote DTE, the incoming call packet contains the values from which negotiation can start.

- The remote DTE may change the negotiated values in its call accepted packet within the bounds depicted in Table 6-4. If it does not counter with a facility request in its call accepted packet, the values in the incoming call packet are assumed to be acceptable.

- The local DCE (because of network constraints) may also modify the values in the call connected packet to the local DTE within the bounds depicted in Table 6-5. The DCE is required to place a value in the call connected packet.

Table 6-4. Valid Facility Requests: A Call Accepted Packet in Response to the Incoming Call Packet

Facility indication	Valid facility request
W(indicated)>=2 W(indicated)=1	W(indicated)>=W(requested)>=2 W(requested)=1 or 2
P(indicated)>=128 P(indicated)<128	P(indicated>=P(requested)>=128 128>=P(requested)>=P(indicated)

Table 6-5. Valid Facility Requests: A Call Connected Packet in Response to the Call Request Packet

Facility indication	Valid facility request
W(requested)>=2 W(requested)=1	W(requested)>=W(indicated)>=2 W(indicated)=1 or 2
P(requested)>=128 P(requested)<128	P(requested>=P(indicated))>=128 128>=P(indicated)>=P(requested)

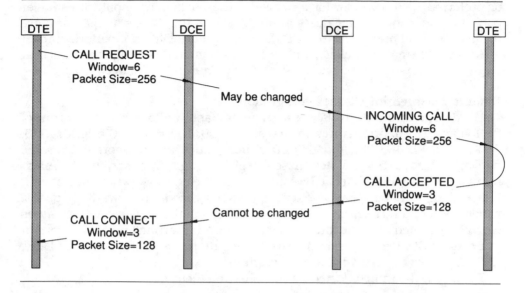

Figure 6-2. Negotiating Facilities

Figure 6-2 shows one example of how the facility operates. DTE A has requested a window size of 6 and a packet size of 256 octets. The packet is transported to the remote DCE and an incoming call packet is sent to the DTE with the same values in the fields. This DTE attempts to negotiate the window size to 3 and the packet size to 128 octets. It places these values in the call accepted packet, which is relayed through the network to the local DTE that originated the call request. The local DCE sends a call connected packet to the DTE.

In this example, the network did not alter the values negotiated between the two DTEs. However, it does have this option. Also, the rules of X.25 require that the negotiation move toward the standard default values of 2 for window size and 128 for packet size.

In summary, window and packet sizes are negotiated on the basis of the following:

- Initial default values

- Values in the call request packet

- Values in the call accepted packet

- Any changes made by the network

A word of caution before leaving this topic. Some X.25 vendors accept a variety of packet sizes from the DTE. If the packets are larger than permitted or preferred by the vendor (or a network), the packets are split into smaller packets and sent to the destination DTE. At the DTE's DCE, they are recombined and presented to the DTE. Some products do not perform packet splitting (into smaller packets) and recombination. In this situation, a call that requests an unsupported packet size will be cleared by the network.

Default Throughput Classes Assignment

The default throughput classes assignment facility allows selection of one of the following throughput rates (in bits/s): 75, 150, 300, 600, 1200, 2400, 4800, 9600, 19,200, 48,000, and 64,000 (other values are supported by some networks, but X.25 stipulates these rates). Throughput describes the maximum amount of data that can be sent through the network, when the network is operating at saturation. Factors influencing throughput are line speeds, window sizes, and the number of active sessions in the network. Other values can be negotiated with the throughput class negotiation facility. Also, throughput class indicates the desired bit-transfer rate between the DTE and DCE. Default values are specified at subscription time.

Throughput can be affected by the following factors:

* Characteristics of the local and remote DTE/DCE interfaces

* Characteristics of the internals of the network (i.e., throughput through the network "cloud")

* Whether the DTEs issue flow-control packets to the network

* Sending data packets of less than the maximum length

* Use of the D bit; if the D bit = 1, throughput is significantly affected by the remote DTE's ability to "turn around" traffic

* Window size

Throughput Class Negotiation

The throughput class negotiation facility allows the throughput rates to be negotiated on a *per-call* basis. A throughput greater than a DTE's default value is not allowed. The allowable rates that can be negotiated are 75, 150, 300, 600, 1200, 2400, 4800, 9600, 19,200, 48,000, and 64,000 bits/s, although many vendors support higher speeds.

If a throughput class is not accepted, the call need not be cleared or blocked. The DCE can lower the requested throughput to the subscribed value.

Negotiation of the throughput class is performed during call setup with the call request, incoming call, call accepted, and call connected packets. The facility is subject to the following rules:

- Throughput classes can be applied independently for each direction or in both directions.

- The calling DTE begins the process by placing the value in its call request packet. The receiving DTE can negotiate at the same rate or a lower rate. It cannot negotiate upward.

Two factors should be considered when using the negotiable services offered by the throughput class facility and flow-control parameter facility, both of which can be used for a single call. First, choosing small window and packet sizes may affect the throughput. Second, using the D bit may also affect throughput.

Transit Delay Selection and Indication

The transit delay selection and indication facility permits a DTE to select a transit delay time through the packet network. This valuable feature gives an end user some control over response time in the network. It is established on a per-call basis. The network must inform both DTEs about the transit delay applied to the call by the incoming call packet to the called DTE, and the call connected packet to the calling DTE. This time may be equal to, greater than, or smaller than the value in the call request packet.

Reliability, Windows, and Acknowledgment Facilities

D-Bit Modification

In the 1970s, some networks implemented procedures that provided a packet acknowledgment to the originating DCE from the receiving DCE. In turn, several of these networks then sent this acknowledgment to the originating DTE. This feature is known as internal network acknowledgment, because the network is responsible for acknowledgment within the network (between the originating and receiving DCEs).

In the 1980 release, a feature was added to X.25 called the D-bit (delivery bit) service. As explained in the introductory section, the D bit set to 1 by the DTE instructs the DCE (the network) to pass the packet to the remote destination DTE and not to acknowledge it. The remote DTE examines the D bit value of 1 and responds with an acknowledgment, which is relayed through the network to the originating DTE. In this manner, X.25 provides end-to-end (DTE-to-DTE) acknowledgment, but this is almost redundant in networks that provide DCE-to-DCE acknowledgment.

The D-bit modification facility is intended for DTEs operating on networks that support end-to-end acknowledgment procedures developed before the 1980 D-bit procedure was introduced. It allows these DTEs to continue to obtain this service *within* the network. This means the P(R) value in the packet has end-to-end significance within the network. The facility applies to all virtual calls and permanent virtual circuits at the DTE/DCE interface.

The facility accepts call request, call accepted, and data packets from the DTE, and changes bit 7 of the GFI from 0 to 1 (see Figure 6-3). For the incoming call,

call connected, and data packets transmitted to the DTE, bit 7 of the GFI is set from 1 to 0. Thus end-to-end significance is obtained within the network.

Using the D Bit during Call Establishment
(Exclusive of the D-Bit Modification Facility)

The D-bit modification facility does not preclude use of the D bit to obtain end-to-end acknowledgment between the DTEs. X.25 permits the calling DTE to set the D bit to 1 in a call request packet to determine if the called DTE will accept a D-bit procedure. This bit is not acted upon by the network, but is passed transparently to the called DTE. This DTE can return a call accepted packet with D = 1 to indicate that it can handle the D-bit confirmation. It passes D = 0 if it cannot handle the procedure.

When the D bit is set to 0 in a data packet, the local DCE is responsible for returning a P(R) value to the DTE in an RR, RNR, reject, or data packet.

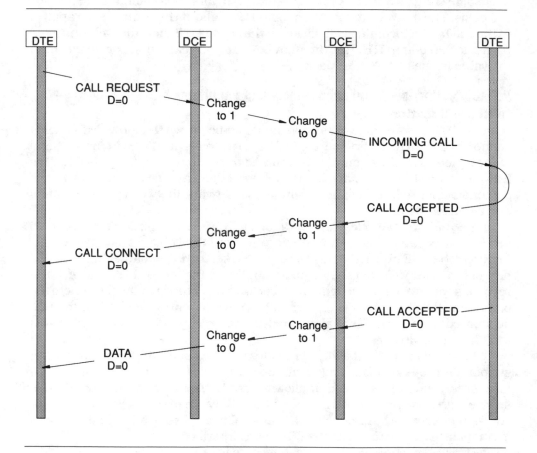

Figure 6-3. D Bit Modification

Therefore, the packet window of the DTE is updated locally. This acknowledgment does not signify any remote acknowledgment.

When the D bit is set to 1 in a data packet, the returned P(R) value indicates that the remote DTE has received a packet. It also indicates that all data bits in a packet have been received in which the D bit had originally been set to 1. Consequently, if the network segments a packet after it leaves the originating DTE, the D bit still confirms the original contents of the packet.

At first, the D-bit procedure seems desirable for all data transmissions. After all, it would guarantee that the data arrived safely at the destination. This contention has merit, but note that the D = 1 means the local DTE must rely on the remote DTE to keep its transmit window open. Since X.25 defaults to a packet window of 2, the remote DTE should be programmed to react to D = 1 quickly, or the local DTE must stop sending packets. Likewise, the local and remote DCEs should be programmed to handle D = 1 packets with minimum delay. Transit delay within the network must also be considered, since this delay may also reduce the number of packets that can be transmitted with D = 1. The problem is certainly alleviated if the DTE negotiates a larger packet-window size, assuming the network and the remote DTE accept larger windows.

Also, the D = 1 may be unnecessary if an upper layer protocol provides end-to-end acknowledgment. For example, protocols that implement the CCITT transport layer (Class 4) provide this service, and the widely used transmission control protocol (TCP) also performs end-to-end acknowledgment.

Figure 6-4 illustrates how the D-bit procedure operates. Notice the effect of the use of D = 1 and D = 0. If a DTE issues packets with D = 1, and then issues packets with D = 0, its local window may not be updated by the local DCE until the remote DCE acknowledges the D = 1 packet. This procedure might reduce throughput, but it could also be used to perform a periodic "checkpoint" with the remote DTE. In other words, the DTE could periodically issue a packet with D = 1 to determine whether all is well at the other side of the cloud.

Packet Retransmission

The packet retransmission facility applies to all logical channels at the DTE/DCE interface. A DTE (but not the DCE) may request retransmission of one to several data packets. The DTE specifies the logical channel number and a value for P(R) in a reject packet. The DCE must then retransmit all packets from P(R) to the next packet it is to transmit for the first time. This facility is similar to the go-back-N technique used by the line protocols at the data-link level (LAPB's reject), except it pertains to the packet level (network level).

The reject facility is not implemented by many networks, because the link level is tasked with error detection and data retransmission. Moreover, X.25 has other conventions for rejecting packets, such as resets.

Extended Packet Numbering

The extended packet numbering facility provides packet sequence numbering using modulo 128 (sequence numbers 0-127) for all channels at the DTE/

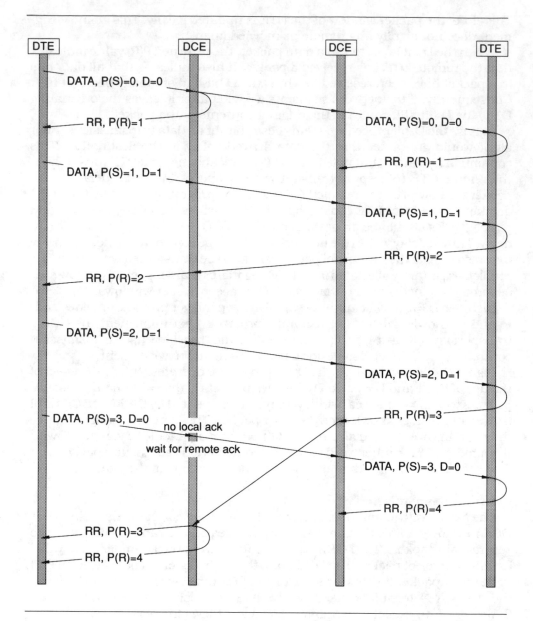

Figure 6-4. D Bit, Exclusive of D Bit Modification Facility

DCE interface. In its absence, sequencing is done with modulo 8 (sequence numbers 0-7). Bits 5 and 6 in the general format identifier (GFI) field are used to request this service (see Chapter 5 for the GFI field).

This 1984 addition was needed to deal with the long propagation time of signals on satellite channels and on other media that have a very high bit-transfer rate, such as optical fiber. In these situations, the sequence numbers P(S) of 0 through 7 are exhausted by the transmitting station before the receiving station has an opportunity to acknowledge the packets.

X.25 does not allow a sequence number to be reused until the first number is acknowledged. In other words, a DTE cannot send a packet with P(S) = 3 if a preceding packet has used this value and is not yet acknowledged. A limited range of sequence numbers might require the DTE or DCE to "shut down" the sending of packets on the channel. As a consequence, the virtual circuit is forced into an idle condition. The extended packet numbering facility simply extends the range of sequence numbers available, allowing the channel to be used more fully. Many networks use the facility for flow control; it places a limit on the number of packets that can be presented to the network.

Call Destination Management Facilities
Hunt Group

The hunt group facility distributes incoming calls across a designated grouping of DTE/DCE interfaces. This 1984 addition lets users allocate multiple ports on a front-end processor or computer. It allows the selection of different front ends or computers at a user site for the X.25 traffic. These multiple ports are managed by the DCE, which is responsible for distributing the calls across them. How they are distributed is not within the purview of X.25.

This facility allows organizations with large computing facilities to direct jobs to different resources. It is similar in concept to the familiar port selector found in most installations.

X.25 specifies that the selection is performed for an incoming call if at least one logical channel is available. This excludes one-way outgoing logical channels. A DTE that is on a DTE/DCE interface belonging to a hunt group originates calls in the normal manner. The calling DTE address in the incoming call packet sent to the remote DTE contains the hunt group address unless other provisions are made, such as the assignment of a specific DTE/DCE address. Permanent virtual circuits may be on the DTE/DCE interface that belongs to a hunt group, and they operate independently of the hunt group operations.

Figure 6-5 illustrates how a hunt group feature could operate. DTE 2 and DTE 3 transmit packets to DTE 1. Instead of using addresses A, B, or C in the packet address field, the sending DTEs use the hunt group address Z. The DCE servicing DTE 1 receives the packets and determines that address Z is actually a hunt group address for ports A, B, and C. It then passes the packets to DTE 1 across one of these links.

People should ascertain how their networks administer a hunt group. Some networks place restrictions on their use in relation to geographic boundaries served by the hunt group. Others require naming conventions for the hunt group addresses. Also, be aware that the hunt group is sometimes related to a group of subscription-time facilities.

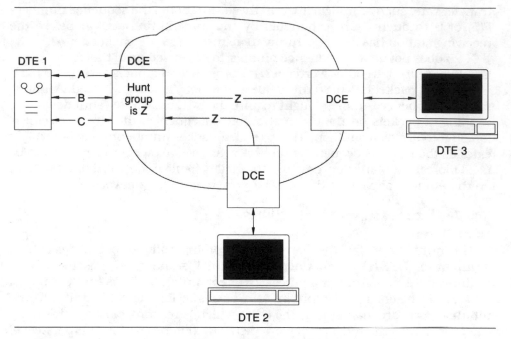

Figure 6-5. Hunt Group

Call Redirection and Call Deflection

The call redirection and call deflection facilities redirect or deflect packet calls when the destined DTE is out of order or busy, or has requested a call redirection. The destination DTE is called the "originally called DTE." The DTE receiving the call is called the "alternative DTE."

These facilities allow a call to be rerouted to a backup DTE, keeping problems and failures isolated from the end user. Call redirection could also permit calls to be redirected to different parts of a country to allow for time zone differences. These facilities are limited to the network of the originally called DTE.

Figure 6-6 shows the basic differences between the call redirection and call deflection services:

- *Call redirection:* The originally called DTE does not receive an incoming call packet when the redirection is performed.

- *Call deflection:* The originally called DTE receives an incoming call packet and then deflects the call.

These services are limited to one call redirection or reflection, although some networks may permit them to be chained to other DTEs. Notwithstanding, X.25

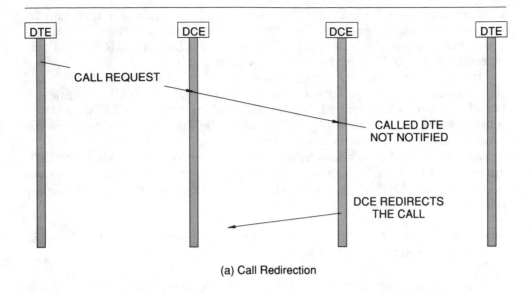

(a) Call Redirection

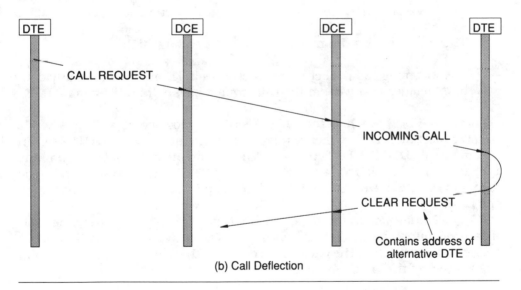

(b) Call Deflection

Figure 6-6. Call Redirection and Call Deflection

requires the call setup (including the redirections/deflections) to be consistent with an established time limit.

The *call redirection* facility redirects calls if the DTE is busy or out of order (see Figure 6-6(a)), but some networks also provide systematic call redirection in other situations. In addition, some networks attempt call redirection by accessing a list of alternative DTEs and trying one DTE at a time or chaining the redirections. In the latter case, a call redirected to, say, DTE B could also be redirected to DTE C, and then to DTE D, and so on.

The call deflection services actually consist of three facilities. The *call deflection subscription* facility permits the DTE to request that an incoming call be deflected to an alternative DTE. The DCE may require the DTE to send this request within a time limit. If the DTE sends the deflection request after the timer expires, the network clears the call.

The *call deflection selection* facility is used on a per-call basis if the DTE subscribes to the call deflection subscription facility. This facility allows the originally called DTE to specify the alternative DTE. The following rules apply to call deflection:

- The originally called DTE that received an incoming call packet returns a clear request packet to its DCE.

- This packet must contain any data and facilities that came along with the incoming call. It must also contain the address of the alternative DTE. It may also contain the call redirection or call deflection notification facility.

- The clear signal is not relayed back to the calling DTE.

- The incoming call packet to the alternative DTE must contain any data and facilities that were in the call request packet from the calling DTE.

Figure 6-6(b) shows how the call deflection service operates. DTE A sends a call request to its DCE, which is relayed through the network to DTE B as an incoming call. DTE B deflects the call with a clear request packet that contains the address of the alternative DTE (which is DTE C). The network relays the signal to the alternative DTE's DCE, which sends an incoming call packet to the DTE.

The *call redirection* or *call deflection notification* facility is used by the DCE in an incoming call packet to inform the alternative DTE that the call is redirected or deflected. The packet also contains the reason for this action and the address of the originally called DTE.

Called-Line-Address-Modified Notification

The called-line-address-modified notification permits the DCE to inform the calling DTE why the called address in a call connected or clear indication packet is different from the DTE's call request packet.

The facility can also be used by the DTE when more than one address is applicable at a DTE/DCE interface (for example, multiple addresses in a hunt group). Assume that the called DTE address in the incoming call packet applies to more than one valid address at the called DTE/DCE interface. The responding DTE uses this facility in the call accepted or clear request packet to indicate that the called DTE address is different from the address in the incoming call packet. The DCE must clear the call if the address is not applicable to this interface.

The DCE at the originating DTE/DCE interface can provide the following reasons for the called-line-address modification:

- Call distribution within a hunt group

- Originally called DTE is out of order

- Originally called DTE is busy

- Prior request that is agreed to by the originally called DTE and the network

- Called DTE originated

- A deflection by the originally called DTE

Miscellaneous Facilities
On-Line Facility Registration

The on-line facility registration facility permits the DTE (with a registration request packet) to request facilities or to obtain the parameters (values) of the facilities at any time. The DCE returns a registration confirmation packet containing the current value of all the facilities applicable to the DTE/DCE interface. Figure 6-7 shows this dialogue between the DTE and the DCE.

Some networks do not offer all the X.25 facilities, and other networks offer their own proprietary facilities. To avoid requesting facilities not available or not allowed, the DTE can transmit a registration request packet to the DCE containing no facilities values. In turn, the DCE sends back the registration confirmation packet containing any facilities that can be negotiated. The DTE can then modify these values in a subsequent registration request packet. When the DCE returns the registration confirmation packet, the facilities are in effect for any subsequent virtual calls.

It is certainly possible that a facility requested by the DTE is not available or not allowed. It may be allowed, but beyond the bounds of a permissible value. If so, the DCE reports in the registration confirmation packet the values allowed and a cause code.

If the DCE cannot accommodate the DTE requests, it will not alter the values of the affected facilities. For example, the request may conflict with other facilities at the DTE/DCE interface, or the request packet may have been issued when a virtual circuit was active at the interface (which would cause a great deal of confusion in the ongoing DTE/DCE dialogue).

Table 6-6 contains the rules for the on-line facility and its use with other facilities.

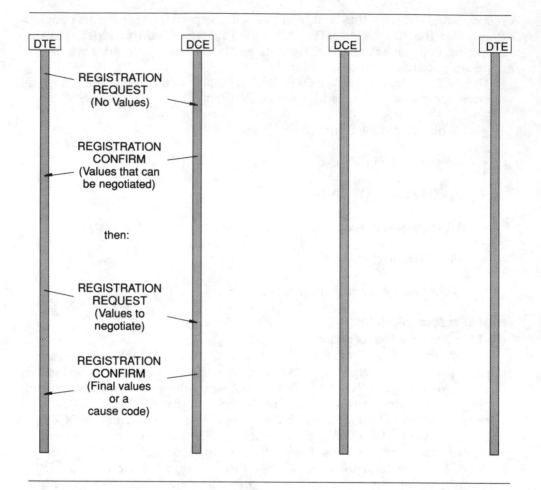

Figure 6-7. On-Line Facility Registration

Fast Select and Fast Select Acceptance

The fast select facility (described in greater detail in Chapter 5) was incorporated into the X.25 Recommendation in 1984. X.25 defines the fast select as an essential facility, which means that vendors or manufacturers implementing X.25 are encouraged to implement the facility. Most vendors have complied.

RPOA

The RPOA facilities allow a calling DTE to specify one or more recognized private operating agencies (RPOA) to handle the packet session. The RPOA is a packet network carrier (a value-added carrier), and acts as a transit network within one country or between countries.

Table 6-6. On-line Facility Registration Facility and Other Facilities

Name of facility or interface parameter	Negotiable in registration request and registration confirmation packets	Indication in registration confirmation packets whether the facility is supported by the DCE	Negotiable only when every logical channel used for virtual calls is in state p1
Extended packet sequence numbering	Yes	Yes	Yes
	(Note 1)		
D bit modification	Yes	Yes	Yes
Packet retransmission	Yes	Yes	Yes
Incoming calls barred	Yes	No	No
Outgoing calls barred	Yes	No	No
One-way logical channel outgoing	(Note 2)		
One-way logical channel incoming	(Note 2)		
Non-standard default packet sizes	Yes	Yes	No
Non-standard default window sizes	Yes	Yes	No
Default throughput classes assignment	Yes	Yes	No
Flow control parameter negotiation	Yes	No	No
Throughput class negotiation	Yes	No	No
Closed user group-related facilities	No	No	—
Bilateral closed user group-related facilities	No	No	—
Fast select	No	No	—
Fast select acceptance	Yes	No	No
Reverse charging	No	Yes	—
Reverse charging acceptance	Yes	Yes	No
Local charging prevention	No	Yes	—
NUI-related facilities	No	No	—
Charging information			
(per interface basis)	Yes	Yes	No
(per call basis)	No	Yes	—
RPOA-related facilities			
RPOA subscription		(Note 1)	
RPOA selection	No	Yes	—

(continued on p. 154)

Table 6-6. On-line Facility Registration Facility and Other Facilities (cont.)

Name of facility or interface parameter	Negotiable in registration request and registration confirmation packets	Indication in registration confirmation packets whether the facility is supported by the DCE	Negotiable only when every logical channel used for virtual calls is in state p1
Hunt group	No	No	—
Call redirection		(Note 1)	
Call deflection-related facilities		(Note 1)	
Call redirection or call deflection notification	No	No	—
Called line address modified notification	No	No	—
Transit delay selection and indication	No	Yes	—
Allocation of logical channel type range	Yes	Yes	Yes

Note 1: Further study is needed.
Note 2: Negotiation of one-way logical channel ranges is accomplished by allocation of logical channel type ranges negotiation.

The *RPOA subscription* facility is used with all virtual calls involving more than one RPOA and one or more gateways. The *RPOA selection* facility is used for an individual virtual call; subscribing is not necessary. With the RPOA selection facility, the call request packet contains a sequence of RPOA transit networks to handle the call. The call is set up and the packets are routed on the basis of this information. The selection facility, if used, overrides the subscription facility, if used.

TOA/NPI Address Subscription

The TOA/NPI address subscription facility supports extended address fields in the call setup and clearing packets. It was added in the 1988 Blue Book release to accommodate an extended E.164 ISDN addressing scheme.

When this facility is in use, the DCE uses the long address format, but the DTE has the option of using or not using it. Chapter 5 covers this subject.

Functions of the CCITT-Specified Facilities

Annex G of X.25 describes a set of facilities required by the OSI network service. They are called DTE facilities, because they are used only between the DTEs and are passed unchanged through the network. Use of these facilities is described in ISO 8208, and they are included in X.25 to encourage consistent coding in systems that use ISO 8208 and a packet network. They are coded following the CCITT-specified DTE facility marker. These facilities are

Calling address extension

Called address extension
Minimum throughput class
End-to-end transit delay
Priority
Protection
Expedited data negotiation

The calling and called address extension facilities provide rules on how to use the CCITT X.213 addressing convention in the facility parameter field (the ISO counterpart, 8348, could also be used). These specifications are examined in Chapter 5. Specifically, encoding conventions are stipulated for the initial domain part (IDP) and the domain-specific part (DSP).

The priority and protection facilities have not yet been approved and are still under study by CCITT. However, ISO 8878/ADD1 describes a procedure for mapping OSI connection-oriented network system priority parameters into the X.25 priority facility, and additional work is proceeding on the use of priorities in X.25. "Use of the X.25 Priority Facility to Provide the OSI CONS with Priority Levels," available from ISO/IEC JTC 1/SC6/WG 2, provides further information.

Facility/Registration Field

The committee that developed the X.25 Recommendation is quite aware of the need to reduce the overhead bits in the X.25 data packet. We learned earlier that the typical data packet contains only three octets in the header. The committee also tried to minimize the length of the facility and registration fields. This section examines their formats.

The facility field is present only in the call setup and clearing packets. The registration field is present in the registration request packet when the DTE asks the DCE to stop a previous agreement for facilities use. It is present in the registration confirmation packet when the DCE indicates to the DTE the facilities available and in effect.

Formats of the Facility/Registration Field

The field contains one to n octets. The codes in the field are divided into four classes and identified by bits 7 and 8 in the first octet of the field. Figure 6-8 shows how the field is formatted. This first octet is called the *facility/registration code field*. The following field is called the *parameter* field. The facility/registration code field is coded to identify four classes of formats:

- *Class A:* One-octet parameter field

- *Class B:* Two-octet parameter field

- *Class C:* Three-octet parameter field

- *Class D:* Variable-length parameter field

If the class D format is used, the octet following the code field indicates the length of the parameter field.

The facility/registration field can contain one or more *facility/registration elements*. An element consists of a facility code, which identifies the facility requested or to be negotiated. Following the facility code is a parameter code with specifics about the request or negotiation. For example, the facility code might indicate the request to negotiate a packet size, and the parameter code would contain the value of the packet size. The next two to *n* octets could be another facility element, and so on.

X.25 specifies the facility/registration field as with extension or without extension. Figure 6-8 depicts the field without extension. This format provides up to 64 codes for classes A, B, and C, and 63 codes for class D. The format is extended by coding 11111111 in the facility/registration field. The second octet is coded as shown in the first octet in Figure 6-8. The extension field can be repeated, allowing for a very long facility field with many facility parameters.

The facility field can contain facilities other than those specified in the X.25

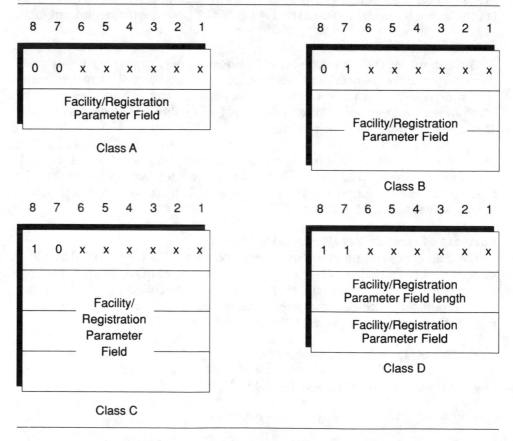

Figure 6-8. The Facility and Registration Formats

Recommendation. For example, CCITT-specified facilities and network-specific facilities can be added. The different facilities are separated from each other by *facility/registration markers*. The marker is an octet set to all zeroes.

The facility/registration parameter field of a marker is set to zeroes when the marker precedes requests for

- Codes specific to the local network

- Non-X.25 facilities for intranetwork calls

- Non-X.25 facilities provided by the network to which the calling DTE is connected

Table 6-7 shows the formats of the code field for the X.25 and CCITT facilities. The succeeding parameter fields are encoded to provide more specific information about what the facility is to do. For example, if the call deflection selection facility is used, the field identifies the alternative DTE and the reason for the deflection. Other examples: The parameter field for the RPOA selection facility identifies the transit network(s). Also, the parameter field uses bits 1, 2, 3, and 4 to indicate the packet size from the calling DTE, and bits 5, 6, 7, and 8 to indicate the packet size from the called DTE.

As suggested by the last example, each facility used during the DTE-to-DTE session must adhere to a specific coding convention within the parameter field. Otherwise, the communicating DTEs and DCEs could not understand each other. Section 7 of the X.25 specification has the coding rules.

Coding of the Registration Code Field

Table 6-8 shows the coding for the registration code field. This field is used only in the registration request and registration confirmation packets. If the field is absent in the registration request packet, the DTE does not wish to modify the previous arrangement for facility usage. If the field is absent in the registration confirmation packet, the facility or facilities are not supported or not open to negotiation.

As with the facility element, a registration element contains the registration code, followed by parameter value(s). The interpretation of the parameters depends on the registration code value. Multiple elements can be coded if necessary. The X.25 Recommendation provides more information on the registration facility coding rules.

Conclusions

The X.25 facilities provide many useful and powerful service features for the packet network user and especially for public data networks tasked with such jobs as redirected calls, reverse charges, and different packet sizes. The X.25 vendors vary greatly in the number of facilities offered within their product lines. The judicious purchaser should carefully check the X.25 facilities in the product.

Table 6-7. Coding of the Facility Code Field

| Facility | \multicolumn{7}{c}{Packet types in which it may be used} | |
	call request	incoming call	call accepted	call con-nected	clear request	clear indi-cation	DCE clear confir-mation	Facility code 87654321
Flow control parameter negotiation	X	X	X	X				
packet size								01000010
window size								01000011
Throughput class negotiation	X	X	X	X				00000010
Closed user group selection	X	X						
basic format								00000011
extended format								01000111
Closed user group with outgoing access selection	X	X						
basic format								00001001
extended format								01001000
Bilateral closed user group selection	X	X						01000001
Reverse charging	X	X						00000001
Fast select	X	X						00000001
NUI selection	X		X					1100110
Charging information								00000100
requesting service	X		X			X	X	
receiving information:								
i) monetary unit								11000101
ii) segment count								11000010
iii) call duration								11000001

(continued on p. 159)

Table 6-7. Coding of the Facility Code Field (cont.)

Facility	Packet types in which it may be used							Facility code 87654321
	call request	incoming call	call accepted	call con- nected	clear request	clear indi- cation	DCE clear confir- mation	
RPOA selection basic format extended format	X							01000100 11000100
Call deflection selection					X			11010001
Call redirection or deflection notification		X						1100011
Called line address modified notification			X	X	X	X		00001000
Transit delay selection and indication	X	X		X				01001001
Marker	X	X	X	X	X	X		00000000
Reserved for extension								11111111

Table 6-8. Coding of the Registration Code Field

Facility	May be used in		Registration code
	Registration request	Registration confirmation	Bits 8 7 6 5 4 3 2 1
Facilities that may be negotiated only when all logical channels used for virtual calls are in state p1	X	X	0 0 0 0 0 1 0 1
Facilities that may be negotiated at any time	X	X	0 1 0 0 0 1 0 1
Availability of facilities		X	0 1 0 0 0 1 1 0
Non-negotiable facilities values			0 0 0 0 0 1 1 0
Default throughput classes assignment	X	X	0 0 0 0 0 0 1 0
Non-standard default packet sizes	X	X	0 1 0 0 0 0 1 0
Non-standard default window sizes	X	X	0 1 0 0 0 0 1 1
Logical channel types ranges	X	X	1 1 0 0 1 0 0 0

X.25 Companion Standards

Goals of Chapter 7

The operating options with X.25 can be a source of confusion because X.25 is implemented with many other CCITT recommendations and ISO standards. Because of X.25's "many relationships," it may be difficult to determine where X.25 fits with other international data communications standards. Therefore, our goal in this chapter is to provide a general survey of the principal standards associated with X.25. The chapter is intended to serve as a general tutorial and convenient reference guide. The reader should obtain the specific standard or recommendation if more detailed information is needed.

The previous chapters have been somewhat detailed in their analysis of the principal aspects of X.25. However, due to the number and complexity of some of the "companion" protocols, in this chapter we restrict ourselves to an overview of the subject. The one exception is X.32. We give it a more thorough examination because of the increased public awareness of the need for network security.

To keep this chapter to a reasonable length, the companion standards for X.25 internetworking are discussed in the next chapter.

Introduction

In addition to the interfaces and protocols residing in the physical, data-link, and network layers, X.25 uses several other standards (recommendations) to support and complement X.25. Some are not cited in the X.25 specification; rather, their use with X.25 is cited within the other (companion) recommendations.

The following CCITT recommendations and ISO standards are discussed in this chapter:

- *X.1:* User classes of service

- *X.2:* User facilities

- *X.10:* Categories of access

- *X.92:* Reference connections for packets with data transmissions

- *X.96:* Call progress signals

- *X.121:* International public data network numbering plan

- *X.134-X.137:* Performance parameters, values, and formula

- *X.213:* Network services

- *ISO 8208:* DTE-to-DTE operations using X.25

X.1. Services and Facilities

For several years, the CCITT has published recommendations for the V Series (which define the data signaling rates on the telephone network and modulation rates for modems). X.1 provides a standard for the signaling rates on public data networks.

X.1 defines 16 classes of service, which depend on whether the DTE operates as an asynchronous start/stop device, a synchronous device, or a packet mode device. The user classes of service and the data signaling rates range from 300 bit/s (bits per second) start/stop asynchronous modes to 64 Kbit/s modes. A vendor or administration may not support all classes of services.

X.25-based networks use the service classes shown in Table 7-1.

X.2. International Data Transmission Services and Optional User Facilities in Public Data Networks

Recommendation X.2 describes the use of facilities, indicating whether a facility is essential (should be used with the network), is an additional (optional) facility, or is applicable to a switched call (VC) or permanent virtual circuit (PVC). The recommendation also specifies the facilities to be used with a circuit-switched network or a packet-switched network.

Table 7-1. Classes of Service

User Class of Service	Data Signaling Rate
Synchronous Mode (X.25 Interface)	
8	2400 bit/s
9	4800 bit/s
10	9600 bit/s
11	48000 bit/s
12	1200 bit/s
13	64000 bit/s
Asynchronous Mode (X.28 Interface)	
20	50-300 bit/s 10 or 11 units/character
21	75/1200 bit/s 10 units/character
22	1200 bit/s 10 units/character

Table 7-2 defines the X.25 facilities as follows: E stands for essential; A, additional; FS, for further study; VC, virtual call; PVC, permanent virtual circuit.

Table 7-2. Facilities

	Facility	User Class of Service			
		8-11		20-22	
		VC	PVC	VC	PVC
1.	**Optional user facilities assigned for an agreed contractual period**				
1.1	Extended frame sequence numbering	A	A	—	—
1.2	Multilink procedure	A	A	—	—
1.3	On-line facility registration	A	—	FS	—
1.4	Extended packet sequence numbering (modulo 128)	A	A	—	—
1.5	D-bit modification	A	A	FS	—
1.6	Packet retransmission	A	A	—	—
1.7	Incoming calls barred	E	—	A	—
1.8	Outgoing calls barred	E	—	A	—
1.9	One-way logical channel outgoing	E	—	—	—
1.10	One-way logical channel incoming	A	—	—	—
1.11	Nonstandard default packet sizes 16, 32, 64, 256, 512,	A	A	FS	FS
	1024, 2048, 4096	A	A	FS	FS
1.12	Nonstandard default window sizes	A	A	—	—
1.13	Default throughput classes assignment	A	A	FS	FS
1.14	Flow Control parameter negotiation	E	—	FS	—
1.15	Throughput class negotiation	E	—	FS	—
1.16	Closed user group	E	—	E	—
1.17	Closed user group with outgoing access	A	—	A	—
1.18	Closed user group with incoming access	A	—	A	—
1.19	Incoming calls barred within a closed user group	A	—	A	—
1.20	Outgoing calls barred within a closed user group	A	—	A	—
1.21	Bilateral closed user group	A	—	A	—
1.22	Bilateral closed user group with outgoing access	A	—	A	—
1.23	Fast select acceptance	E	—	FS	—
1.24	Reverse charging acceptance	A	—	A	—
1.25	Local charging prevention	A	—	FS	—
1.26	Network user identification subscription	A	—	A	—
1.27	NUI override	A	—	—	—
1.28	Charging information	A	—	A	—
1.29	RPOA selection	A	—	A	—
1.30	Hunt group	A	—	A	—
1.31	Call redirection	A	—	FS	—
1.33	TOA/NPI address substitution	A	A	FS	—
1.34	Direct call	FS	—	A	—

(continued on p. 164)

Table 7-2. Facilities (cont.)

	Facility	User Class of Service 8-11 VC	8-11 PVC	20-22 VC	20-22 PVC
2.	**Optional user facilities on a per-call basis**				
2.1	Flow control parameter negotiation	E	—	—	—
2.2	Throughput class negotiation	E	—	—	—
2.3	Closed user group selection	E	—	E	—
2.4	Closed user group with outgoing access selection	A	—	FS	—
2.5	Bilateral closed user group selection	A	—	FS	—
2.6	Reverse charging	A	—	A	—
2.7	Fast select	E	—	FS	—
2.8	Abbreviated address calling	FS	—	A	—
2.8	Network user identification selection	A	—	A	—
2.9	Charging information	A	—	A	—
2.10	RPOA selection	A	—	A	—
2.11	Call deflection selection	A	—	—	—
2.12	Call redirection or deflection notification	A	—	FS	—
2.13	Called line address modified notification	A	—	FS	—
2.14	Transit delay selection and indication	E	—	—	—
2.15	Abbreviated address calling	FS	—	A	—

X.10. Categories of Access for DTEs

The X.10 Recommendation was adapted in the 1984 CCITT release to define the different categories of access for DTEs into different kinds of networks. Specifically, the standard defines how DTEs interface into circuit-switched networks, packet-switched networks, and leased circuit networks.

In addition, the standard defines how terminals interface into an Integrated Services Digital Network (ISDN). X.10 stipulates the data signaling rate and the physical interface requirements (such as X.21, EIA-232-D, etc.). Table 7-3 explains aspects of X.10 relevant to X.25 systems.

X.92. Hypothetical Reference Connections for Public Synchronous Data Networks

The X.92 Recommendation establishes the specific connections available for DTEs into data networks. The following links are permitted within the standard:

- *Link A:* Data-link between two adjacent data-switching exchanges in a national network

- *Link A1:* Data-link between two adjacent gateway data-switching exchanges (DSE) in an international connection

- *Link B1:* Data-link between a local DSE and a gateway DSE

Table 7-3. Categories of Access

Category of access	Data signaling rate	DTE/DCE interface requirements
Start-stop direct connection to a packet-switched data transmission service		
C1	110 bit/s	
C2	200 bit/s	
C3	300 bit/s	See Recommendation X.28
C4	1200 bit/s	
C5	75/1200 bit/s	
C6	2400 bit/s	
Synchronous direct connection to a packet-switched data transmission service		
D1	2400 bit/s	
D2	4800 bit/s	
D3	9600 bit/s	See Recommendation X.25 and X.31 (Case A)
D4	48000 bit/s	
D4	64000 bit/s	
Start-stop switched connection by means of a Circuit Switched Public Data Network to a packet-switched data transmission service		
K1	300 bit/s	See Recommendation X.28
Start-stop switched connection by means of a Public Switched Telephone Network to a packet-switched data transmission service		
L1	110 bit/s	
L2	200 bit/s	
L3	300 bit/s	See Recommendation X.28
L4	1200 bit/s	
L5	75/1200 bit/s	
L6	2400 bit/s	
Synchronous switched connection by means of a Circuit Switched Public Data Network to a packet-switched data transmission service		
O1	2400 bit/s	
O2	4800 bit/s	
O3	9600 bit/s	See Recommendation X.32
O4	48000 bit/s	
O5	64000 bit/s	
Synchronous switched connection by means of a Public Switched Telephone Network to a packet-switched data transmission service		
P1	1200 bit/s	
P2	2400 bit/s	See Recommendation X.32
P3	4800 bit/s	
P4	9600 bit/s	

(continued on p. 166)

Table 7-3. Categories of Access (cont.)

Category of access	Data signaling rate	DTE/DCE interface requirements
Synchronous switched access by means of an ISDN B channel to a packet-switched data transmission service		
Q1	2400 bit/s	
Q2	4800 bit/s	
Q3	9600 bit/s	See Recommendation X.31
Q4	48000 bit/s	
Q5	64000 bit/s	
Synchronous direct connection via the B channel to a packet-switched data transmission service		
T1	2400 bit/s	
T2	4800 bit/s	See Recommendation X.25
T3	9600 bit/s	and X.31 (maximum
T4	48000 bit/s	integration)
T5	64000 bit/s	
Synchronous direct connection via the B channel to a packet-switched data transmission service		
U1	2400 bit/s	
U2	4800 bit/s	
U3	9600 bit/s	See Recommendation X.31
U4	48000 bit/s	
U5	64000 bit/s	
Synchronous switched connection by means of an ISDN B channel to a packet-switched data transmission service		
Y1	2400 bit/s	
Y2	4800 bit/s	
Y3	9600 bit/s	See Recommendation X.25 and X.31 (Case B)
Y4	48000 bit/s	
Y5	64000 bit/s	

- *Link G1:* Data-link between a source gateway DSE and a destination gateway DSE in an international connection

- *Link C:* Data-link between source DTE and destination DTE

- *Link D:* Data-link between source DTE and the source local DSE or the data link between destination DTE and destination local DSE

- *Link E:* Data-link between communicating processes

As discussed in Chapters 6 and 8, X.25 and X.75 use the X.92 Recommendation for their links and reference connections.

X.96. Call Progress Signals in Public Data Networks

This standard establishes the signals that may be used to inform DTEs (such as calling DTEs) about the progress of a connection or connection request through a public network. X.96 defines the signals to be returned to the caller to indicate connections that were not made (and why) and to report on the progress of a call through a network. X.96 can be very valuable to a calling DTE. It establishes mechanisms for the DTE to know if there is a problem detected at the DTE/DCE interface, if a virtual call has been reset or cleared, or if a permanent virtual circuit has been reset. The entries in Table 7-4 pertaining to X.96 are relevant to X.25: M stands for mandatory; (M), mandatory when relevant facility is used; and FS, for further study. (A hyphen means not applicable.)

X.121. International Numbering Plan for Public Data Networks

The X.121 Recommendation has received considerable attention throughout the world because its intent is to provide a universal addressing scheme, allowing users to communicate with each other through multiple networks. X.121 establishes a standard numbering scheme for all countries' networks and individual users within those networks.

A DTE within a public data network is addressed by an international data network address. The international data network address consists of a data network identification code (DNIC) plus a network terminal number (NTN). Another option is to provide the international data number as the data country code (DCC) plus a national number (NN).

The four codes have identifiers as follows: The DNIC consists of four digits—the first three digits identify the country and can be regarded as a data country code (DCC). The fourth digit identifies a specific data network within a country. The network terminal number can consist of 10 digits or if a national number (NN) is used in place of the NTN, 11 digits are allowed.

The international numbering scheme is summarized as

$$P + DNIC + NTN$$
$$(1) \quad (4) \quad (10)$$

or

$$P + DCC + NN$$
$$(1) \quad (3) \quad (11)$$

Chapter 5 examines X.121 and other addressing standards in greater detail.

The X.134, X.135, X.136, and X.137 Recommendations

The X.134, X.135, X.136, and X.137 Recommendations provide guidance on defining and using performance parameters and values on a packet-switched network. Many networks use these specifications to support their X.25- and X.75-based products. The documents are named as follows:

- *X.134: Apportionment Boundaries and Packet Level Reference Events for Defining Packet-Switched Performance Parameters*

Table 7-4. X.96 Call Progress Signals

Call Progress Signal	Definition	Category	VC	PVC
Registration/ cancellation confirmed	The facility registration or cancellation requested by the calling DTE has been confirmed by the network.	B	(M)	(M)
Local procedure error	A procedure error caused by the DTE is detected by the DCE at the local DTE/DCE interface. Possible reasons are indicated in relevant Series X interface Recommendations.	D1	M	M
Network congestion	A congestion condition exists in the network.	C2	M	M
Network out of order	Temporary inability to handle data traffic.	C2	—	M
Invalid facility request	A facility requested by the calling DTE or the called DTE is detected as invalid by the DCE at the local DTE/DCE interface.	D1	M	—
RPOA out of order	The RPOA nominated by the calling DTE is unable to forward the call.	D2	(M)	—
Not obtainable	The called DTE address is out of the numbering plan or not assigned to any DTE.	D1	M	—
Access barred	The calling DTE is not permitted the connection to the called DTE.	D1	M	
Reverse charging acceptance not subscribed	The called DTE has not subscribed to the reverse charging acceptance facility.	D1	(M)	—
Fast select acceptance not subscribed	The called DTE has not subscribed to the fast select acceptance facility.	D1	(M)	—
Incompatible destination	The remote DTE/DCE interface or the transit network does not support a function or facility requested.	D1	M	M
Ship absent	The called ship is absent.	D1	M	—
Out of order	The remote number is out of order. Possible reasons include: DTE is uncontrolled not ready; DCE power off; Network fault in the local loop; In packet switches only (X.25 level 1 not functioning, X.25 level 2 not in operation).	D1 or D2	M See Note 1	M
Network fault in the local loop	The local loop associated with the called DCE is faulty.	D2	See Note 1	
DCE power off	Called DCE has no main power or is switched off.	D1	See Note 1	
Uncontrolled not ready	Called DTE is uncontrolled not ready.	D1	See Note 1	
Note 1	Although the basic out-of-order call progress signal is transmitted for these conditions, the diagnostic field in the clearing or resetting packet may give more precision.			

(continued on p. 169)

Table 7-4. X.96 Call Progress Signals (cont.)

Call Progress Signal	Definition	Category	VC	PVC
Controlled not ready	Called DTE is signaling controlled not ready.	D1	FS	FS
Number busy	The called DTE is detected by the DCE as engaged on other call(s) and therefore as not being able to accept the incoming call.	C1	M	—
Remote procedure error	A procedure error caused by the DTE or an invalid facility request by the remote DTE is detected by the DCE at the remote DTE/DCE interface. Possible reasons are indicated in relevant Series X interface Recommendations.	D1	M	M
Long term network congestion	A major shortage of network resource exists.	D2	—	—
Network operational	Network is ready to resume normal operation after a temporary failure or congestion.	C1	—	M
Remote DTE operational	Remote DTE/DCE interface is ready to resume normal operation after a temporary failure or out of order condition (e.g., restart at the DTE/DCE interface). Loss of data may have occurred.	C1	—	M
DTE originated	The remote DTE has initiated a clear, reset, or restart procedure. See Note 2.	B or D1	M	M
PAD clearing	The call has been cleared by the local PAD as an answer to an initiation from the remote DTE.	B	M (X.28 only)	
Note 2	Possible reasons for this include reverse charging not accepted.			

- *X.135: Speed of Service (Delay and Throughput) Performance Values for Public Data Networks When Providing International Packet-Switched Services*

- *X.136: Blocking Aspects of Grade of Service for Public Data Networks When Providing International Packet-Switched Services*

- *X.137: Availability Performance Values for Public Data Networks When Providing International Packet-Switched Services*

X.134 sets the framework for the other specifications. It contains information on the boundaries for national and international virtual circuit connections and establishes the monitor points for performance analysis. It also describes in detail events significant for performance in the use of the various X.25 packets, such as call request and receive not ready (RNR). X.134 also contains a detailed state diagram that explains the rules for flow control across the X.25 DTE/DCE interface and the X.75 STE-X/STE-Y interface.

X.135 specifies the parameters and tools for measuring delay and throughput across multiple X.25 and X.75 networks. It defines four parameters:

1. Call setup delay

2. Data packet transfer delay

3. Throughput capacity

4. Clear indication delay

X.136 provides the specifications to define and measure network blocking. It contains permissible probability thresholds for the following X.25 blocking situations:

1. Virtual call request rejection

2. Virtual call clearing

3. Virtual call reset

4. Permanent virtual call reset

5. DTE restart

Here is an example of how X.136 is applied: The probability that a DTE receives a clear indication packet because the network path is not available is not to exceed 9×10^{-3}.

X.137 uses eight performance parameters to compute the availability of an X.25 or X.75 virtual connection. Several formulas are provided to calculate mean time between service outages (MTBSO), mean time to service restoration (MTTSR), failure rate, and unavailability. The performance parameters are as follows:

1. Call setup failure probability

2. Call setup error probability

3. Throughput capacity

4. Residual error rate

5. Reset probability

6. Reset stimulus probability

7. Premature disconnect probability

8. Premature disconnect stimulus probability

X.213. Network Service Definitions

As with all OSI layers, services are invoked with primitives. Table 7-5 shows the primitives used by the network service. The parameters required in primitives are also shown. In various sequences these primitives perform network establishment, network release, and, of course, data transfer. X.25 uses them to create the various packets (call request, reset, etc.) and the fields within the packets.

The addresses in the parameters are all NSAP addresses. These addresses have variable lengths, with a maximum of 32 characters. The called address identifies the receiving NSAP. The calling address parameter identifies the requesting address of the NSAP. The responding address identifies the address of the NSAP to which the actual network connection has been established. X.25

Table 7-5. Network Service Primitives (X.213)

Primitive	Parameters
N-CONNECT request	(Called Address, Calling Address, Receipt Confirmation Selection, Expedited Data Selection, Quality of Service Parameter Set, NS User-Data.)
N-CONNECT indication	(Called Address, Calling Address, Receipt Confirmation Selection, Expedited Data Selection, Quality of Service Parameter Set, NS User-Data.)
N-CONNECT response	(Responding Address, Receipt Confirmation Selection, Expedited Data Selection, Quality of Service Parameter Set, NS User-Data.)
N-CONNECT confirm	(Responding Address, Receipt Confirmation Selection, Expedited Data Selection, Quality of Service Parameter Set, NS User-Data.)
N-DATA request	(NS User-Data, Confirmation request.)
N-DATA indication	(NS User-Data, Confirmation request.)
N-DATA ACKNOWLEDGE request	
N-DATA ACKNOWLEDGE indication	
N-EXPEDITED-DATA request	(NS User-Data.)
N-EXPEDITED-DATA indication	(NS User-Data.)
N-RESET request	(Reason.)
N-RESET indication	(Originator, Reason.)
N-RESET response	
N-RESET confirm	
N-DISCONNECT request	(Reason, NS User-Data, Responding Address.)
N-DISCONNECT indication	(Originator, Reason, NS User-Data, Responding Address.)

may use the NSAPs for the calling and called DTE addresses, but this aspect of addressing is the network administrator's concern.

The receipt confirmation selection parameter stipulates whether the network connection will use receipt confirmation. If this parameter is accepted by the local and remote network service users, subsequent data primitives can request the confirmation of actual data through the confirmation request parameter of the N-data request protocol data unit. The expedited data selection parameter stipulates the use of expedited data transfer during the actual network connection. Expedited data are used for higher priority traffic. The quality-of-service (QOS) parameters are invoked during session establishment. These parameters can be mapped into the X.25 facilities.

X.223. Providing the X.25 Packet Layer
Procedures from the X.213 Service Definitions

The 1988 Blue Books include X.223, which describes the mapping between X.25 and the primitives of X.213. X.223 provides the rules for mapping the connection-mode primitives and the X.25 packet elements. In its simplest form, it describes how the primitives are used to create the various packet types and how the parameters and the primitives are used to create the fields within the packets.

Table 7-6 shows the use of X.223 for call establishment, with the X.213 connection primitives and their mapped counterparts in the X.25 packet procedures. The table also shows the X.213 primitive parameters and how they are mapped to the fields in X.25 connection management packets. The X.213 quality-of-service parameters are mapped into X.25 packet-level procedures, principally through X.25 facilities. Table 7-6 also shows the mapping relationship of the QOS subparameters and how they relate to the X.25 packets and the X.25 facilities.

The X.25 data packets are created from the X.213 data primitives. These are the N-data request primitive and the N-data indication primitive. These primitives carry two parameters, which are mapped into the X.25 packet fields. First, the NS-user-data parameter is used to create the X.25 user-data field and perhaps the M bit. Second, the X.213 confirmation request primitive is mapped into the X.25 D bit and the P(S) field.

As might be expected, the X.25 interrupt packet is created from the X.213 expedited data request primitives, and the X.213 reset primitives are mapped into the X.25 reset packets. Finally, the disconnect primitives are mapped into the X.25 clear packets, also shown in the table.

ISO 8208 Using X.25 Directly between Computers

X.25 was published to define the operations between a user device (DTE) and a packet-switched data network (a DCE in X.25 terminology). Several years ago it was recognized that X.25 could prove quite useful in managing sessions and connections between two computers without an intervening network. That is to say, X.25 could be used for a DTE-to-DTE operation. Consequently, ISO

Table 7-6. X.213 Connection Management Primitives and X.25 Call Management Packets

X.213 Primitives	X.25 Packets
N-CONNECT request	Call Request
N-CONNECT indication	Incoming Call
N-CONNECT response	Call Accepted
N-CONNECT confirm	Call Connected
N-DISCONNECT request	Clear Request
N-DISCONNECT indication	Clear Indication, Restart Indication or Clear Request
N-DATA request	Data
N-DATA indication	Data
N-EXPEDITED DATA request	Interrupt
N-EXPEDITED DATA indication	Interrupt
N-RESET request	Reset Request
N-RESET indication	Reset Indication, Reset Request
N-RESET response	
N-RESET confirm	
Primitive Parameters	**Fields in the Packets**
Called Address	Called DTE address field or Called address extension facility
Calling Address	Calling DTE address field or Calling DTE address extension facility
Responding Address	Called DTE address field or Called DTE address extension facility
Receipt Confirmation Selection	General format identifier (GFI)
Expedited Data Selection	Expedited data negotiation facility
QOS Parameters	These X.25 facilities: Throughput class negotiation Minimum throughput class negotiation Transit delay selection and indication End-to-end transit delay
Originator and Reason	Cause code and diagnostic code
NS-User Data	User data field in a Fast Select packet
NS-User Data	User data field in a data packet
Confirmation Request	D bit with the P(S)

published ISO 8208, *X.25 Packet Level Protocol for Data Terminal Equipment.*

For the most part ISO 8208 mirrors the X.25 Recommendation and therefore describes operations quite similar to those described in Chapters 5 and 6. However, we saw that X.25 specifies different types of packets, different timers, and different state logic for the DCE and the DTE. Consequently, a main feature of ISO 8208 is its definition of how the DTEs can use the basic X.25 interface without having to assume the responsibility of a network DCE.

With considerable detail, 8208 defines how the X.25 protocol can be used as a direct interface between two DTEs, using the X.25 rules as much as possible. For the most part the DTE is unaware that it is connected directly to another DTE. However, certain procedures within the X.25 protocol not required of a DTE are required with 8208. Some principal differences between X.25 and 8208 revolve around the rules that the DTE must adhere to in any connection with another DTE. They are summarized in this section.

Whether the DTE is connected to a DCE or another DTE must be considered. ISO 8208 provides the following rules and considerations:

- One of the DTEs must emulate a DCE for logical channel selection during virtual call setups and for the resolution of virtual call collisions.

- A DTE must be able to accept a restart indication packet, with a restarting cause field "DTE originated." Of course, this event does not occur in the DTE/DCE environment.

- In a DTE/DCE environment, a DTE might receive a restart, clear, or reset indication packet with a cause field other than "DTE originated." ISO 8208 requires that the DTE be able to handle such a packet as it normally would in a DTE/DCE environment, or treat it as an error.

- Under 8208 a DTE may transmit a diagnostic packet.

- A DTE can ignore or treat as an error the reception of facility codes that do not apply to a direct DTE-to-DTE session. In a conventional X.25 DTE/ DCE environment a DTE will never receive a registration request packet. However, with 8208, an initiating DTE can transmit a registration request packet and the responding DTE must process it.

- In an X.25 DTE/DCE environment, a DTE will not receive a reject packet. ISO 8208 permits a destination DTE to transmit a reject packet and requires the receiving DTE to process it.

- In an X.25 DTE/DCE environment, a fast select facility does not require prior agreement. That is to say, a DTE may use the facility during the call setup. ISO 8208 requires that the optional use of the fast select facility be agreed upon by both communicating DTEs before any call setup that uses this facility.

- In an X.25 DTE/DCE environment, the flow-control parameter negotiation facility and the throughput class negotiation facility are always present if the DTE has subscribed to them. The facility request is not necessarily required in the call request packet.

Obviously, many X.25 rules must be changed to accommodate a direct DTE-to-DTE session. Other rules are required as well, and you should obtain the ISO 8208 specification if you are tasked with using the X.25 protocol for direct DTE-to-DTE operations.

X.32. DTE/DCE Interface through Dial-Up Networks, ISDNs, and Circuit-Switched Data Networks

Introduction

X.32 is published by CCITT to provide guidelines for the interface of packet mode user devices (DTE) and data circuit terminating equipment (DCE) for operations through a switched telephone network, an integrated services digital network (ISDN), or a circuit-switched data network. More simply, X.32 defines the arrangements for using an X.25 interface with these networks.

Figure 7-1 provides a functional view of X.32. The operations depicted here are called dial-in by the DTE and dial-out by the packet switched public data network (PSPDN). The dial-in operation is used by the packet mode DTE to access the data network through X.32-based selection procedures. The DTE uses automatic or manual dial-up ports and modems. The dial-out operation from the packet network to the user device uses automatic answering procedures. Optionally, the DTE can use manual answering.

When communications are to be established on dial-up switched links, it is often a good idea to require identification procedures between the calling and called parties. X.32 stipulates procedures for establishing both a DTE and DCE *identity*. When a DTE dials in to a network or is accessed by the network, the network may require identification of the DTE to the DCE. Likewise, the DTE may wish to have the DCE's identity before proceeding with the data exchange.

For DTE identification, X.32 provides four options. Identification is provided by

- The public switched network

- The HDLC XID (exchange identification frame), at the link layer

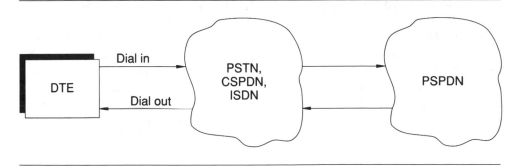

Figure 7-1. X.32 Functional View

- The X.25 packet-layer registration facility

- The X.25 network user identification (NUI) facility in the call setup packet

For DCE identification, X.32 stipulates three choices. Identification is provided by

- The public switched network

- The link-level XID frame

- The X.25 packet-layer registration facility procedure

In both the DTE and DCE identification procedures, X.32 permits the identity of these devices to become known with one of two procedures. The first procedure allows the identification to be established before any virtual call establishment. No X.25 call-management package can be exchanged between the DTE and the DCE until the identification is completed. The second choice allows the identification to be performed per virtual call by the NUI (network user identification) facility. With this method, DTE identity is coded in the facility field within the call request packet.

In establishing the DCE identity, X.32 stipulates that the identification before virtual call establishment can be provided by a public switched network through the ISDN number or the circuit-switched public data network number that identifies the DCE. As we just mentioned, the DCE identity procedure can also be provided by the HDLC XID frame procedure. The CCITT X.32 Recommendation cites the option for DCE identification per virtual call as needing further study.

X.25 and X.32

X.32 provides several options for dial-in and dial-out procedures, as summarized above. Because this book is about X.25, we focus on the X.25 packet layer and its relationship to X.32. If X.32 is used for identification on authentication for dial-in and dial-out procedures and if these services are performed at the packet layer, the X.25 protocol provides two operations.

The first operation is the use of registration packets for identifying either the DTE or DCE. As with the conventional X.25 registration packet procedure, the registration request packet is used to carry the identification of the DTE to the DCE. The registration confirmation packet then carries the identification of the DCE to the DTE. The second option is the use of the network user identification (NUI) selection facility, carried in the connection setup packets. As mentioned earlier, the NUI selection facility can be used on a per-call basis.

X.32 Identification Protocol

An important X.32 procedure deals with the *identification protocol*, used for exchanging identification and authentication information. X.32 defines the *questioning* party and the *challenged* party. The questioning party challenges other party to provide sufficient identification and authentication. The identification protocol elements are passed between the parties with XID or registration packets.

Several definitions will help us examine this protocol:

- *Identity element* (ID): A string of octets representing the challenged party's identity.

- *Signature element* (SIG): A string of octets representing another identity, such as a password or a result of an encryption process.

- *Random number* (RAND): An unpredictable range of octets.

- *Signed response element* (SRES): Reply of the challenged party to the questioning party.

- *Diagnostic element* (DIAG): Result of the identification process, transmitted by questioning party at the end of the identification process.

In its identification protocol, X.32 stipulates two security options: security grade 1 and security grade 2. Security grade 1 involves two messages exchanged between the challenged and questioning parties. Both options are in effect for the switched call. Any new identification process must first be preceded with a link disconnection.

As depicted in Figure 7-2(a), the challenged party must first send its identity (ID) and, if required, some type of signature (SIG). In turn, the questioning party

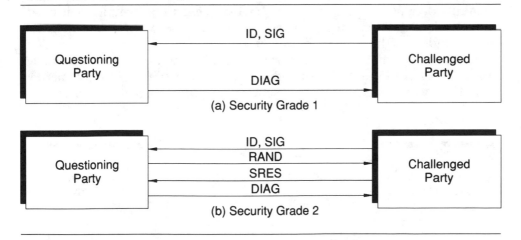

(a) Security Grade 1

(b) Security Grade 2

Figure 7-2. X.32 Authentication Procedures

responds with the diagnostic message (DIAG), which reports the result. If the exchange is not successful, security grade 1 permits up to three retries, before a disconnection.

Security grade 2 involves a more enhanced authentication exchange (see Figure 7-2(b)). Basically, if the initial identification and signature of the challenged party are valid, the questioning party returns a message with a random number (RAND), which the challenged party must encrypt and return as its signed response (SRES). The questioning party then decrypts the SRES. If the result of its decryption equals the value in the RAND, an appropriate diagnostic message (DIAG) is sent to the challenged party, and the two parties have completed authentication and identification. If the encryption and identification process does not succeed, the error diagnostic message is returned and a connection is not made. X.32 permits only one attempt when the network is the questioning party.

Both security grades are established with the network by subscription. They are not available on a per-call basis.

X.32 Secure Dial-Back Facility

X.32 also includes a commonly used feature for dial-in systems, called the dial-back facility. This optional X.32 feature allows the dialing in DTE to identify itself and then disconnect. In turn, the network uses the identity information provided in the dial-in procedure to dial back the DTE. The DCE is required to identify itself and the DTE must once again identify itself. This very useful and relatively simple procedure enhances security, ensuring that the calling party is physically located at a registered public switched network number. Figure 7-3 illustrates the procedures for the dial-back facility.

Conclusions

We have learned that X.25 refers to several "companion" standards and recommendations, and most vendors have implemented them in their products. Reading these companion specifications is essential for gaining a full understanding of the X.25 Recommendation.

The X.32 Recommendation is now used in X.25 dial-up configurations as well as X.25/ISDN interfaces. In addition, most countries have implemented the X.121 international addressing scheme for public packet networks.

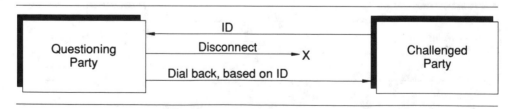

Figure 7-3. The X.32 Dial-back Facility

Chapter 8

Internetworking X.25 with Other Systems

Goals of Chapter 8

The introductory remarks in the previous chapter can be repeated for this chapter: X.25 can be a source of confusion because it is used with other CCITT recommendations and ISO standards. Chapter 7 provided a survey of companion standards to X.25. Our goal in this chapter is to continue the survey and to focus on the principal internetworking recommendations and standards associated with X.25.

Like the previous chapter, this chapter is intended as a general tutorial and convenient reference guide. The reader should obtain the specific standard or recommendation if more detailed information is needed. Due to the breadth of the topic, we restrict this chapter to an overview of the subject.

In addition, we explore the IBM and DEC approaches to X.25 internetworking. My intent is not to imply that these vendors are better than others that are not included. Rather, they are included because of their positions in the industry.

Introduction

X.25-based networks were developed to allow users to share computer and information resources, as well as a common communications system. As organizations have brought the computer into almost every facet of business, it has become obvious that a single network, while very useful, is also inadequate to meet burgeoning information needs. For example, a user of one network often needs to access computers and databases that "belong" to another network. It is prohibitively complex and expensive to merge all resources into one network.

An alternative to the "one network for all" approach is interconnecting networks to obtain the required resources for the user. With this approach, a network remains relatively independent from other networks and is not concerned with their internal operations.

Hereafter, a network is also called a *subnetwork*. The term is used with another new term in this book, the *internet*. The term subnetwork conveys the idea that a network is a part of several other networks. The subnetworks form the internet.

The subnetwork is an autonomous whole. It consists of collections of equipment, physical media, and software used to support the user community.

Examples of subnetworks are privately owned networks, public networks (such as Telenet, Tymnet, Datapac, and various Department of Defense networks, which are semiprivate), and local area networks.

Internetworking is not simple; it requires considerable analysis and forethought before it is implemented. Yet the task is usually not insurmountable. As we shall see in this chapter, vendors and standards organizations have developed and implemented many effective internetworking techniques for X.25 interfaces. Indeed, many vendors now support X.25 through their proprietary products. In addition, several standards have been published to provide guidelines on how to internetwork X.25 with such networks as local area networks, ISDNs, circuit-switched networks, and maritime satellite networks.

Dividing the Layers

Before we explore specific products and standards, we should note that several standards organizations and telecommunications manufacturers divide the OSI communications layers into sublayers. This approach offers more flexibility and options to users and further separates discrete (but complementary) functions. The next three sections explain the sublayering of the transport, network, and data-link layers.

Dividing the Transport Layer

The CCITT and ISO standards now divide the transport layer into five protocol classes numbered 0 through 4 (see Figure 8-1). Each class contains a specific set of user support functions. The lower numbered classes provide a somewhat limited set of services, and the higher numbered classes offer more services. This approach allows both user and vendor to adapt to different requirements, yet stay within an "umbrella" of standards.

The transport layer sits on top of the X.25 layers. Since X.25 is designed to handle many network interface problems, it is not necessary to implement the full features of the transport layer. Therefore, transport protocol class 2 is often used with X.25, because a class 2 protocol resynchronizes as a result of X.25 resets and restarts.

The provision for protocol classes within the transport layer also gives the user several options in obtaining services through an internet. For example, a user might choose the class 4 protocol to obtain end-to-end reliability through a connectionless-mode internet. Also, class 4 is sometimes used with X.25.

Dividing the Network Layer

In its ISO DIS 8648 specification, ISO divides the network layer into three functional groups (see Figure 8-1). This division provides a convenient method for identifying internetworking operations. Moreover, several vendors now use this convention in their commercial offerings. At the top of the network layer is the subnetwork independence convergence protocol (SNICP), which provides relay and routing services for internetworking. This sublayer contains the

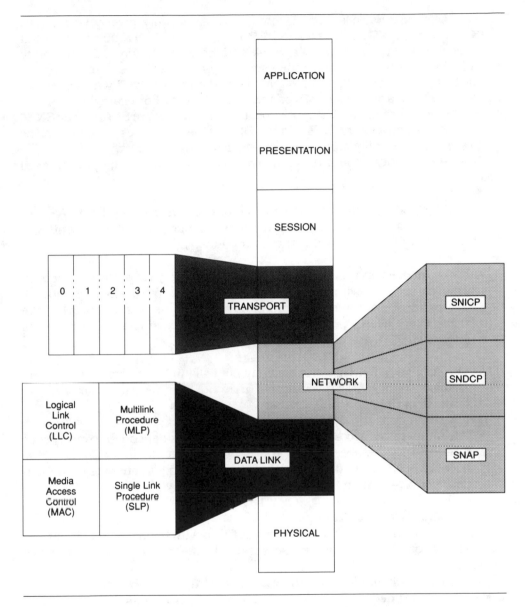

Figure 8-1. The Internetworking Layers

internetwork protocols to effect data transfer between networks.

The middle group is the subnetwork dependent convergence protocol *(SNDCP)*, which can be used to bring the interconnecting networks to a level needed for the interconnection. The interconnecting networks (subnetworks) may not provide a needed service, so SNDCP provides a "mapping" of the required service, or it may operate an explicit protocol to provide the convergence. At its most basic level, SNDCP serves as a network protocol converter.

ISO publishes DIS 8878 as an SNDCP to support a 1980 X.25 network that does not have all the features of a 1984 X.25 network. It adds information to the 1980 packet to obtain the added services of the 1984 version.

The lowest sublayer is the subnetwork access protocol (SNAP), which contains the services relevant to each interconnecting network. For example, SNA, the X.25 network interface, and Ethernet local area networks are SNAPS. The SNAP transfers data between the DTE and the DCE. It also manages the connections and receives the quality-of-service requests from the end user.

Several other ideas about these internetworking concepts are summarized below:

- The SNDCP may perform some or all of the functions of the SNAP. For example, the network service provisions may be completely absent, and SNDCP would then assume these functions.

- Two subnetworks may transmit using the same form of protocol data unit. This is possible with the following situations: the same subnetwork independent convergence protocol is used in both subnetworks, the subnetwork access protocol provides identical or similar services, or all subnetworks layers are the same.

- The subnetwork access protocol may not exist in the network layer. Local area networks (LANs), for example, may not use the subnetwork access protocol in the network layer.

- The subnetwork access protocol and subnetwork dependent convergence protocol may be absent from the network layer. In this situation, the network service functions can be performed by the subnetwork independent convergence protocol using the data-link layer.

Dividing the Data-Link Layer

The network sublayers should not be confused with the data-link sublayers. Several vendors and standards also subdivide the data-link layer into two sublayers.

One approach is published by IEEE as part of the IEEE 802 LAN specifications. The MAC (media access control) sublayer is protocol-specific to a LAN, such as Ethernet. The LLC (Logical Link Control) serves as an interface to an upper layer protocol, typically the network layer, and isolates it from the specific actions of the MAC sublayer. LLC uses many of the features of HDLC.

In an IEEE LAN network, the LLC relinquishes some of its data-link functions to the MAC. For example, it relies on MAC to insert framing signals (in HDLC, flags; in Ethernet, preambles). It also relies on MAC for the frame check sequence (FCS) operations. Conversely, LLC assumes some of the functions of the network layer. For example, it uses the N(R) and N(S) values in the control field to flow control LAN workstations in a manner similar to X.25's use of the P(R) and P(S) fields in the packet header. It can also establish logical connections between workstations with the HDLC SABME command, in a manner similar to X.25's packet-level procedures with the call request packet.

LLC can also be configured to perform none of these services. In this case, it uses the HDLC unnumbered information frame (UI) as a connectionless link-layer protocol.

Another approach is to divide the data-link layer into the following sublayers:

- *Single Link Procedure* (SLP): The use of a single communications link between two computers.

- *Multilink Procedure* (MLP): The use of more than one link between two computers.

With this approach, the MLP sits above several SLPs and manages them as if they were one logical link, providing the end user with additional capacity and better reliability. MLP is examined in the section dealing with X.75.

Internetworking X.25 and SNA

IBM has developed several major products to internetwork SNA and X.25. They fall into two categories: products that use X.25 as the primary transit network between SNA and X.25 devices and products that use SNA as the primary transit network between SNA and X.25 devices. This section discusses the use of X.25; the next section, the use of SNA.

X.25 as the Transit Network

The IBM X.25 NCP packet-switching interface (NPSI) provides an interface for SNA users to (and through) a packet-switched data network. NPSI appears to SNA as a series of switched or nonswitched SDLC links. When used as an interface to an X.25 network, NPSI provides communications between the following DTEs:

- SNA host node to SNA peripheral node

- SNA host node to SNA host node

- SNA host node to non-SNA X.25 node

- SNA host node to X.28 node

- SNA host node to other non-SNA node

NPSI provides a key service called the virtual circuit manager (VCM). This manager supervises all virtual circuits at the NPSI packet-switched interface and manages all connections using switched virtual circuits. It is also responsible for error recovery on the virtual circuits. The virtual circuit manager functions are controlled by the systems services control point (SSCP) or by X.25 control packets from the packet network. VCM allows the SNA user to communicate with either remote SNA nodes or remote non-SNA nodes.

SNA as the Transit Network

IBM's X.25 SNA Interconnect (XI) gives a user the ability to use SNA as the transit network. In other words, it provides the "cloud" between X.25 and SNA devices. The XI network is made up of a set of communicating devices with the XI node residing in a front-end processor using the network control program (NCP) and NPSI. The X.25 packets or SNA protocol data units are routed between XIs using the conventional SNA network services. XI is not needed at SNA intermediate nodes; XI is installed only where the X.25 DTE interfaces connect to the 3725 front-end processor.

XI has a several important characteristics:

- All SNA functions are retained (however, XI does require additional storage and machine cycles).

- XI can connect to X.25 DTEs on a single LAPB link and communicate with IBM hosts.

- XI provides a gateway to other X.25 networks.

- XI does not support the X.75 interface.

- All IBM equipment that supports an X.25 interface can be connected to XI.

Use of X.25 Features. The XI interface uses all the 1984 "essential" facilities of X.25 except fast select, throughput class negotiation, and transit delay selection and indication.

The closed user group (CUG) facilities allow up to 100 CUGs in one XI network. The following features are supported:

- Call allowed only within the CUG

- Called only within CUG but outgoing call allowed outside CUG (outgoing access)

- Incoming and outgoing calls barred within CUG

X.25 facilities are transparent to XI, except for the address extension facility. XI uses this facility as follows: The called address extension facility is provided by coding the called DTE address extension in the facility field. It is used by a DTE/PDN (Public Data Network) to call an XI/DTE. The calling address extension facility is used by a gateway DTE for outgoing calls to identify the calling XI/DTE.

Session Pipe. In providing a transit network with SNA, a fundamental question had to be addressed. How are logical units (LUs) to be used, since the logical unit concept is integral to SNA? It might appear that a logical unit session could be related to each X.25 virtual call. However, LU-to-LU sessions provide more functions for the user than does an X.25 logical channel connection. An SNA session entails considerable setup and management resources, which a comparable X.25 VC does not require. As a consequence, setting up an LU for each virtual call is impractical, because of the prohibitive cost.

The XI concept is based on the idea of a session being a "pipe." The X.25 logical channel networking procedures are performed completely within XI. All these logical channel communications occur through a single session between two XIs supporting the process. Consequently, the system services control point (SSCP) resources are not needed for each VC.

As stated earlier, the LU is simply a pipeline for the virtual calls. Once these sessions are established between two logical channels, they can be switched only between each other. XI does not permit switching to another LC on another session. Of course, this would be a very powerful capability, but it would be extraordinarily complex and costly.

XI/X.25 Call Setup. When a call request packet is received at the XI node, XI examines the address fields in the packet header to determine the correct outbound trunk on which to route the traffic. It then allocates a logical channel (LC) on the outbound interface, and updates the LC tables to "map" the logical channels together. The LC tables are also flagged to indicate a call setup state. The call request packet is updated to contain the outbound LCN and is then queued for transmission.

When the destination XI receives the packet, it examines a routing table to determine the proper XI/DTE interface. It updates the LC tables, and places the LCN in the packet. It maps the call request packet to an incoming call packet and queues the packet for transmission to the DTE.

If the DTE accepts the call, it returns a call accepted packet to XI, which uses the LCNs previously mapped to route this packet to the origination DTE. During this return, it changes the LC tables to indicate that the call has been accepted. Lastly, the originating XI node maps the call accepted packet to a call confirm packet and queues it for return to the originating DTE.

Internetworking DECnet and X.25
Introduction
DEC provides two major gateway products for connecting DEC equipment (which may or may not use DECnet) to an X.25 network. The two products are VAX PSI and VAX PSI Access.

The VAX PSI system operates in one of two modes, native mode and multihost mode. The native mode allows a direct access to one or more X.25 packet networks from a single VAX system. The multihost mode provides direct access into one or more X.25 public networks. It also provides indirect access for other systems. DEC requires that all systems have the VAX PSI system installed and all systems run DECnet.

The VAX PSI Access software operates in one mode: access mode. The access mode provides system access to any X.25 packet data network to which the system is connected. DEC requires that both systems use DECnet.

DEC also provides a combination system that permits the same VAX machine to run both VAX PSI and VAX PSI Access.

Another very useful feature in the DEC X.25 gateway is the ability to configure the VAX to operate as either a DTE or a DCE. This approach, which other vendors have as well, is very useful for communicating with another system that may not have X.25 DCE software.

A single VAX PSI provides considerable flexibility because it permits a VAX to connect to more than one packet network. Moreover, the gateway provides the ability to use multiple physical lines into one or more networks.

When the VAX is to operate as a DCE rather than a DTE, DEC has established that it use the ISO 8208 protocol. The VAX ISO 8208 profile supports all the X.25 optional facilities. Table 8-1 describes the system parameter values used with VAX PSI on the ISO 8208. (Chapter 7 provides information on ISO 8208).

DECnet manages X.25 virtual circuits (switched and permanent) through its network management layer. The network management commands the routing

Table 8-1. VAX PSI DCE Mode (ISO 8208)

CCITT Parameter	ISO 8208 Default value
Frame Control	
Retransmission Timer (TI) (milliseconds)	2000
Maximum Number of Transmissions (N2)	20
Maximum Number of Unacknowledged Frames (K)	7
Packet Control	
Call Requests Packet Timer (T21) (seconds)	200
Restart Request Packet Timer (T20) (seconds)	180
Reset Request Packet Timer (T22) (seconds)	180
Clear Request Packet Timer (T23) (seconds)	180
Maximum Retransmission for Restarts	1
Maximum Retransmission for Resets	1
Maximum Retransmission for Clears	1
Packet size (bytes)—default	128
Window size—default	2
Interrupt Response Timer (T26) (seconds)	180

layer to initialize X.25 circuits. This is performed by DECnet's routing initialization sublayer, which contains a database maintained by network management. The database maps the routing layer circuits to X.25 permanent and switched circuits. It contains such information on X.25 calls as addresses, the X.25 packet sizes, and call attempts. An outgoing call to an X.25 network is serviced by the routing initialization sublayer, which provides the necessary parameters to the X.25 header. These parameters are used to communicate directly with the X.25 network node.

Routing initialization determines whether to accept an incoming X.25 call or reject it, principally by examining the DTE addresses in the X.25 incoming call packet. The routing initialization sublayer may also segment and combine DNA datagrams in the packets. The sublayer also appends an error check field to every packet to check for transmission errors at the other end of the link.

The routing initialization sublayer also monitors the X.25 connections. Some events monitored are X.25 clears, restarts, and resets. If any of these packets is transmitted to the routing initialization sublayer, it sets the circuit as inoperable, informs its routing control sublayer, and then attempts to reinitialize the X.25 circuit.

DECnet X.25 Gateways

VAX PSI uses VAX specific I/O calls to manage an X.25 gateway interface. These calls are actual implementations of the abstract primitives in the OSI Model and are used to

- Assign a logical channel for transmission

- Set up a virtual circuit

- Reject a call request

- Transmit data

- Transmit an interrupt

- Receive and confirm an interrupt

- Reset a virtual circuit

- Confirm a virtual circuit

- Confirm a restart

- Clear a virtual call

Table 8-2 shows the basic function codes (primitives).

Table 8-2. VAX PSI I/O Calls (a partial list)

FORMAT	*$ASSIGN.(*)*
DESCRIPTION	Assign a channel
FORMAT	*$CANCEL chan*
DESCRIPTION	Clear a virtual call on a channel
FORMAT	*$DASSGN chan*
DESCRIPTION	De-assign the channel
FORMAT	*$QIO[efn],chanfunc=IO$_ACCESS(*)*
DESCRIPTION	Set up a virtual call circuit
FORMAT	*$QIO[efn],chanfunc=IO$ACCESS!IO$M_ACCEPT(*)*
DESCRIPTION	Accept a request to set up a virtual circuit
FORMAT	*$QIO[efn],chanfunc=IO$_DEACCESS(*)*
DESCRIPTION	Clear a virtual circuit
FORMAT	*$QIO[efn],chanfunc=IO$_NETCONTROL(*)*
DESCRIPTION	Reset a virtual circuit or confirm receipt of a reset
FORMAT	*$QIO[efn],chanfunc=IO$_READVBLK(*)*
DESCRIPTION	Receive data
FORMAT	*$QIO[efn],chanfunc=IO$_WRITEVBLK(*)*
DESCRIPTION	Transmit data
(*): Additional I/O Parameters	

A key aspect of the VAX PSI system is the network control block (NCB), which is constructed to support a virtual call and contains (at a minimum) the following:

- The remote DTE address for switched virtual calls

- The permanent virtual circuit name for PVCs

- The remote DTE subaddress

- The local subaddress

- User data

- Diagnostic codes

- Network name

- Access control information

- The facilities invoked for the session

VAX PSI also uses the concept of a "mailbox" for each logical call. The facility permits the user to handle incoming calls, associating a mailbox with a specific session. When incoming calls arrive at the user DTE, the user program reads the NCB and the mailbox associated with a logical channel.

VAX PSI also makes extensive use of return status codes. They determine whether the various I/O requests into the X.25 network were successful; for example, whether a call request was successfully received.

Internetworking an X.25 Station on a LAN
Introduction

At first glance, placing an X.25 station onto a local area network might appear relatively simple. After all, if all components use standard primitives with the LAN and perform encapsulation and decapsulation functions, the process should be fairly straightforward. Unfortunately, the problem is more involved. Consider the following:

- Since X.25 is written from the network (DCE) perspective, a user must define some specific DTE actions.

- LAN stations generally communicate symmetrically (i.e., on a DTE-to-DTE basis). We have learned that X.25 is asymmetrical: DTE-to-DCE on each side of the network cloud.

- X.25 is basically point-to-point, with the DTE and DCE as the two points. Many LANs are broadcast systems, and the LAN DTEs connect logically through the broadcast medium.

- X.25 uses the very reliable, connection-oriented data-link layer, LAPB. Most LANs use the Logical Link Control, type 1 specification from the IEEE (IEEE LLC1, 802.2). LLC1 is connectionless, and allows unnumbered information (UI) frames. Consequently, LLC1 differs significantly from LAPB.

- Many X.25 public packet network vendors administer the X.25 facilities. LAN stations often need to control some of the facilities directly. Moreover, some X.25 DCEs are very powerful, offering several thousand simultaneous virtual calls to the attached DTEs. Many LANs do not have this capacity.

- With a connectionless link-level LAN (LLC1), the idea of an X.25 level 2 (LAPB) link connection does not exist. Reinitializing the link from the context of X.25 is simply not in the repertoire of LLC1's commands and responses.

- If the SABME option of LLC is exercised, LLC is designated as type 2 (LLC2). This option allows LLC to perform acknowledgment and flow-control functions between two workstations on a LAN. Therefore, the X.25 packet-level procedures for flow control and acknowledgment become redundant.

Nonetheless, internetworking X.25 with LANs is possible. Fortunately, the ISO 8881 (Annex A) provides several scenarios for internetworking X.25 LAN stations. These four possibilities are some of the more common:

- One gateway between a LAN and an X.25 WAN (wide area network)

- Two gateways between a LAN and an X.25 WAN

- One gateway that connects two LANs

- Two gateways that connect two LANs

As an example, a LAN station in Figure 8-2 is to communicate with another station not on its LAN. It must communicate with an internetworking unit (IWU) located on its LAN. The IWU provides gateway functions to support the internetworking. As discussed in the introductory section of this book, the protocols below X.25 PLP on the right and left sides of each other are independent of each other. ISO 8881 (Annex A) describes how the right and left sides of the X.25 PLP levels can be coupled, but it does not address the lower levels.

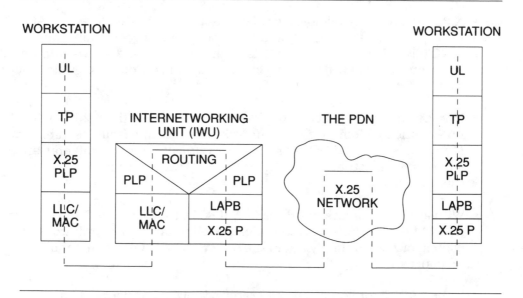

Figure 8-2. Internetworking X.25 Devices on a LAN

The LAN station acts as an X.25 DTE, and each station communicates in a point-to-point mode as stipulated by ISO 8208. The packet-level (PL) entity of the DTE-to-DTE session is identified by the media across control (MAC) address of the two LAN stations.

The IWU maps the logical channel numbers across the two sides of the PLP levels. This task is the same as in any wide area X.25 network that must map the LANs across both sides of the network cloud. However, the IWU performs two different roles: It emulates a DCE on the terminal side and a DTE on the network side.

Call Setup and Clearing

The IWU performs the functions of an X.25 network cloud, receiving call setup and clear packets from both sides of the gateway, performing several editing functions, and mapping the packet types to other packet types.

During a call setup, the IWU receives an incoming call packet from either the LAN or an X.25 network. (These networks have already processed the request from a user, created the call request packet, and sent it to the X.25 PLP, where it is mapped to the incoming call packet.) The IWU checks the packet (including facilities requests). It matches the window sizes and packet sizes to relate the incoming call packet to those available on the other interface. If the IWU does not have segmentation and reassembly capabilities, it must ensure the packet sizes on the two interfaces are equal or clear the call. If segmenting and reassembly is supported by the IWU, it dictates the sizes. It maps the MAC addresses at the LAN interface and the X.25 address at the packet interface (X.25 address fields and address extension fields).

The IWU determines the recipient of the packet and maps the address across both sides of the IWU. It must also select a free logical channel on the other side of the IWU and store the association of the two logical channels to transfer the ongoing data packets to the proper recipient during data transfer. It then transmits a call request packet to the outgoing side of the IWU. The receiving station maps this packet into an incoming call packet.

If the call request is successful, the IWU receives a call connected packet from the called station. It then transmits a call accepted packet to the calling interface, using the logical channel corresponding to the original incoming call packet. The IWU handles unsuccessful calls with clear request and clear indication packets.

Thus, the IWU acts as an intermediary between the two communicating stations. For example, it recreates the call request packet from the originating station in one direction and recreates the call accepted packet in the other direction.

Internetworking X.25-Based Networks with X.75
Introduction

X.25 is designed to allow users to communicate with each other through one network. However, two users operating on two separate X.25 networks may need to establish communications to share resources and exchange data. X.75 is designed to meet this need. It can also connect packet exchanges within a network. The standard has been in development for more than 10 years; it was published as a provisional recommendation in 1978 and amended in 1980, 1984, and 1988.

The objective of X.75 is to allow internetworking. It provides a gateway for a user to communicate through multiple networks with another user (see Figure 8-3). It is also used to connect exchanges within a network. The standard works best when user stations, networks, and packet exchanges use X.25 packets, because X.75 uses the X.25 packet headers created at the user/subnetwork interface. The end user of an X.25 connection never sees X.75.

X.75 is quite similar to X.25; it has many of its features, such as permanent virtual circuits, virtual call circuits, logical channel groups, logical channels, and several of the control packets. The architecture is divided into physical, link, and packet levels with X.75 PLP in the network layer.

X.75 defines the operation of international packet-switched services. It describes how two terminals are connected logically by an international link, while each terminal operates within its own packet mode data network. X.75 uses a slightly different term for the network interface. In the description of X.25, we used the term data circuit-terminating equipment (DCE) to describe an X.25 packet exchange. The X.75 terminology defines this device as signaling terminal equipment (STE), even though it may be the same as the X.25 device.

Like X.25, the physical level can be implemented with appropriate V Series recommendations (such as V.35). X.75 requires the signaling to be performed at 64 Kbits/s. (An optional rate is 48 Kbits/s.) Of course, many vendors use other link speeds (56 Kbits/s, 1.544 Mbits/s, etc.). The second level of X.75 uses the HDLC subset LAPB. X.75 does not support LAP.

X.75 and Multilink Procedures (MLP)

The X.75 link level frequently uses the multilink procedure (MLP), which permits multiple links between STEs. MLP establishes the rules for frame transmission and frame resequencing for delivery to and from the multiple links. With multilink operations parallel communications channels between STEs appear as one channel with a greater capacity. The arrangement provides more reliability and throughput than could be achieved on a single channel.

Multilink procedures exist at the upper part of the data-link level (see Figure 8-1). The X.25 network layer perceives that it is connected to a single link, and the LAPB single links operate as though they are connected directly to the network layer. MLP is responsible for flow control between layers 2 and 3, as well as for resequencing the data units for delivery to the network layer. The network layer operates with a perceived higher bandwidth in the data link-layer.

X.75 Packet Types

X.75 does not use the variety of packet types found in X.25, primarily because the STE-to-STE communications has no relationship to the "other side of the cloud." In X.75 there is no other side, since communication is only

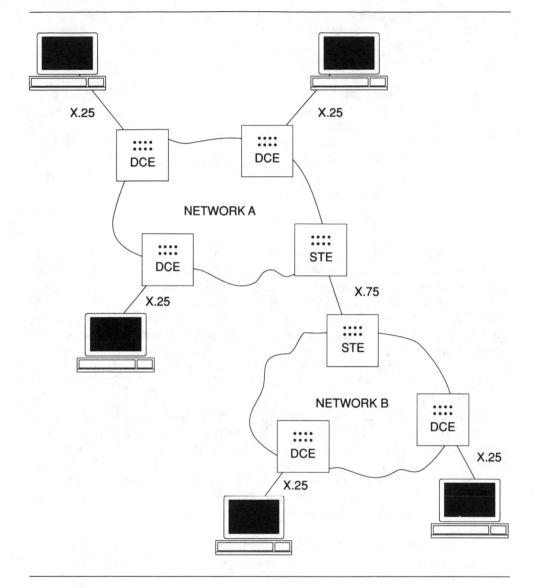

Figure 8-3. X.75 Gateways

between two STEs and not two sets of DCEs/DTEs. The X.75 protocol uses the following packet types:

    Call setup and clearing
        Call request
        Call connected
        Clear request
        Clear confirmation

Data and interrupt
    Data
    Interrupt
    Interrupt confirmation

Flow control and reset
    Receive ready
    Receive not ready
    Reset
    Reset confirmation

Restart
    Restart
    Restart confirmation

The X.75 packet format is almost identical to the X.25 format. The address fields are specifically defined as international data numbers (X.121). The logical channels have significance only for the STE/STE interface.

Figure 8-4 shows the similarities and differences between X.25 and X.75. The DTE in Network A initiates a call to a DTE in Network C. The call setup packet and logical channel relationships are depicted for each phase of the connection establishment. Note that X.75 does not use the incoming call and call accepted packets needed by X.25 on the "other side" of the network cloud.

X.75 Utilities

The X.75 packet carries an additional field called network utilities (see Figure 8-5). It provides for network administrative functions and signaling. In many situations, a request in the X.25 user packet facility field invokes an X.75 network utility. The X.25 facilities that do not require any STE action remain in the facilities field and are relayed transparently through the STE. Other user facilities that require STE action are mapped into the X.75 utilities field. The utilities are described below.

- The *transit network identification* contains the first four digits of the international data number of the transit network controlling a portion of the virtual circuit. If more than one transit network is involved in the call traversal of the networks, this identification is also present in the call connected packet.

- The *call identifier* is an identifying name established by the originating network for each virtual circuit. When used with the DTE address, it uniquely identifies the call.

- The *throughput class indication* specifies the throughput classes applying to the call.

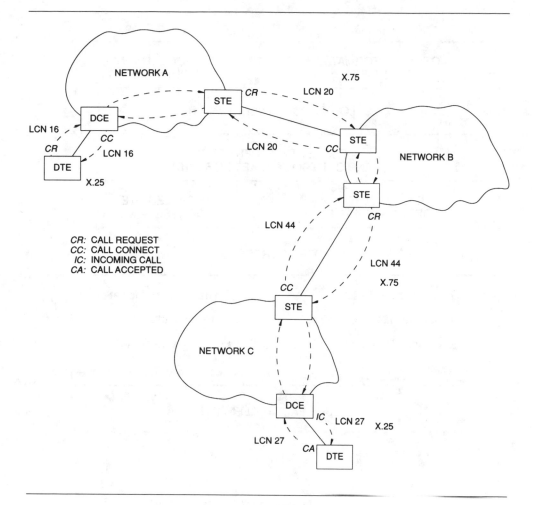

Figure 8-4. Internetworking with X.75

- The *window size indication* identifies the negotiated window size between the STEs.

- The *packet size indication* identifies the negotiated packet size between the STEs.

- The *fast select indication* indicates that a fast select is requested for the call.

- The *closed user group indication* establishes calls between DTEs that are members of an international closed user group. X.75 also supports closed user group with outgoing access indication.

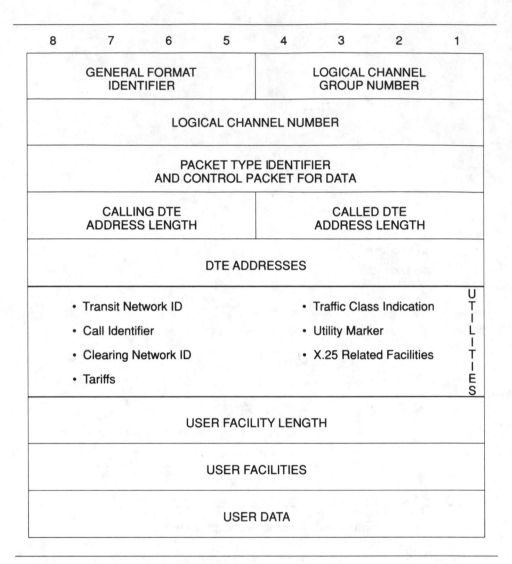

| 8 | 7 | 6 | 5 | 4 | 3 | 2 | 1 |

GENERAL FORMAT IDENTIFIER

LOGICAL CHANNEL GROUP NUMBER

LOGICAL CHANNEL NUMBER

PACKET TYPE IDENTIFIER AND CONTROL PACKET FOR DATA

CALLING DTE ADDRESS LENGTH

CALLED DTE ADDRESS LENGTH

DTE ADDRESSES

- Transit Network ID
- Call Identifier
- Clearing Network ID
- Tariffs

- Traffic Class Indication
- Utility Marker
- X.25 Related Facilities

UTILITIES

USER FACILITY LENGTH

USER FACILITIES

USER DATA

Figure 8-5. The X.75 Packet

- The *reverse charging indication* allows reverse charging of calls to be established across the networks.

- The *called line address modified notification*, used with hunt groups and call redirections, identifies the specific reason for the called address to be different from the address in the call request packet.

- The *clearing network identification code* provides additional information on the origin of the clear request packet.

- The *traffic class indication* identifies such service information as terminal, facsimile. This utility has not yet been fully defined.

- The *transit delay selection and indication* identifies the transit delay on the virtual circuit in accordance with X.135.

- The *utility marker* separates X.75 utilities from non-X.75 utilities. Its use is subject to bilateral agreements between networks.

- *Tariffs* could be used for billing, but this utility is defined by each network.

- The *network user ID* (NUI) provides supplementary information for billing, accounting, etc.

- The *recognized private operating agencies* (RPOA) is used to designate the transit network.

Accessing X.25 Networks through an ISDN

The motivation for using X.25 and ISDN may not be obvious, especially since ISDN is still limited in use. Nonetheless, as the number of ISDN installations grows, some means must be provided to convey data to a packet network through the local ISDN node, since the user workstation may be physically attached to an ISDN channel.

The ISDN CCITT Recommendation X.31 provides two scenarios for the interface of an X.25 packet mode terminal into an ISDN node: Case A describes access to a packet network, and Case B describes the use of an ISDN virtual circuit service.

Case A: Access to a Packet Data Network

Figure 8-6 illustrates Case A, which supports a rudimentary service. The ISDN node transfers packet calls transparently from the DTE to the X.25 network's access unit (AU). This scenario supports only B-channel access. Moreover, if two local DTEs wish to communicate with each other, their packets must be transmitted through the ISDN and through the X.25 network, before one DTE's packets can be relayed to the other DTE. This minimum integration scenario uses the B channels for all call management, which is performed using ISDN signaling procedures before initiating the X.25 level 2 and level 3 procedures. In essence, the ISDN node passes the X.25 call transparently to the X.25 network.

Case A supports an X.25 permanent access or an X.32 demand access. The demand access is shown in Figure 8-6 with the switched connection between the two exchange termination points (ET). Both provide a 64-Kbits/s connection between the packet network port and the X.25 user device.

Figure 8-6 shows two options available with Case A. Note that in this figure

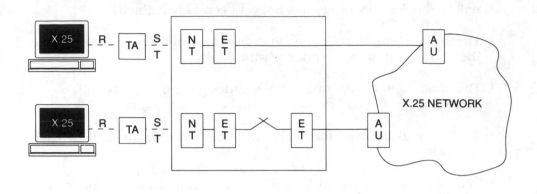

Figure 8-6. Minimum Configuration Scenario (Case A)

(and in all ISDN specifications), an X.25 network and its terminal adapter (TA) are considered equivalent to a packet mode TE1 at the ISDN S/T interface. The top part of the figure illustrates how the permanent, nondemand option is used. The X.25 DTE and TA or the TE1 is connected to the ISDN port at the packet data network ISDN access unit port (AU). The ISDN Q.931 messages are not used, and the TA is tasked with physical rate adaptation (bit rate changes) between the R reference point and the 64 Kbits/s B-channel rate.

The bottom part of Figure 8-6 shows the second option, called demand access. Before any X.25 functions, ISDN signaling procedures set up a B channel. Typically, an ISDN Q.931 setup message identifies the access port of the packet data network, and the called DTE field in the X.25 packet identifies the remote user device.

Case B: Using the ISDN Virtual Circuit Service

The Case B scenario provides several additional functions (see Figure 8-7). The ISDN provides a packet handling (PH) function within the node. Actual implementations of Case B use two separate facilities for the interconnection. The ISDN switch is provided through a vendor's ISDN NT1 product, and the packet handler function is provided by the vendor's packet switch itself.

Case B permits two options: access via the B channel and access via the D channel. With the first option, the X.25 packet- and data-link layer procedures are conveyed through the B channel. Access through the D channel is the implementation used in more vendor's products today. All active logical channels are established through a D-channel connection, and all X.25 packets—including connection setups, connection disconnects, and data packets—must be transmitted on the D channel on the LAPD link. In effect, the D channel access provides the preferred method for out-of-channel (out-of-band) signaling.

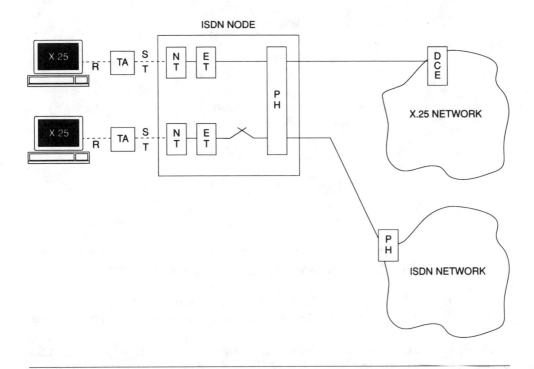

Figure 8-7. Maximum Configuration Scenario (Case B)

X.25 states that a DTE operating with Case B of X.31 must adhere to the following addressing rules:

- Before 1997: Addresses will be a maximum of 12 digits from E.164.

- After 1966: Addresses may have 15 digits based on E.164.

Example of X.25 and ISDN Q.931 Connection Establishment

Figures 8-8 and 8-9 illustrate the use of X.25 across an ISDN using the B channel. As illustrated in Figure 8-8, an ISDN terminal adapter (TA) is required to provide the protocol translations. This section provides a general review of X.25 and ISDN operations. For the reader who needs a more detailed view of the these figures, X.31, Appendix III, is a good source.

The originating user device (DTE A on the left side of Figure 8-9) communicates with the TA with the three layers of X.25. Before the DTE begins any X.25 operations, its TA sets up an LAPD link (if one does not exist). Upon receiving a UA frame, it then sets up an ISDN Q.931 network-level connection between the TA and the ISDN node by exchanging several ISDN messages labeled "Set Up Q.931 Connection" in Figure 8-9.

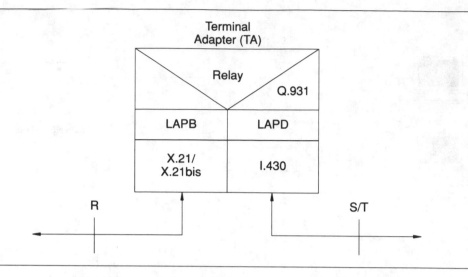

Figure 8-8. ISDN Terminal Adapter Support for X.25

Next, an LAPB link is established with the exchange of LAPB frames, labeled "Set Up LAPB Link" in Figure 8-9. Then, the TA issues a call request packet.

The effect of this packet is the establishment of an X.25 logical channel between the ISDN node, the TA, the DTE, and the DCE. Once the B channel is available, it is used to pass the X.25 connection management packets back and forth between the DTE and DCE. These operations are shown in Figure 8-9 with the arrows between the DTE and DCE.

The bottom part of the figure shows the effect of the X.25 clear procedures, which cause the release of the D and B channel sessions.

Example of an Operating ISDN/X.25 Internetworking System

Here we discuss Northern Telecom's ISDN/X.25 internetworking system to illustrate an actual product providing the X.25/ISDN service. Northern Telecom's ISDN packet handler supports several packet mode services through the ISDN node. It supports X.25 service on either the B or D channel, as well as synchronous and asynchronous support solely on the B channel. Currently four types of X.25 packet mode service can be obtained through the packet handler. Some options require the establishment of layer 3 only; others require the establishment of layers 1 and 2 through the D channel, and then the establishment of layer 3 through the B channel. Table 8-3 summarizes the options, the channels, and the layers invoked.

X.300 Interworking Recommendations

CCITT publishes a series of recommendations about the internetworking of various types of networks. These standards were published in the 1988 Blue

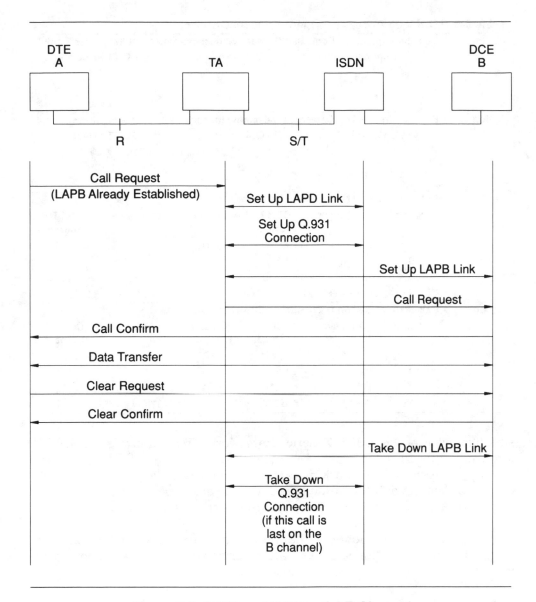

Figure 8-9. Q.931 and X.25 on the B Channel

Books as the X.300 Series. They actually encompass several documents numbered X.300 through X.370, generally called the X.300 interworking recommendations. Notice that we have introduced a new word, *interworking*; CCITT uses this word in place of internetworking.

Perhaps the most useful feature of X.300 is its explanation of how the X Series recommendations (such as X.25) fit into interworking. Figure 8-10 is a

Table 8-3. ISDN X.25 Access (Northern Telecom Options)

Option 1:	Establishing call on Dedicated B Channel (necessary to establish Layer 3 only).		
	Channel	**OSI Layer**	**CCITT Protocol**
	B	3	X.25
	B	2	LAPB
	B	1	I.430
Option 2:	Establishing Call on Dedicated D Channel (necessary to establish Layer 3 only).		
	Channel	**OSI Layer**	**CCITT Protocol**
	D	3	X.25
	D	2	LAPB
	D	1	I.430

Option 3:	Establishing Call on Switched B Channel.					
	Channel	**OSI Layer**	**CCITT Protocol**	**Channel**	**OSI Layer**	**CCITT Protocol**
	D	3	Q.931	D	3	X.25
	D	2	LAPD	D	2	LAPD
	D	1	I.430	D	1	I.430
	(ESTABLISH LAYERS 1 and 2)			(AND THEN LAYER 3)		

Option 4:	Establishing Call on D Channel on Demand.					
	Channel	**OSI Layer**	**CCITT Protocol**	**Channel**	**OSI Layer**	**CCITT Protocol**
	D	3	Q.931	D	3	X.25
	D	2	LAPD	D	2	LAPD
	D	1	I.430	D	1	I.430
	(ESTABLISH LAYERS 1 and 2)			(AND THEN LAYER 3)		

simplified view of the X.300/X-Series framework. The standards are divided into three categories:

1. Aspects of interworking pertinent to different cases
2. Aspects of interworking pertinent to each case
3. Aspects of internetwork signaling interfaces

The X.300 Recommendations that pertain to X.25-based packet-switched public data networks "for each case" are described in this section. They are as follows:

- *X.322:* Circuit-switched public data networks (CSPDN)

- *X.323:* Packet-switched public data networks (PSPDNs)

- *X.324:* Mobile systems

- *X.325:* Integrated services digital networks (ISDNs)

- *X.326:* Common channel signaling networks (CCSNs)

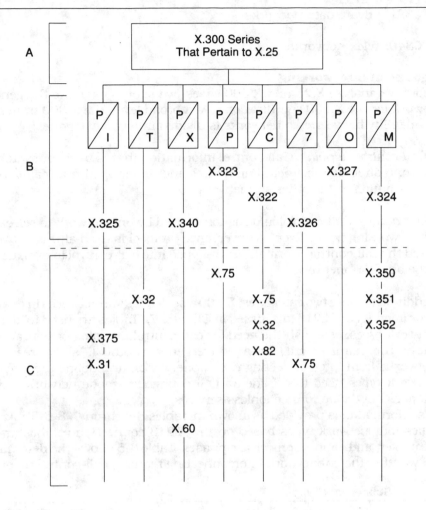

LEGEND:
A: ARRANGEMENTS GENERIC TO DIFFERENT CASES
B: ARRANGEMENTS FOR EACH CASE
C: INTERWORK SIGNALLING INTERFACES

ABBREVIATIONS:
C: CIRCUIT SWITCHED DATA NETWORK
 I: ISDN
M: MOBILE NETWORK
O: PRIVATELY OWNED NETWORK
P: PACKET SWITCHED DATA NETWORK
T: TELEPHONE NETWORK
X: TELEX NETWORK
7: SIGNALLING SYSTEM NO 7

Figure 8-10. X.25 and the X.300 Recommendations

- *X.327:* Private data networks

- *X.340:* Telex networks

Categories of Interworking

Before we analyze X.25 and X.300 cases, we should examine the general framework for the X.300 specifications. At a broad level, the X.300 transmission capability between two networks is divided into two categories:

- *Call-control mapping.* Call-control information that is used for switching in one subnetwork (including addressing) is mapped into call-control information in the other subnetwork.

- *Port access.* Call-control information is used by one network to select the interworking point. Then a convergence protocol is used at this network, and the call-control information is mapped into call-control information in the other subnetwork.

In addition to these two categories, X.300 also defines subnetworks in relation to Recommendation X.213 (discussed in Chapter 7). Tables are used to identify subnetwork types, establish the need for call-control mapping or port access, stipulate the requirement for a convergence protocol, show resulting subnetworks from interconnecting two subnetworks, and define the different subnetwork types used to provide an OSI connection-mode network service (X.300 does not define connectionless services).

This information is provided as shown in Tables 8-4 through 8-6. Table 8-4 identifies four network types based on the X.213 connection-establishment, data-transfer, and connection-release phases. Table 8-5 shows the determination of whether the subnetwork interconnecting requires call-control mapping

Table 8-4. Subnetwork Types

Phase of the Call	Connection Establishment	Data Transfer Phase	Connection Release Phase
Subnetwork Type			
I	M	M	M
II	M	P	M
III	S	P	S
IV	M or S	F	M or S
Legend:			
M	All mandatory elements required for the provision of the OSI Network Service are signaled through the subnetwork by means of its signaling capability.		
P	The functionality of the subnetwork corresponds to that of a physical connection.		
S	A subset of all mandatory elements required for the provision of the OSI Network Service are signalled through the subnetwork by means of its signaling capability.		

Table 8-5. Interconnecting Two Networks=Categories of Interworking

Subnetwork Type	I	II	III	IV
I	Interworking by call control mapping	Interworking by call control mapping or by port access	Interworking by call control mapping or by port access	Interworking by call control mapping or by port access
II	Interworking by call control mapping or port access	Interworking by call control mapping	Interworking by call control mapping or by port access	Interworking by call control mapping or by port access
III	Interworking by call control mapping or by port access	Interworking by call control mapping or by port access	Interworking by call control mapping	Interworking by call control mapping or by port access
IV	Interworking by call control mapping or by port access	Interworking by call control mapping or by port access	Interworking by call control mapping or by port access	Interworking by call control mapping

Table 8-6. Providing OSI Connection-mode Network Service with Different Subnetwork Types

Phase of the OSI-NS Call Connection	Connection Establishment Phase	Data Transfer Phase	Connection Release Phase
Subnetwork Type			
I	No Convergence Protocol Required	No Convergence Protocol Required	No Convergence Protocol Required
II	No Convergence Protocol Required	Convergence Protocol Required	No Convergence Protocol Required
III	Convergence Protocol Required	Convergence Protocol Required	Convergence Protocol Required
IV	Convergence Protocol Required	Convergence Protocol Required	Convergence Protocol Required

or port access. Finally, Table 8-6 shows whether a convergence protocol is required by the four network types for the X.213 phases.

Transfer of Addressing Information

X.301 includes rules for the transfer of addressing information. In Chapter 5 we learned about the various X.25 addressing schemes. X.301 defines how X.121 and E.164 addresses are used between two networks.

Figure 8-11 with Table 8-7 depicts the permissible address forms for the call-establishment phase. The prefixes P1 through P6 are not passed over the IWF, and their form and use is an internal network matter. The escape digits E1 and

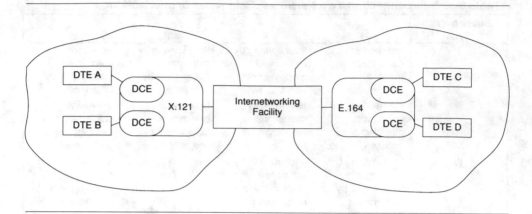

Figure 8-11. X.301 Addressing Domains

Table 8-7. Call Establishment Phase Address Forms

Direction	Form of Address	Extent of Validity
A to B	NTN	Network
A to B	P1+NTN	Network
A to B	DNIC+NTN	Internetwork
A to B	P2+DNIC+NTN	Internetwork
A to B	NTN+[NPI/TOA]	Network
A to B	DNIC+NTN+[NPI/TOA]	Internetwork
C to D	SN	Network
C to D	P3+SN	Network
C to D	CC+(NDC)+SN	Internetwork
C to D	P4+CC+(NDC)+SN	Internetwork
C to D	SN+[NPI/TOA]	Network
C to D	CC+(NDC)+SN+[NPI/TOA]	Internetwork
A to C	E1+CC+(NDC)+SN	Internetwork escape to E.164/E.163
A to C	P5+E1+CC+(NDC)+SN	Internetwork escape to E.164/E.163
A to C	CC+(NDC)+SN+[NPI/TOA]	Internetwork
C to A	E2+DNIC+NTN	Internetwork escape to X.121
C to A	P6+E2+DNIC+NTN	Internetwork escape to X.121
C to A	DNIC+NTN+[NPI/TOA]	Internetwork

E2 indicate that the succeeding address is a different numbering plan. The prefixes may or may not precede the escape digit.

It is also permissible to use another field to indicate the type of address present. This element in the protocol is called the number plan indentification/ type of address (NPI/TOA). Its form depends on the specific network access protocol used.

Internetworking X.25 and Maritime Satellite Systems. X.324, X.350 – X.352

In the past, ships at sea were equipped with high-frequency radio systems, using telephony and telex transmission schemes. The earlier systems also relied on Morse code. While high-frequency systems are still used (with signal reflection across the ionized atmospheric layers) most maritime users now use satellite systems for transmission and reception of data, video, and voice.

In 1979 the International Maritime Satellite Organization (INMARSAT) was founded to foster standards and operational facilities for at-sea communications. It became operational in 1982 and now provides continuous communications services to properly equipped ships in all parts of the world.

INMARSAT operations are governed by several CCITT recommendations. Here we discuss the operations of a maritime-ship communication system as well as the CCITT mobile data transmissions specifications.

An at-sea ship's communications process with a satellite is controlled by an earth station (obviously a misnomer in this case). The ship's antenna dish is quite small, only 0.9 meters in diameter. To prevent signal interference it is mounted on the ship's superstructure. A stabilization system keeps the dish pointed directly at the communicating satellite.

CCITT has developed these recommendations to govern maritime communications. The 1988 CCITT Blue Books include them as part of the X.300 interworking recommendations:

- *X.324:* General arrangements for interworking packet-switched public networks with mobile systems

- *X.350:* General requirements for maritime satellite service

- *X.351:* Packet assembly/disassembly facilities (PADs) in association with maritime services

- *X.352:* Internetworking public packet networks and maritime satellite systems

- X.353: Routing principles for maritime satellite systems and public data networks

The X.324 Recommendation is a very brief document that describes the relationships of these specifications and defines the requirements for the use of other standards, such as X.1, X.2, and X.10 (Chapter 7 describes these standards).

The maritime local circuit is between the ship's DTE and the ship's earth station. The maritime satellite circuit is the satellite channel between the ship's earth station and the coastal earth station. The maritime terrestrial circuit is the circuit connecting the coastal earth station to the maritime satellite data switching exchange (MSDSE). This exchange provides the internetworking between the satellite system and the public data network, handling routing as well as call control to and from ships at sea. It also manages the charging of the calls.

X.350 specifies several options for the interface between the components. For example, Recommendations X.21 *bis* and X.22 are permitted for circuit-switched public data networks, and X.25 is permitted for interfacing into packet networks. An interface through an X.25 public data network is best, because this specification provides many functions and is used throughout the world.

Recommendation X.121 is used to address the ships at sea. The format for the shipboard DTE is the DNIC plus a ship station identity (Recommendation E.210/F.120) plus optional digits identifying the on-board DTE. Three DNICs have been assigned the Atlantic Ocean, Pacific Ocean, and Indian Ocean; they are 1111, 1112, and 1113, respectively.

In addition to the X.121 identification scheme, the transmission type is identified by a prefix code. A two-digit code describes the type of call—telephone, telex, or data—and the category of call within those transmission types. Table 8-8 shows some examples.

X.351 specifies implementation of PAD support for the maritime service. Essentially, Recommendations X.3 and X.29 are used; Chapter 9 discusses these specifications. Generally speaking, the PAD parameter settings are similar to the settings of X.3, but some parameter values do differ, so refer to the specific X.351 specification for more detail.

Other X.300/X.25 Interworking Recommendations

Here is a brief look at other X.300/X.25 interworking recommendations.

Table 8-8. Examples of Maritime Satellite Service, Prefix & Access Codes

Code	Application
15	Radiogram service
20	Access-to-Maritime PAD
24	Telex letter service
32	Medical advice
34	Person-to-person call
36	Credit card calls
38	Medical assistance
39	Maritime assistance
41	Meteorological reports
42	Navigational hazards and warnings
43	Ship position reports
51	Meteorological forecasts
55	News, international
56	News, national

X.322. Interworking X.25 with Circuit-Switched Public Data Networks (CSPDN)

X.322 is a rather terse description of call-control arrangements between a packet network and a circuit network. It defines the arrangements for this call by referencing CCITT X.301 and X.302, specifications described earlier in this section.

X.322 requires the interworking between the packet and circuit networks to be performed in accordance with X.75, C.32, and/or X.82.

X.323. Interworking Packet Networks

The X.323 specification is also quite terse, simply setting the requirements for X.75 use in interworking arrangements between two packet networks. As with the other X.300 specifications, it describes the use of user classes of service with X.1 and user facilities with X.2. It also stipulates the use of X.29, X.31, X.32, and X.96 for this internetworking arrangement. In addition, it stipulates the use of logical links A1 and G1, as defined in X.92 (X.92 is described in Chapter 7).

X.325. Internetworking ISDNs and Packet Networks

The X.325 specification establishes the procedures for internetworking ISDNs and packet networks that use the X.25 interface. X.325 requires X.75 and X.31 for the specific internetworking signaling interfaces. As might be clear at this point in our discussion of the X.300 Recommendations, X.325 also stipulates the specific transmission services as defined in X.1 and X.2. X.325 is a bit more detailed than some of its counterparts.

Since ISDNs and packet networks use different addressing and numbering plans (for example E.164 and X.121), X.301 describes the mapping of the addresses between the two different types of networks, as described earlier in this section.

X.326. Internetworking X.25 with Common Channel Signaling Networks (CCSN)

X.326 defines the internetworking between common channel signaling systems and packet networks in the context of the OSI (Open Systems Interconnection) Model. X.326 recommends the packet network offer the full capability of the OSI network-layer service (as defined in X.213 and X.223). Furthermore, the standard stipulates that an OSI connection-oriented network-layer service is to be provided for the interworking of these two networks. X.326 stipulates the use of X.75 as the internetworking protocol between the packet networks and the common channel signaling networks.

X.327. Internetworking X.25 with Private Data Networks

As might be expected, X.327 has little to say about interworking between public and private networks, since CCITT's orientation is toward public internetworking. However, X.327 does provide guidance on the interconnection of X.25 devices through public and private X.25-based networks. Basically, the major aspect of X.327 is its description of the mapping of connection-oriented services (as defined in X.213) to the X.25 packets.

The Internet Protocol (IP)

Introduction

The Internet Protocol (IP) is an internetworking protocol developed by the Department of Defense. The system was implemented as part of the DARPA internetwork protocol project and is widely used throughout the world. IP is a connectionless service, permitting the exchange of traffic between two host computers without any prior call setup. (However, these two computers do share a common connection-oriented transport protocol.)

Figure 8-12 shows the relationship between IP and X.25. The IP is used at the IP gateway to determine the route of the datagram to (in this example) subnetworks A, B, or C. X.25 is invoked only at the entrance and exit of the internet, that is to say, between DTE 1 and subnet A, DTE 2 and subnet B.

The IP header and the X.25 header are used for different operations. The IP header identifies the address of the receiving network and host computer with an IP address called the *internet address*. IP addresses may also be used to identify the gateways that are to participate in routing the data unit. Generally, the IP address is not used between the host DTE and the network. The X.25 address is used instead. The IP datagram and header may be encapsulated further into the specific protocol of the transit network. For example, a transit

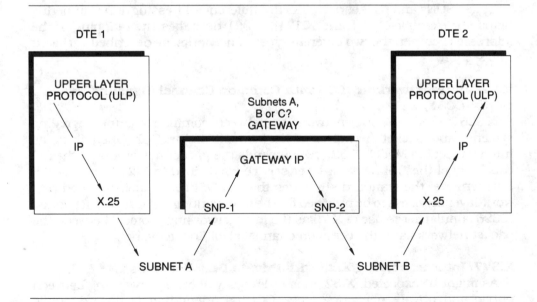

Figure 8-12. IP and X.25

network could be an SNA network. IP is not concerned with the internal operations of the transit networks.

After the transit network (subnet A) has delivered the traffic to an IP gateway, its internal control information is stripped away. The gateway then uses the destination address in the datagram header to determine where to route the traffic. At the receiving network (subnet B), it then passes the datagram to the network interface protocol (as with X.25), where it is delivered to the receiving station.

IP Source Routing

IP uses a mechanism called *source routing* as part of its routing algorithm. Source routing allows an upper layer protocol (ULP) to determine how the IP gateways route the datagrams. Indeed, the ULP could be X.25, but in most systems, the upper layer protocol is a vendor-specific protocol. The ULP has the option of passing a list of internet addresses to the IP module. The list contains the intermediate gateways to be transited during the routing of the datagrams to the final destination.

When a gateway IP receives the datagram, it uses the addresses in a source routing field to determine the next intermediate transit network. The gateway IP then replaces the source route entry with its own address. This address is the address known to the subnet that is next receiving the datagram.

The IP gateway makes routing decisions based on the routing list. If the destination host resides in another network, the IP gateway must decide how to route to the other network. Indeed, if multiple hops are involved in the communications process, each gateway must be traversed and the gateway must make decisions about routing the traffic.

Since IP is connectionless, the datagrams could be lost between the two end users' stations. For example, the IP gateway generally enforces a maximum queue length; if this queue length is violated, the buffers will overflow. In this situation, the additional datagrams are discarded in the network. For this reason, the higher level transport layer is essential.

IP does not become involved in the user-to-network interface; this part of the internet work is the task of X.25. Consequently, an internet implementer attempts to keep X.25 transparent to IP and vice versa.

Conclusions

X.25 is used in many different internetworking and interworking configurations, but most commonly with X.75 in public data networks. Increasingly, it is being implemented with IP networks as part of the GOSIP protocol suite (see Appendix A). CCITT has published a number of X.25 interworking recommendations in the X.300 and X.31 Recommendations. Also, many vendors now use X.25 within proprietary products.

The PAD Standards

Goals of Chapter 9

The goals of this chapter are to describe the CCITT packet assembler/ disassembler (PAD) recommendations and to examine some options for using them on an X.25-based network. The reader who wants more detailed information on PAD operations should consult Appendix F, X.3 Parameters in More Detail.

Introduction to the Triple X Recommendations

As the X.25 Recommendation developed in the 1970s, standards groups recognized that most operating terminals were (and are) asynchronous devices. Obviously, an interface was needed to connect these terminals to synchronous packet networks. Consequently, standards were developed to provide *protocol conversion* and *packet assembly-disassembly* (PAD) functions for the asynchronous terminal. After the initial 1976 draft of the X.25 Recommendation, the standards committees followed up in 1977 with recommendations for three specifications to support X.25 interfaces with asynchronous terminals: X.3, X.28, and X.29. These recommendations have been enhanced with the 1988 release (the 1988 version of X.3 provides a user with the flexibility to tailor additional characteristics for a particular terminal).

The idea of a PAD is to provide protocol conversion for a user device (DTE) connecting to a public or private packet data network, and a complementary protocol conversion at the receiving end of the network (if necessary). The goal is a transparent service to user DTEs through the network. While X.3 and its companion standards X.28 and X.29 address asynchronous devices (which constitute many devices in operation today), some vendors offer other PAD services to support protocols such as binary synchronous control (BSC) and synchronous data link control (SDLC).

The asynchronous-oriented PAD performs the following functions:

- Assembly of characters into the user-data field in the packets

- Disassembly of the user-data field back to individual characters at the other end

- Handling of virtual call setups, clearings, resettings, and interrupts

- Generation of service signals (status signals from the PAD to the terminal)

- Mechanism for forwarding packets (full packet or timer expires and partial packet sent)

- Editing of PAD commands

- Automatic detection of terminal's data rate, code set, type of parity, and other operational characteristics

X.3

The 1988 version of X.3 defines a set of 22 parameters that the PAD uses to identify and control each terminal communicating with it (see Figure 9-1). When a DTE/DCE connection is to be established, the PAD parameters are used to determine how the PAD communicates with the user DTE and vice versa. The user DTE also has the option of altering the parameters after the logon to the PAD device is complete.

Each of the 22 parameters consists of a reference number and parameter values. Table 9-1 explains these parameters and references in general terms. Again, Appendix F gives more detailed information.

X.28

X.28 defines the procedures to control the session between the user terminal (DTE) and the PAD (see Figure 9-2). Upon receipt of an initial logon transmission from the user DTE, the PAD establishes a connection with the DTE and subsequently provides services in accordance with X.28.

X.28 supports the procedures for

- Session establishment

- Service initialization

- Data exchange

- Control information exchange

- Session termination

Messages sent from the terminal to the PAD are called *command signals*. During a command state, the terminal can set up and take down calls and reconfigure the X.3 table. The messages sent from the PAD to the terminal are called *service signals*, and they are also used to manage the call and the X.3 table. X.28 requires the PAD to return a service signal when a terminal issues a command to it.

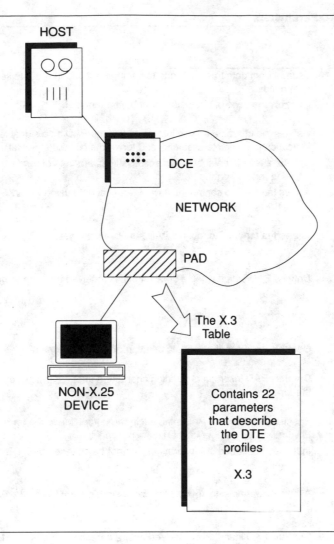

Figure 9-1. The PAD and X.3

X.28 specifies two profiles for providing service to the user DTE. The *transparent* profile means the servicing PAD is transparent to both DTEs; the DTEs perceive that they have a direct virtual connection to each other. In this situation, the remote DTE is responsible for some PAD functions; for example, error checking. The *simple* profile uses the fully defined X.3 Recommendation and the parameter functions to satisfy the user DTE requests.

X.28 Physical-Level Requirements

X.28 defines the use of the CCITT V Series or X Series modems for the physical-layer interface. Lower speed interfaces use the V.21, V.22, and V.23

Table 9-1. PAD Parameters

X.3 Parameter Reference Number	Description
1 Pad recall	Escape from data transfer mode to command mode in order to send PAD commands.
2 Echo	Controls the echo of characters sent by the terminal.
3 Data forwarding	Defines the characters to be interpreted by the PAD as a signal to forward data. Indication to complete assembly and forward a complete packet.
4 Idle timer delay	Selects a time interval between successive characters of terminal activity as a signal to forward data.
5 Ancillary device control	Allows the PAD to control the flow of terminal data using XON/XOFF characters.
6 Control of PAD signals	Allows the terminal to receive PAD service messages.
7 Operation of the PAD on receipt of breaking signal from DTE	Defines PAD action when a break signal is received from the terminal.
8 Discard output	Controls the discarding of data pending output to a terminal.
9 Padding after carriage return	Controls PAD insertion of padding characters after a carriage return is sent to the terminal.
10 Line folding	Specifies whether the PAD should fold the output line to the terminal. Predetermined number of characters per line.
11 Binary speed of DTE	Indicates the speed of the terminal. Cannot be changed by DTE.
12 Flow control of the PAD	Allows the terminal to flow control data being transmitted by the PAD.
13 Line feed insertion	Controls PAD insertion of line feed after a carriage return is sent to the terminal.
14 Line feed padding	Controls PAD insertion of padding characters after a line feed is sent to the terminal.
15 Editing	Controls whether editing by PAD is available during data transfer mode (parameters 16, 17, and 18.)
16 Character delete	Selects character used to signal character delete.
17 Line delete	Selects character used to signal line delete.

(continued on p. 217)

Table 9-1. PAD Parameters (cont.)

X.3 Parameter Reference Number	Description
18 Line display	Selects character used to signal line display.
19 Editing PAD service signals	Controls the format of the editing PAD service signals.
20 Echo mask	Selects the characters which are not echoed to the terminal when echo (Parameter 2) is enabled.
21 Parity treatment	Controls the checking and generation of parity on characters from/to the terminal.
22 Page wait	Specifies the number of lines to be displayed at one time.

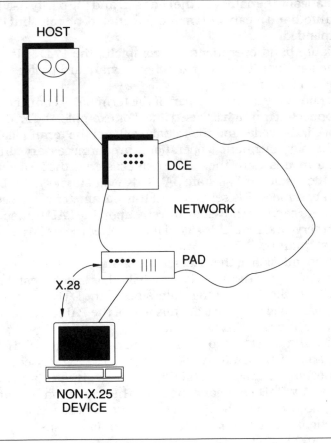

Figure 9-2. The X.28 Protocol

standards (300-1200 bit/s). Medium-speed interfaces use V.22 *bis* (2400 bit/s). V.28 is also stipulated for use, an unnecessary requirement, because the V Series interfaces cite the use of V.28 within their own respective standards. Automatic dial-in and dial-out uses V.25, although in North America the EIA 366-A standard is more prevalent. X.28 does not cite the use of any other higher speed V Series interfaces for the physical level.

Call Establishment between the DTE and the PAD

X.28 describes the DTE and PAD call-establishment procedures through state logic and state diagrams. This section provides a brief overview of the call-establishment state logic.

After the physical path between the DTE and DCE has been established, the DTE and the PAD exchange binary 1s between the DTE/DCE interface. The interface is then in an active link state. At this time the DTE is permitted to transmit characters indicating a service request to initialize the PAD.

The PAD is configured to be an *auto-baud* port, meaning that the PAD can detect automatically the data rate, the code set, and the parity used by the DTE. In the past, auto-baud meant automatic detection of bit rate, but the definition has been expanded.

After the auto-baud operations are complete, the PAD selects the initial profile for the terminal. The PAD may choose standard profiles, described in X.28, for the X.3 parameters.

Certain actions may be unnecessary if the terminal is connected to the PAD directly or connected through a leased line. For example, the PAD may already know the speed, the code, and the initial profile of the terminal. Obviously in this case, the aforementioned operations are unnecessary. In any event, following the transmission of the service request signal, the DTE enters the DTE wait state (which is defined as state 3A). This wait state is actually stipulated if the value of parameter 6 is set to zero. If this parameter is not set to zero, the interface enters a service ready state directly upon the PAD transmitting a PAD identification service signal. This signal is sent after the PAD receives a service request signal from the DTE.

After the transmission of the PAD service signal, the interface enters a PAD waiting state, unless a virtual call is established or is being established. Even when the PAD is in the PAD waiting state (state 5) the DTE may transmit a PAD command signal. Following the transmission of the PAD command signal, the DTE must enter into the DTE wait state.

If parameter 6 is not set to zero, the PAD, upon receiving a valid PAD selection command signal, will transmit an acknowledgment PAD service signal and will enter a connection in progress state (state 7). During this period the PAD cannot accept any PAD command signals. The transition to state 8 (service signals state) occurs when the PAD receives a call destined for the DTE. The PAD service signals state allows a transition to data transfer, connection in progress, or PAD waiting.

Other scenarios allow the PAD and the terminal to move from the data-transfer state back to the service signal state or the waiting for command state.

X.28 PAD Service and Command Signals

Tables 9-2 through 9-4 list the PAD service and command signals. Be aware that each service and command signal in these tables is defined in X.28 with a specific sequence of IA5 characters. The X.28 document provides more detailed information.

The X.28 protocol is quite simple and is not considered very user friendly (in addition, the X.28 document is a monument to obfuscation). Consequently, several PAD vendors have developed proprietary PAD-to-user interfaces. Some products use the X.28 Recommendation behind a vendor package to isolate the user from the X.28 protocol.

Table 9-2. PAD Command Signals

PAD command signal		Function	PAD service signal sent response
STAT		To request status information regarding a virtual call connected to the DTE	FREE or ENGAGED
CLR		To clear down a virtual call	CLR CONF or CLR ERR (in the case of local procedure error)
PAR?	List of parameter references	To request the current values of specified parameters	PAR (list of references with their current values or INV)
SET?	List of parameter references and corresponding values	To request changing or setting of the current values of the specified parameters and to request the current values of specified parameters	PAR (list of parameter references with their current values or INV)
PROF (identifier)		To give to PAD parameters a standard set of values	Acknowledgement
RSET		To reset the virtual call	Acknowledgement
INT		To transmit an interrupt packet	Acknowledgement
SET	List of parameters with requested values	To set or change parameter values	Acknowledgement or PAR (list of invalid parameter references followed by INV)
Selection PAD command signal		To set up a virtual call	Acknowledgement
ICLR		To invite remote PAD to clear down a virtual call	CLR PAD
RPAR?	List of parameter references	To request the current values of specified parameters in remote pad	RPAR (list of parameter references with their current values or INV)
RSET?	List of parameter references	To request changing or setting of the current values of the specified parameter(s) and to request the current value of specified parameter(s)	RPAR (list of parameter references with their current values or INV)

Table 9-3. PAD Service Signals

Standard format of the PAD service signal			Explanation
RESET	DTE	1, 2, or 3 characters which represent the decimal value of the diagnostic code	Indication that the remote DTE has reset the virtual call
	ERR		Indication of a reset of a virtual call due to local procedure error
	NC		Indication of a reset of a virtual call due to network congestion
	RPE		Indication of a reset of a virtual call due to remote procedure error
CLR			Indication of clearing
CLR	CONF		Confirmation of clearing
		The characters to be sent are network dependent	PAD identification PAD service signal
ERR			A PAD command signal is in error
XXX			Indication of line delete function completed for printing terminals
PAGE			Indication that a page wait condition has occurred
BS SP SS			Indication of character delete function completed for video terminals
ENGAGED			Response to status PAD command signal when a call has been established
FREE			Response to status PAD command signal when a call is not established
PAR		Decimal value of parameter: parameter value, INV, or list of invalid parameters	Response to set and read PAD command signal and to set PAD command signal, if at least one parameter is invalid
*			Prompt PAD service signal
Format effector			Acknowledgement PAD service signal
TRANSFER TO		DTE address and facilities	Indication that a called DTE reselection by the PAD is in progress
RPAR		Decimal value of parameter: parameter value, INV, or list of invalid parameters	Responses to remote set and real PAD command signal

X.29

X.29 provides the procedures for the PAD and a remote DTE or PAD to exchange control information on an X.25 call. X.29 is quite useful in allowing a host computer (DTE) to change the PAD parameters of the terminals connected to it. X.29 allows information exchange to occur at any time, either at a data-transfer phase or any other phase of the virtual call. Figure 9-3 shows the relationship of X.29 to the other related standards.

As discussed earlier in this book, the X.25 Q bit controls certain functions of X.29. An X.25 packet contains user-data fields and may also contain the Q bit. The Q bit (or data qualifier bit) is contained in the header of the data packet.

Table 9-4. Clear Indication PAD Service Signals

Clear indication PAD signal	Possible standard mnemonics	Explanation (See Recommendation X.96 in Chapter 7)
Number busy	OCC	The called DTE is detected by the DCE as engaged and not able to accept the incoming call.
Network congestion	NC	A congestion condition exists within the network.
Invalid facility request	INV	Invalid facility requested by the calling DTE.
Access barred	NA	The calling DTE is not permitted to obtain connection to the called DTE.
Local procedure error	ERR	A procedure error caused by the DTE is detected by the PAD.
Remote procedure error	RPE	A procedure error caused by the DTE is detected by the DCE at the remote DTE/DCE interface.
Not obtainable	NP	The called DTE address is out of the number plan or is not assigned to any DTE.
Out of order	DER	The called number is out of order.
PAD clearing	PAD	The call has been cleared by the local PAD as an answer to an invitation to clear from the remote DTE.
DTE clearing	DTE	The remote DTE has cleared the call.
Reverse charging acceptance not subscribed	RNA	The called DTE has not subscribed to reverse charging acceptance.

The remote device uses it to distinguish between a packet containing user information (Q = 0) or one containing PAD information (Q = 1).

X.29 defines eight control messages called PAD messages. They are summarized in Table 9-5 and described in more detail below.

The set message is sent to the PAD to instruct it to change one to n of the X.3 parameters. If this message contains no values, the PAD restores the X.3 parameters to the values before the call.

The read message is used by a host computer to instruct the PAD to return the current values of the X.3 parameters stored at the PAD. If the read message has no values, the PAD returns all 22 parameters.

The set and read message is used first to change the X.3 parameters, and second to return the changed values to the host computer. When a PAD receives a set, read, or set and read message, it must first deliver any outstanding data to the terminal before acting on these messages. Table 9-6 shows the rules for using these messages.

The parameters indication message is sent in response to the set or set and read messages. The message contains a parameter reference, which identifies the specific X.3 parameter. This code is followed by the current value for the X.3 parameter.

The invitation to clear is an instruction to the PAD to clear the call. This message is typically used when a terminal attached to a PAD issues a host computer logoff message to the PAD, which relays the message to the host. The

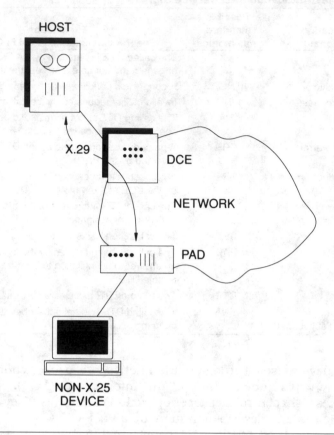

HOST

X.29

DCE

NETWORK

PAD

NON-X.25
DEVICE

Figure 9-3. The X.29 Protocol

Table 9-5. X.29 Messages

Message Type	Purpose of Message
• Set:	Changes an X.3 value.
• Read:	Read an X.3 value.
• Set and Read:	Change an X.3 value and require PAD to confirm the change.
• Parameters Indication:	Returned in response to above commands.
• Invitation to Clear:	Allows X.25 call clear by remote DTE. PAD clears to local terminal.
• Indication of Break:	PAD indicates terminal has transmitted a break.
• Error:	In response to an invalid PAD message.
• Reselection:	Instructs PAD to call a different address.

Table 9-6. X.29 Set, Set & Read, and Read PAD Messages

PAD message sent from the DTE		Action upon the PAD's parameters	Indication PAD message transmitted to the DTE
Type	Parameter field		
SET	Blank	Reset all the implemented X.3 parameters to their initial profile values	None
	List of selected parameters with the desired values	Set selected to given values a) If no error b) PAD fails to modify some parameters	 a) None b) List these invalid parameters
SET & READ	Blank	Reset all the implemented X.3 parameters to their initial profile values	List the implemented X.3 parameters and their initial values
	List of selected parameters with the desired values	Set selected parameters to given values	List of these parameters with new values
READ	Blank	None	List all implemented X.3 parameters with their current values
	List of selected parameters	None	List of selected parameters with their current values

host will then issue this message back to the PAD. At this time the PAD will clear this call. The procedure ensures that no data are lost in transit.

The triple X standards use the X.96 specification to define several service signals relating to a clear. Table 9-7 lists and describes these signals.

The indication of break message sent by the terminal is used in a variety of ways. One approach is for the host computer to issue a reset upon receiving the break message.

The error message is sent if a PAD message is in error. The X.29 Recommendation defines six types of error messages, coded to indicate the following:

- No additional information

- Parameter reference does not exist or is not implemented in the PAD

- Parameter value is invalid or is not implemented in the PAD

- Parameter value cannot be altered from the current setting

- Parameter is read only

- Parameter follows an invalid parameter separator

Table 9-7. Clear Indication PAD Service Signals

Clear indication PAD signal	Possible standard mnemonics	Explanation (See Recommendation X.96 in Chapter 7)
Number busy	OCC	The called DTE is detected by the DCE as engaged and not able to accept the incoming call.
Network congestion	NC	A congestion condition exists within the network.
Invalid facility request	INV	Invalid facility requested by the calling DTE.
Access barred	NA	The calling DTE is not permitted to obtain connection to the called DTE.
Local procedure error	ERR	A procedure error caused by the DTE is detected by the PAD.
Remote procedure error	RPE	A procedure error caused by the DTE is detected by the DCE at the remote DTE/DCE interface.
Not obtainable	NP	The called DTE address is out of the number plan or is not assigned to any DTE.
Out of order	DER	The called number is out of order.
PAD clearing	PAD	The call has been cleared by the local PAD as an answer to an invitation to clear from the remote DTE.
DTE clearing	DTE	The remote DTE has cleared the call.
Reverse charging acceptance not subscribed	RNA	The called DTE has not subscribed to reverse charging acceptance.

The X.29 protocol can be used to change a terminal's profile. Often the terminal user (an accountant, an automated teller machine customer, etc.) has no idea about the network and its many PAD parameters. The X.29 feature gives a host computer the capability to reconfigure certain characteristics of the devices that communicate with it through a PAD. Of course, how the PAD facilities are used is largely up to the creativity of the network managers and designers.

X.29 Packet Format

Figure 9-4 shows the format of an X.29 packet. Note the Q bit is used and the data field contains the values for the parameters. The data field contains the protocol identifier and the X.29 control data. The protocol identifier field consists of four octets, with octets 2, 3, and 4 set to 0 (they are reserved for future use). The first octet is coded with bits 8 and 7 set to the following values:

- 00 = For CCITT use

- 01 = For national use

- 10 = Reserved for international user bodies

- 11 = For DTE-DTE use

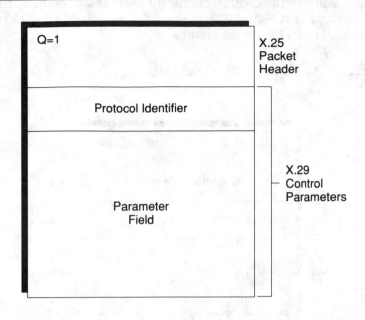

Figure 9-4. The X.29 Control Packet

The octets of the call user-data field contain the user characters received by the PAD from the user terminal during call establishment. The control messages exchange the control signals between the host computer and the PAD. To keep our details on the coding schemes relatively simple, we examine the packet format for the read, set, and set and read messages. The coding rules for the other messages are in the X.29 specification.

Figure 9-5 illustrates the parameter field of the packet. It contains the coding for the message code, the parameter references, and the parameter values. The parameter reference field is a decimal number of the X.3 parameter (see Table 9-8). The parameter value field contains the X.3 parameter values.

Table 9-8. Type and Coding of Octet 1 of PAD Messages

Message Type	Message Code (Bits)			
	4	3	2	1
Set PAD message	0	0	1	0
Read PAD message	0	1	0	0
Set and read PAD message	0	1	1	0
Parameter indication PAD message	0	0	0	0
Invitation to clear PAD message	0	0	0	1
Indication to break PAD message	0	0	1	1
Reselection PAD message	0	1	1	1
Error PAD message	0	1	0	1

Table 9-8 shows the coding scheme for the message code. In the case of the packet illustrated in Figure 9-5, the permissible values are 0010 for set, 0100 for read, and 0110 for set and read.

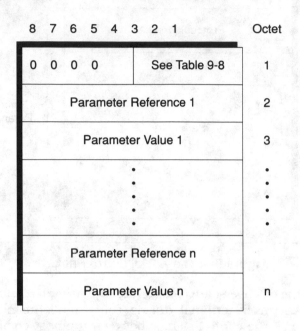

Figure 9-5. The X.29 Message Format

Conclusions

The use of X.3, X.28, and X.29 has been instrumental to the success of X.25, because they have allowed simple, inexpensive terminals to interface with a sophisticated X.25-based packet network. However, as the use of X.25 chips increases and vendors develop virtual terminals (VT), the need for the triple X recommendations will diminish.

X.25's Future

Introduction

Some people in the industry believe that X.25 is outdated and will fall into disuse as the industry adopts connectionless protocols and relatively error-free links. Only time will tell. However, X.25 use is increasing, as we will discuss in this chapter.

X.25 Market Shares and Market Trends

The 1988 U.S. market for X.25 products has been estimated at $392 million. Of this market, the U.S. federal government accounted for about 20 percent, and the private sector (private networks) accounted for about 55 percent. The remainder was in the public network sector and other value added networks.

X.25 equipment accounts for approximately 7 percent of the wide area network equipment market. However, the X.25 share of the wide area market is expected to increase to about 13 percent by 1993. The relative number of PADs is expected to decrease in comparison to native-mode X.25 interfaces. There are several reasons for this trend.

- Most private networks are using X.25 as the primary interface standard for host computers (or front-end processors). This trend should continue, because more computer vendors are introducing X.25-related features into their product lines.

- X.25 is one of the very few data communications network interface standards with world-wide acceptance. It is viewed as a "universal" protocol and is used by many companies simply because it is widely used and widely understood. Therefore, users and vendors will continue to expand the use of the standard. (The only network-level protocol for data communication networks that approaches the number of installations of X.25 is the Internet Protocol (IP). It is designed to perform internetworking functions, not to be a network interface protocol.)

- X.25 is certified for conformance and interoperability in practically all the public networks. End users find this service very attractive, because it gives them some assurance of compatibility between different vendors' products.

- ISDN contains several services that allow X.25 users to use the X.25 features through an ISDN node.

- Several personal computer manufacturers are introducing X.25 boards into their product lines. In addition, the personal computer LAN software vendors are placing X.25 in their protocol suites.

- Several offerings now available incorporate X.25 into the T1 technology.

- Vendors are starting to introduce the ISO 8208 DTE-to-DTE X.25 convention into their products. This standard allows the use of X.25 as a nonnetwork interface. For example, two host computers can interconnect using X.25 at the lower three levels for flow control, user identifications, etc.

- Vendors are also starting to use the ISO 8881 LAN X.25 Recommendation. This protocol permits an X.25 device to access a remote X.25 DCE through a local area network, such as Ethernet or a token ring.

- Knowledgeable end users have begun to realize that X.25 software has a wide variety of uses. Anything that can be assigned a logical channel number can avail itself of the X.25 features. In fact, some organizations use X.25 as a session layer protocol. This is not the intent of X.25, but it works well enough at this upper layer. Other organizations have implemented X.25 with a subset of the full protocol, and then have designed specialized modules to tailor X.25 to their specific needs. Again, this was not CCITT's intent, and such a system will not pass a certification test. (I have examined several systems that were called X.25 interfaces, but they were quite "skeletal," or had so much code tacked onto the original code that they could not interoperate with a certified system. They were X.25 in name only.)

- Some manufacturers think that the CCITT X.25 Recommendation is "settling down" in that the changes (every four years) are relatively minor. They see opportunities for building X.25 chip sets that incorporate all three levels of X.25. Currently, most vendors build X.25 chips with only the lower two levels. The third level is implemented with software. Implementing all three levels in hardware should significantly reduce the cost of X.25.

- Emerging standards from federal governments specify X.25 use for connection-oriented wide area network (WAN) interfaces. For example, the United States government has published the *US Government OSI Profile* (GOSIP). The United Kingdom has published a similar requirements specification. The Canadian government has released *Canadian Open Systems Applications Criteria* (COSAC). These standards specify the use of X.25 for connection-oriented (WANs).

A number of people have complained about X.25 because of its connection-oriented nature, and in some technical papers on X.25 the writers actually appear to have an "ax to grind" about X.25. I have attended meetings in which the connectionless and connection-oriented zealots lost all sense of logic in their discussion of the trade-offs between the two approaches.

Without question, the overhead of maintaining state tables and timers on each X.25 connection can be significant, and fast select still requires connection-oriented operations. Most applications need some type of connection-oriented service to account for data transfer. Perhaps it can be obtained in a better way in other protocols, perhaps operating at another layer in the OSI stack.

Certainly valid concerns are the lack of multipoint features and the duplicate sequencing, flow control, and acknowledgment operations that exist at layer 2 (LAPB) and layer 3. The approach works well on WAN interfaces but is quite cumbersome for use on LANs. A viable approach for using X.25 on LANs is to replace LAPB with LLC type 1. Yet another approach is to use LLC type 2 for the X.25 layers 2 and 3. Of course, this latter approach effectively eliminates X.25, which is fine if the situation so warrants.

It has been stated in several journals and articles recently that X.25 is antiquated because it is "slow". This statement shows a lack of understanding of both X.25 and layered protocols. The "speed" of X.25 is

a) Based principally on the physical layer, which only stipulates speeds to 64 Kbit/s. However, nothing precludes the user from replacing this layer with a "higher speed" physical layer such as a fiber distributed data interface (FDDI), a T1 carrier, or an 802.6 metropolitan area network (MAN) system (and probably altering or eliminating LAPB at layer 2).

b) Based only somewhat on the data link layer, in that the connection-oriented aspect of LAPB may not make effective use of relatively error-free, high-speed media such as fiber, FDDI, T1, MANs, or broadband ISDN (BISDN). As stated before, LAPB can be removed from X.25 without affecting X.25 layer 3 operations.

c) Based somewhat on layer 3, in that the connection-oriented, virtual circuit aspect of this layer requires maintaining tables, state diagram, etc. for each virtual connection. Again, X.25 is designed for operations that need connection-oriented network interfaces.

It should be emphasized that any connection-oriented protocol will consume resources and will likely "slow things down". Be it X.25 at the network layer, TCP and TP4 at the transport layer, or X.400 at the application layer—services rarely come without cost. But it seems rather silly to criticize X.25 for merely doing what it was designed to do. The answer is simple. If X.25 is not needed, then don't use it. But don't become caught-up in the ongoing debates between the connectionless and connection-oriented zealots. Go play a game of tennis, or golf. It's more productive and more fun.

Finally, it should also be stated that if X.25 does reach obsolescence, its use has paved the way for better and more efficient virtual circuit technologies: a) ISDN, b) prearbitrated access slots in 802.6 MANs, and c) the emerging virtual circuit concept in the asynchronous transfer mode (ATM), the signaling digital hierarchy (SDH), and synchronous optical network (SONET). If nothing else, X.25 will leave behind an impressive legacy.

Using X.25 as a Tool to Administer the Network

Because X.25 is a connection-oriented network protocol, it must keep rather extensive records about a user session. Several vendors have developed software to take advantage of the session-oriented aspect of X.25 to record network usage, and to calculate network charges for generating invoices or cost allocation reports to the users. Most vendors' software systems collect network usage data and provide billing and management information in a variety of formats, in both batch and on-line forms. For example, the NetCharge™ service from DHD Services of McLean, Virginia, provides the network manager with a variety of services, summarized in Table 10-1.

Internally, the DHD system uses the Automatic Message Accounting standards developed and administered by Bellcore (document TR-TSY-000301). This approach keeps the user's transactions in formats widely used throughout the industry, and accounting records and files are more easily transported across different administrative systems in different networks. This system supports non-X.25 networks as well.

Conclusions

X.25 is appropriate for systems needing a connection-oriented network interface. Moreover, X.25 is somewhat technology independent. Even though the standard stipulates a low-speed interface (up to 64 Kbits/s), the data-link and packet layers can operate with high-speed media. Also, several vendors do not use LAPB at the link level, but place the X.25 packet into T1 frames, ISDN B channels, etc. Nothing precludes users who want a connection-oriented network protocol from using X.25 on optical fibers.

X.25 is somewhat complex and contains a considerable amount of logic oriented toward low-speed and error-prone networks (for example, the negotiation of transit delay and throughput, and the use of a D bit for end-to-end acknowledgment). However, the end user is not required to select those features of X.25.

Table 10-1. Example of X.25-Based Management Services (Source NetCharge™)

Usage Data Processing and Rating
• Captures usage data, manages unbillable call records.
• Manages multi-day calls, and calls-in-progress during a switch reading.
• Edits and error checks usage on volume, duration, or per-transaction basis, as specified.
• Supports different rates structures for each customer and service; handles several options on reverse charging and fast selects.
• Supports per-call discounts linked to promotions and incentives linked to time-of-month, other special options.
• Identification of X.25 logical channel numbers in relation to originating and terminating calls.
Invoice Generation
• Generates and manages invoices with services such as balance forwarding, usage displays, credits, adjustments, prorations, taxations, multiple billing, journals, and summary reports.
Database Access
• Provides authorized users on-line access to data for various jobs such as reporting, menus for batch job scheduling, correction of usage data errors.
Report Generation
• Provision for some 60 reports relating to invoices, sales, accounting, ratings, edits, updates, usage.
Other Features
• Support of other services, such as restart and recovery, security, currency exchange for foreign accounts, salespersons' commissions, traffic statistics, and data archiving.

The packet level interface operations of X.25 are similar to the ISDN network layer. Some people hope to integrate network-layer functions of these two standards into one product that would be more efficient and consume less memory and cycle time on a machine.

X.25 will continue to be used for the foreseeable future because of its wide base of users and its proliferation into other standards and products. Perhaps its greatest values are that it provides a standard network interface convention, and it has served as a pioneer to other virtual circuit technologies.

Examples of Packet Networks

Introduction

This appendix provides an overview of several packet networks. It focuses on the routing operations at the packet switches inside the network and some other aspects of the networks of particular interest. Although X.25 does not define how the packets are routed within the network, a few examples here illustrate its use for controlling some internetwork functions.

The networks and products in this appendix were chosen because of their prevalence in the industry and/or their unique attributes.

Systems Network Architecture (SNA)

IBM introduced Systems Network Architecture (SNA) in September 1973. Today, thousands of licensed SNA sites are in operation. Even if you do not use SNA, understanding its basic features is a good idea because it is so pervasive. The chapter on internetworking (Chapter 8) explains the possible interconnectivity of SNA and X.25 in more detail, and that chapter assumes the basic understanding of SNA concepts given here. We begin our analysis of SNA with an explanation of how a user obtains the SNA services.

To use the SNA network, a user class of service (COS) must first be defined; that is, the user must define a preferential route and a preferential level of service. For example, the preferential route could be land lines instead of satellite links because of response time considerations, use of certain links that are more secure than others, and the bypassing of certain nodes.

The class of service (COS) defines a list of preferential routes, called virtual routes (VR) (see Figure A-1). A virtual route is a logical route between two end points. A user session is assigned the first operational VR in the COS table. Each virtual route is then mapped into a table to create explicit routes (ERs). An explicit route is a sequence of intermediate nodes from the originating to terminating stations. Each explicit route is also defined in a transit routing table. The routing table contains the destination addresses as well as explicit route numbers.

Routing through SNA is session oriented and fixed at the time the user's profile is generated into the routing table. As with all packet-switching networks, the table provides alternate routing entries in the event of problems with nodes or channels.

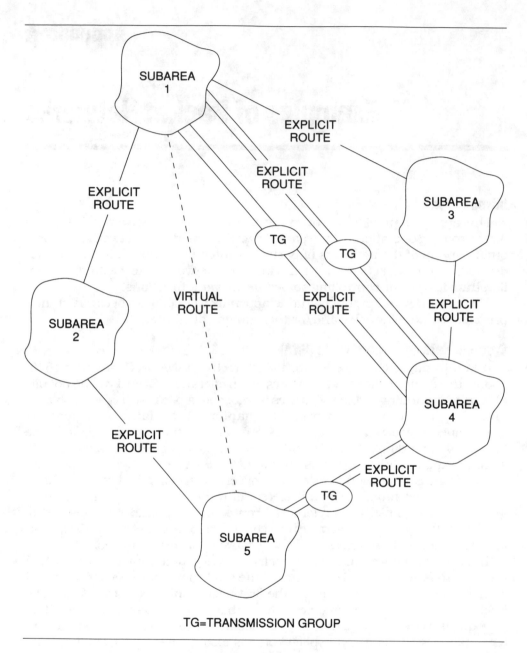

TG=TRANSMISSION GROUP

Figure A-1. SNA Routes

The SNA directory is partial—no single switching facility has an understanding of the complete end-to-end path. The switch knows only the adjacent nodes to which it is to route traffic. The explicit routes are broken down into route segments. A change in network configuration and topology (for example, adding new nodes or removing nodes from the network) necessitates changing only the transaction routing tables of the adjacent nodes. No other nodes are affected.

All these activities take place outside the purview of X.25. Indeed, many X.25-based networks use X.25 as the interface into and out of the network, and then invoke the SNA routing protocols to manage the traffic inside the network.

Tymnet

Tymnet uses a session-oriented directory within its "cloud" and is also an example of centralized routing. It provides a control center (the "supervisor") that determines the route through the network for each user session. The route is selected when each user logs on to the network. The network supervisor sets up a session by sending a "needle" packet to the requesting node. The needle packet identifies all the intermediate nodes needed to complete the packet transfer to the end site. When the needle packet arrives at the source node, the packet is then sent along the path to the intermediate nodes, where buffers are set up and reserved for a two-way session between the two users.

Tymnet establishes the needle packet on the basis of a "link cost": link capacity load conditions of each line, type of link, and the type of application session (interactive, batch, etc.). Thereafter, a session traverses the same path while the users are logged on to the network. The network supervisor maintains an awareness of the entire network by requiring that each node send status packets to it every few seconds. These packets contain the operational status of each node and provide information on packet delay through the nodes. To terminate the session, a "path zapper" packet releases the channels and buffers through the path.

Each Tymnet node is allocated logical channels, and the channels are reserved for transmissions when the session is set up with the needle packet. The logical channel number identifies the session and the packets belonging to the session. The term "logical channel" is not to be confused with the X.25 term. Although the Tymnet and X.25 logical channels perform similar functions (user identification), they are not compatible.

ARPANET

ARPANET is an example of adaptive or dynamic directory routing. Each node is aware of the entire network topology and independently computes the optimum (shortest) path to each destination node and the final node. Adaptive networks such as ARPANET function on the concept of node-adjacency knowledge; that is, a particular node is aware of the status of those nodes adjacent to it. The process is depicted in Figure A-2, which shows the routing table for node D. The routing table consists of several entries. Three illustrated are final destination (FD), next node (NN), and a calculated overall delay (OD). If node D wishes to transmit packets to node A, it performs a table lookup to final destination A and determines that the next node to route the packets is C. The overall delay from D to C to B to A is seven units of time—shorter than any other path to A.

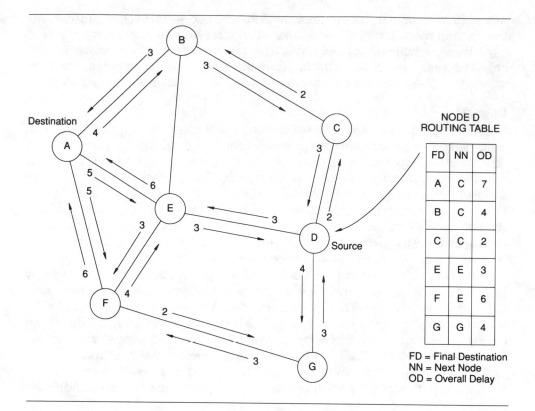

Figure A-2. Adaptive Routing

As the packets are sent out from node D to its adjacent nodes (C, E, and G), the software at D keeps records of the time required to receive an acknowledgment from the adjacent nodes. In addition, each node knows how many packets it has outstanding for other nodes. Every 10 seconds the node calculates the delay on each of its outgoing links. Information on significant changes in delay time is sent by packet flooding to all other nodes. The nodes then use the information to recompute the routing table. Hence the name dynamic or adaptive routing: Routing logic changes according to network conditions.

Telenet

Telenet, one of the largest public packet networks in the world, has a unique approach to network routing. First, the network has a two-level routing hierarchy. A backbone network covers the United States; the second-level lines fan out from the backbone network throughout geographical areas. Each hub in the Telenet topology consists of the backbone switches as well as the lower level switches.

The unique aspect of Telenet is that it uses virtual circuit routing based on the X.75 protocol. This protocol was designed primarily for internetworking, but it has some useful features for session-oriented routing protocols.

X.75 is invoked to establish an end-to-end path through the network. A call is established by the transmitter sending a call request packet. This packet threads through the network setting up an appropriate route. During the call setup, the routing paths are determined by the network control center, which sends appropriate routing tables to the backbone switches. These tables consist of primary choices, typically shortest path routes, and less optimal alternate routes. A secondary choice is used during call setup if a primary choice is not available.

The network control center actually provides a set of choices. The local node determines the specific outgoing link on the basis of an assessment of line use and the total number of virtual calls passing through each direction on the link. Thus, Telenet uses locally determined information as well as centralized information to build the route. This approach is similar to the French network Transpac (discussed next).

If the call setup cannot be completed because outgoing links are unavailable, a call clear packet is issued back to the preceding node. The node is required to try an alternate path using the same process. This process continues until a path is found or until it is determined that none exists.

X.75 provides an additional field in its packet called the utility field. As the call request packet traverses through the network, a count field is incremented in the utility field. This allows the nodes to detect excessive loop counts and clear the call if necessary, or attempt route selection once again.

The X.25/X.75 connection-oriented approach with mapping of logical channel numbers at each node presents an interesting problem with a session disestablishment node or link failure. If any of these problems occurs, each virtual circuit end point must determine the need to set up a new path. Telenet provides for a problem to be noted by a clear indication packet sent in both directions from the point of the problem. This clears the virtual call between the two end users. The originating source node can then recreate the session by establishing a reconnect request packet. The connection is completed by the destination site sending a reconnect accept packet.

This is one of the few instances of the X.25/X.75 protocol being used as an integral part of route management in the network. The earlier Telenet approach was based on datagram routing. However, the X.75 packet header is only 3 bytes long (for a data packet); the previous Telenet datagram packet required 16 octets for each header. This overhead created significant line use problems.

Note that Telenet also uses the multilink procedures (MLP) for handling a virtual call, providing for load sharing across multiple links. MLP increases throughput and enhances reliability.

Transpac

Transpac is the French public data network. With operations beginning in December 1978, it was one of the first networks of this type. It uses the X.25

interface protocol for handling virtual call setup and data transfer within the network cloud.

Transpac assigns routes on a single-path basis using a virtual call. The virtual call setup establishes the subsequent data packet route through the network. The call request packet is routed using routing tables in each node. The tables and routing logic in each node map a destination node to a specific outbound link.

Transpac uses two types of nodes. The first provides alternate routing capability. The second has no alternate routing capability, but connects directly to the first type of node. This approach provides a flexible yet cost-effective feature, allowing Transpac to configure alternate routing for critical nodes and nonalternate routing for less important tertiary nodes.

Transpac manages network routing by calculating and analyzing the shortest path and minimum costs. As with many networks, costs mean factors other than actual costs. Transpac defines costs in terms of link resources and link use. Each node's control unit (CU) gathers resource data from each of its switching units (SUs). The resource data are based on the capacity and use of the buffers and links. The cost data are sent to a network management center (NMC) whenever a change occurs. The NMC compares these values with the costs currently understood by the source and sink nodes.

Routing control takes place mainly at the NMC. However, an individual node can choose the next hop in the overall virtual path. It chooses the next node that equals or reduces the NMC's calculation of the minimum-cost path between the source and sink nodes. This decision permits the node to adjust to the changing link and buffer conditions between it and its adjacent nodes.

Thus, like Telenet, Transpac uses both centralized and distributed procedures. Network routing is actually a minimum-hop protocol with adjustments made for nodal link and buffer use.

Datapac

Datapac is the largest public data network in Canada. It is administered by Telecom Canada and has some similarities to Telenet and Transpac. However, it uses different options at the interface and within the network cloud.

An end user is provided access to the network on a virtual circuit basis. The user receives an end-to-end virtual circuit connection, which requires the packets to be resequenced at the other end in the same order as they were transmitted through the cloud. However, inside the network the packets are routed independently through the network. This means the sink node is responsible for resequencing packets, restoring lost packets, or discarding duplicates if they occur.

Upon receiving data from the customer, the source packet node buffers the traffic for subsequent transmittal on a network trunk. Each packet is sent through the network and is individually acknowledged at the destination source. Datapac provides end-to-end service. If the acknowledgment is not received within three seconds, the source node retransmits the data.

Inside the network, Datapac routing is based on two major factors. First, a routing table provides the optimum outgoing trunk route for each destination site. Second, a table is used to establish the overall end-to-end delay to reach a destination node via the particular outgoing trunk. Datapac changes the routing decision when the delay exceeds a preestablished threshold. When this new information is available, the neighboring nodes receive the information. This technique is similar to the ARPANET routing algorithm.

Datapac offers a set path (preferred path) as an option. This approach allows a path to be selected from the entire network. However, if a preferred path is not selected, the routing system will pick the best existing route. As stated earlier, there can be alternate routing, principally when a node detects overflow on a trunk route or a trunk.

The route selection for the overflow link follows the same rules as in the preferred routing. Additionally, an option for overflow routing can be selected network-wide. Nonetheless, the Datapac routing system determines the alternate route. If the overflow route is not appropriate, Datapac reverts to the minimum-delay routing discussed above. The principal purpose of overflow routing is to allow load sharing between adjacent nodes in the network.

Datapac also supports a concept called trunk group metric. For example, a group of trunks (say, three trunks each operating at 56 Kbits/s) might be preferred over a single trunk. The default logic might choose the trunk route because it has an overall greater capacity. The trunk group metric is not used if the preferred-path option is in effect.

A Tutorial on Link Protocols

Introduction

This appendix provides a tutorial on link protocols. The following interrelated topics are covered:

- Asynchronous and synchronous transmission

- Flow control of traffic between computers

- Sequencing of traffic and accounting

- Actions to be taken in the event of error detection

Data-link controls (DLCs, also called line protocols) manage dataflow across the communications path or link. Their functions are limited to the individual link. That is to say, link control is responsible only for the traffic between adjacent nodes or stations on a line. Once the data are transmitted to the adjacent node and an acknowledgment of the transmission is returned to the transmission site, the link control task is complete for that transmission.

Asynchronous Line Protocols

Asynchronous DLCs place timing bits around each character in the user-data stream (see Figure B-1). The start bit precedes the data character and notifies the receiving site that data are on the path (start bit detection). The line is idle before a start bit arrives and remains idle until a start bit is transmitted. The start signal initiates mechanisms in the receiving device for sampling, counting, and receiving the bits of the data stream. The data bits are represented as the mark signal (binary 1) and the space signal (binary 0).

The user-data bits are placed in a temporary storage area, such as a register or buffer, and are later moved into the terminal or computer memory for further processing.

Stop bits, consisting of one or more mark signals, provide the mechanism to notify the receiver that all bits of the character have arrived. Following the stop bits, the signal returns to idle, thus guaranteeing that the next character will begin with a 1-to-0 transition. Even if the character is all zeros, the stop bit returns the link to a high or idle level.

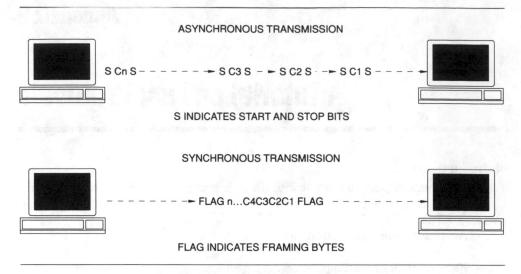

ASYNCHRONOUS TRANSMISSION

S Cn S − − − − − − → S C3 S − → S C2 S −→ S C1 S − − − − →

S INDICATES START AND STOP BITS

SYNCHRONOUS TRANSMISSION

− − − − − − − → FLAG n...C4C3C2C1 FLAG − − − − − − − →

FLAG INDICATES FRAMING BYTES

Figure B-1. Line Control Formats

This method is called asynchronous transmission, because of the absence of continuous synchronization between the sender and receiver. The process allows a data character to be transmitted at any time without regard to any previous timing signal; the timing signal is a part of the data signal. Asynchronous transmission is commonly found in such machines as teletypes or teleprinters and low-speed computer terminals. The vast majority of personal computers use asynchronous transmission. Its value lies in its simplicity.

Since X.25 uses synchronous lines, an asynchronous device must first connect to an intermediate device, which converts the asynchronous stream into a synchronous stream. This device, called a packet assembler-disassembler or PAD, is discussed in Chapter 9.

Synchronous Line Controls

Synchronous DLCs do not surround each character with start/stop bits, but place a preamble and *postamble* bit pattern around the user data. These bit patterns are usually called a SYN (synchronization) character, an EOT (end of transmission) character, or simply a flag (flag is the term used in the X.25 documentation). They notify the receiver that user data are arriving and that the last user-data character has arrived. Figure B-1 also depicts the format for synchronous line controls.

X.25 uses bit-oriented synchronous lines, although some offerings are available that support the character- and count-oriented techniques. However, use of these nonstandard approaches is gradually decreasing.

Character-Oriented Protocols

The character-oriented synchronous data-link controls were developed in the 1960s and are still widely used today. The binary synchronous control (bisync) family consists of character-oriented systems. These protocols rely on a specific code set (ASCII, EBCDIC) to interpret the control fields; thus, they are code dependent.

The character-oriented protocols have dominated the vendors' synchronous line protocol products since the mid-1960s. While still widely used, they are being replaced by count and bit protocols.

Count-Oriented Protocols

In the 1970s, count-oriented protocols (also called block protocols) were developed to address the code-dependence problem. Their principal advantage over character-oriented protocols is their more effective means of handling user-data transparency: They simply insert a count field at the transmitting station. This field specifies the length of the user-data field. As a consequence, the receiver need not examine the user-field contents. It need only count the incoming characters as specified by the count field.

Bit-Oriented Protocols

Bit-oriented data-link control protocols were developed in the 1970s and are now quite prevalent throughout the industry. They form the basis for most of the new link-level systems in use today, and the X.25 LAPB protocol uses this technique (Chapter 4).

Bit protocols do not rely on a specific code (ASCII/IA5 or EBCDIC) for line control. Individual bits within an octet are set to effect control functions. An eight-bit flag pattern of 01111110 is generated at the beginning and end of the frame to enable the receiver to identify the beginning and end of a transmission. Chapter 4 explains how the X.25 link level uses bit-oriented protocols.

Link-Level Operations

This section examines the major concepts of link-level operations. Figure B-2 will get us started, illustrating several important points about data-link (level 2) communications. The DTE (a user device) is to transmit data (in X.25, the

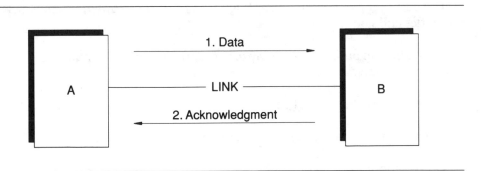

Figure B-2. Link Layer Operations

data on the link is called a frame) to the DCE (the packet exchange). Event 2 is important in the process: The DCE sends to the DTE an acknowledgment of the data received. This acknowledgment means that the DCE has checked for possible errors occurring during frame transmission, and as best it can determine, the frame has been received without corruption. It so indicates by transmitting another frame on the return path indicating acceptance.

The data communications industry uses two terms to describe this response. The term ACK denotes a positive acknowledgment; the term NAK, a negative acknowledgment. A NAK usually occurs because the signal was distorted by faulty conditions on the channel (noise, etc.). The frame in event 2 will be either an ACK or a NAK. In the event of a transmission error, the DTE must receive a negative acknowledgment (NAK) so it can retransmit the data.

If the DTE receives an ACK in event 2, it assumes the data have been received correctly at the DCE, and the data-link control system at the DTE can purge this data from its queue. (The application process often saves a copy on disk or tape for accounting, auditing, or security.)

Note that the level 2 data-link protocols do not provide end-to-end acknowledgment through multiple links. Some systems provide this service at level 3, the network layer. However, the OSI Model intends that end-to-end accountability be provided by the transport layer (level 4).

Functions of Timers

Most line protocols use timers to verify that an event has occurred within a prescribed time. When a transmitting station sends a frame onto the channel, it starts a timer and enters a wait state. The value of the timer, usually called T1 (no relation to a digital T1 carrier), is set to expire if the receiving station does not respond to the transmitted frame within the set period. When the timer expires, one to n retransmissions are attempted, each with the timer T1 reset, until a response is received or until the link protocol's maximum number of retries is met. If transmission still fails, the link level attempts recovery or problem resolution. If unsuccessful, recovery is performed by a higher level protocol or by manual intervention and trouble-shooting efforts. (The retry parameter is usually designated as parameter N2.)

The T1 timer just described is designated as the acknowledgment timer. Its value depends on

- Round trip propagation delay of the signal (usually a small value, except for very long and very high speed circuits)

- The processing time at the receiver (including queuing time of the frame)

- The transmission time of the acknowledging frame

- Possible queue and processing time at the transmitter when it receives the acknowledgment frame

The receiving station may use a parameter T2 with T1. Its value is set to ensure an acknowledgment frame is sent to the transmitting station before the T1 at the transmitter expires. This action keeps the transmitter from resending frames unnecessarily.

The timing functions can be implemented by a number of individual timers. The protocol designer/implementer determines how the timers are set and restarted.

Automatic Request for Repeat (ARQ)

When a station transmits a frame, it places a send sequence number in a control field (see Figure B-3). The receiving station uses this number to determine whether it has received all other preceding frames (with lower numbers). It also uses the number to determine its response. For example, after it receives a frame with send sequence number 1, it responds with an ACK with a receive sequence number 2, which signifies that it accepts all frames up to and including 1 (inclusive acknowledgment) and expects 2 to be the send sequence number of the next frame. The send sequence number is identified as N(S); the receive sequence number, N(R).

The automatic request for repeat or ARQ is the process by which a receiving station requests a retransmission. For example, receipt of a NAK with receive sequence number 2 indicates that frame 2 is in error and must be retransmitted. The process is automatic, without human intervention (a somewhat anti-quated term today). A stop-and-wait ARQ is a simpler half duplex protocol that waits for an ACK or NAK before sending another frame.

Another technique, continuous ARQ, can use full duplex (two-way simulta-neous) transmission; in other words, transmission in both directions between the communicating devices. This approach was developed in the 1970s, when better channel use became more important (satellite links, fast-response packet networks). Because continuous ARQ has several advantages over a stop-and-wait, half duplex system, its use has increased in the industry during the past several years.

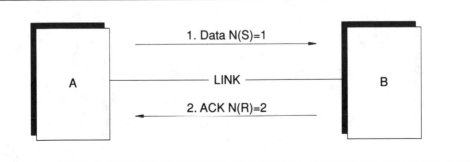

Figure B-3. Sequencing and Acknowledging Frames

Piggybacking

The newer line protocols permit the inclusion of the N(S) and N(R) field within the same frame. Figure B-4 illustrates this technique, called piggybacking. The protocol "piggybacks" an ACK (the N(R) value) onto an information frame (sequenced by the N(S) value). For example, assume a DCE sends a frame with N(R) = 5 and N(S) = 0. The N(R) = 5 means all frames up to a number 4 are acknowledged, and the N(S) = 0 means the DCE is sending user information in this frame with a sequence of 0.

Flow Control with Sliding Windows

Continuous ARQ devices use transmit and receive windows to aid in link management. A window is established on each link to provide a reservation of resources at both stations. These resources may be the allocation of specific computer resources or the reservation of buffer space for the transmitting device. In most systems, the window provides both buffer space and sequencing rules. When a link session is initiated between the stations (handshake), a window is established. For example, if two stations A and B are to communicate with each other, station A reserves a receive window for B, and B reserves a receive window for A. Windowing is necessary for full duplex protocols because they entail a continuous flow of frames into the receiving site without the intermittent stop-and-wait acknowledgments. Consequently, the receiver must have a sufficient allocation of memory to handle the continuous incoming traffic.

The windows at the transmitting and receiving sites are controlled by state variables (another name for a counter). The transmitting site maintains a send state variable V(S). It is the sequence number of the next frame to be transmitted. The receiving site maintains a receive state variable V(R), which contains the number expected to be in the sequence number of the next frame. The V(S) is incremented with each frame transmitted and is placed in the send sequence field N(S) in the frame.

Upon receiving the frame, the receiving site checks for a transmission

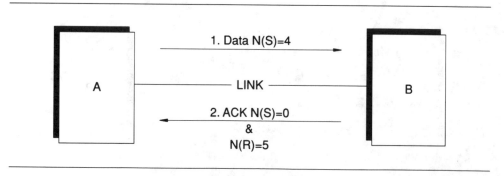

Figure B-4. Piggybacking

error. It also compares the send sequence number N(S) with its V(R). If the frame is acceptable, it increments V(R) by one, places it into a receive sequence number field N(R) in an acknowledgment (ACK) frame, and sends it to the original transmitting site to complete the accountability for the transmission.

If an error is detected or if the V(R) does not match the sending sequence number in the frame, a NAK (negative acknowledgment) with the receiving sequence number N(R) containing the value of V(R) is sent to the original transmitting site. This V(R) value informs the transmitting DTE of the next frame that it is expected to send. The transmitter must then reset its V(S) and retransmit the frame whose sequence matches the value of N(R).

The sliding window scheme allows the receiving station to restrict the flow of data from the transmitting station by withholding the acknowledgment frames. This action prevents the transmitter from opening its windows and reusing its send sequence number values until the same send sequence numbers have been acknowledged. A station can be completely "throttled" if it receives no ACKs from the receiver.

Many data-link controls use the numbers 0 through 7 for V(S), V(R), and the sequence numbers in the frame. Once the state variables are incremented through 7, the numbers are reused, beginning with 0. Because the numbers are reused, the stations must not be allowed to send a frame with a sequence number that has not yet been acknowledged. For example, the station must wait for frame number 6 to be acknowledged before it uses a V(S) value of 6 again. The use of 0-7 permits seven frames to be outstanding before the window is "closed." Even though 0-7 gives eight sequence numbers, the V(R) contains the value of the next expected frame, which limits the actual outstanding frames to seven.

The High Level Data Link Control standard (HDLC) and similar link protocols use sequence numbers and state variables to manage the traffic on a link (see Table B-1).

Table B-1. Functions of State Variables and Sequence Numbers

Functions
Flow Control of Frames (Windows)
Detect lost Frames
Detect Out-of-Sequence Frames
Detect errored Frames
Uses
N(S): Sequence number of transmitted frame.
N(R): Sequence number of the acknowledged frame(s). Acknowledges all frames up to N(R)-1.
V(S): Variable containing sequence number of next frame to be transmitted.
V(R): Variable containing expected value of the sequence number N(S) in the next transmitting frame.

Examples of Link-Level Operations

This section should tie together several of the concepts discussed earlier in this appendix. It also adds some additional concepts to previous points. Earlier figures have been expanded in this section to show the transmit and receive windows between the two machines. To keep the discussion relatively simple, the figures here show the transmit and receive windows in alignment with each other. However, in an actual operation, the windows' updates lag slightly behind each other, depending on which machine initiates the action.

Figure B-5 shows two protocol data units (PDUs, or frames) being transmitted from machine A to machine B. This example assumes that the transmit window is 7.

The notations in Figure B-5 mean the following:

- TLWE: The *transmit lower window edge* denotes the last PDU sent and acknowledged (PDU 0) and the smallest numbered PDU that has been sent and not acknowledged (PDU 1).

- TUWE: The *transmit upper window edge* denotes the last PDU transmitted (PDU 2) and the next PDU to be sent (PDU 3). This latter value of 3 is the value of LAPB's V(S).

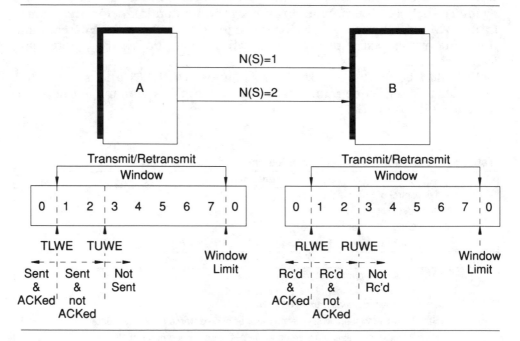

Figure B-5. Effect of Sending Two PDUs

- RLWE: The *receive lower window edge* denotes the last PDU received and acknowledged (PDU 0) and the smallest numbered PDU that has been received and not acknowledged (PDU 1).

- RUWE: The *receive upper window edge* denotes the last PDU to be received (PDU 2) and the next expected PDU (PDU 3). This latter value of 3 is the value of LAPB's V(R).

Figure B-6 shows that machine B has returned an acknowledgment to machine A with N(R) = 2. As discussed earlier, this means all PDUs up to and including N(S) = 1 are acknowledged, and PDU 2 is expected next.

The effect of the ACK is to "slide" the transmit window at A and the receive window at B by a value of 1. Therefore, PDU 2 has not yet been ACKed and remains outstanding (usually because machine B has not yet performed error checking).

In Figure B-7, machine A has sent machine B four more PDUs numbered N(S) = 3, 4, 5, and 6. The transmit and receive windows are updated to indicate that machine A is permitted to send two more PDUs (PDU 7 and PDU 0) before the windows are closed. Remember that PDUs 2, 3, 4, 5, and 6 are not yet acknowledged. Therefore, with a window of 7, two more PDUs can be sent.

In Figure B-8, machine B returns an ACK of 7, which inclusively acknowledges all PDUs up to and including 6. Since PDU 6 was the last PDU outstanding, machine A now has a transmit window of 7.

As discussed earlier in the appendix, the use of sequence numbers ranging from 0 to 7 permits seven PDUs (frames) to be outstanding before the window is "closed." Even though 0 to 7 gives eight sequence numbers, the V(R)

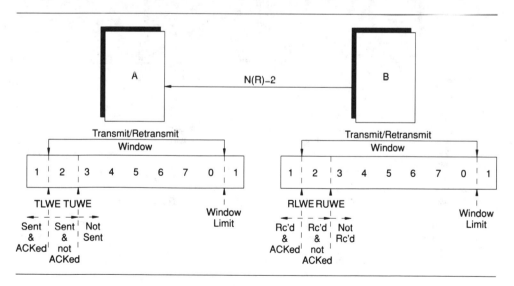

Figure B-6. Effect of an Acknowledgment

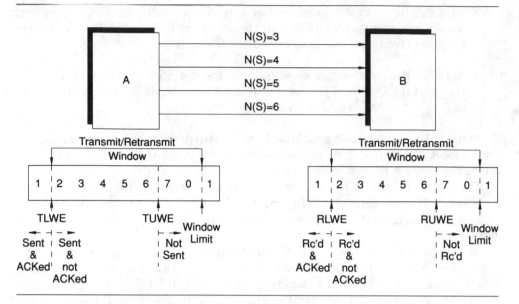

Figure B-7. Sending More PDUs

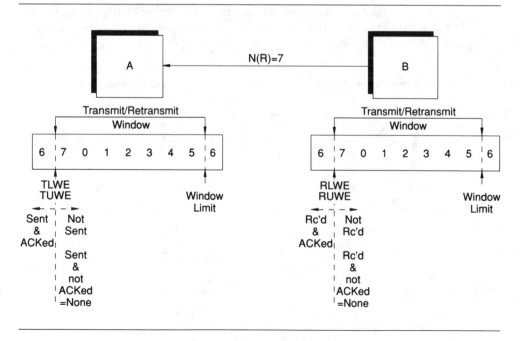

Figure B-8. ACKing all Traffic

contains the value of the next expected frame, which limits the actual outstanding frames to 7. Figure B-9 illustrates this concept. If eight PDUs were sent to machine B, the return of N(R) = 7 would be ambiguous. Machine A would not know (a) if the N(R) = 7 meant machine B was still expecting to receive the PDU 7 that was transmitted as the first PDU in the figure, or (b) if the N(R) = 7 acknowledged all the PDUs, from 7 through 6.

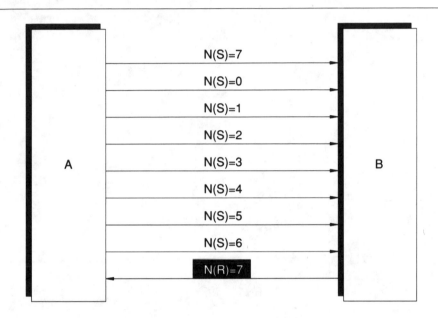

Does this state:
(1) Still Expecting N(S)=7?
(2) ACKing 7-6 and Expecting Next N(S)=7?

Figure B-9. Rationale for Window Restrictions

X.25 Conformance Testing, Interoperability Testing, and Product Certification Analysis

Introduction

Ideally, an organization will ensure a product conforms to a specification such as X.25 before it acquires it. In reality, most organizations are not equipped to meet this goal, but the products must be tested by some means. Several organizations in the U.S., Europe, and Japan are tasked with the important job of conformance testing; that is, testing whether or not the product performs in accordance with the international recommendation or standard.

Fortunately, X.25 "certification" has been going on for several years. The leaders in this endeavor have been the public packet networks, such as Telenet and Tymnet. Moreover, organizations such as the Corporation for Open Systems (COS) in the U.S. and SPAG in Europe are providing leadership roles for OSI protocol testing.

Differences between Conformance and Interoperability Testing

A protocol that has been "certified" by a testing organization will not necessarily operate with another seemingly "likc" protocol. Conformance certification means that the product has been implemented in accordance with the standard and that it processes the relevant packets as stated in the standard (see Figure C-1). This means it operates satisfactorily with a testing machine.

Because of differences in other aspects in a product's implementation (timers, retries, etc.), two conformance-certified products may still not "interoperate." Consequently, some organizations also conduct tests (called interoperability tests) between two real systems to determine whether they can communicate (see Figure C-2). The public networks actually perform a combination of the two procedures: conformance and interoperability testing.

Some tests consist of a paper evaluation wherein the vendor's implementation conformance statement is evaluated against the standard. This approach works well enough if its limits are recognized, but the next step should be to

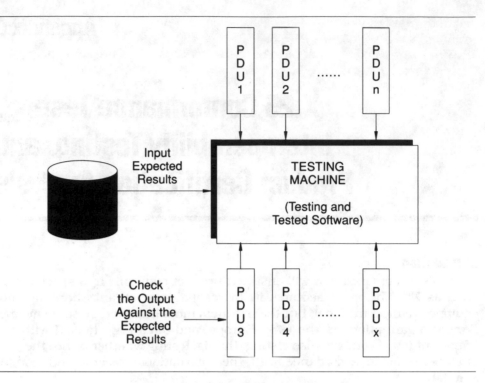

Figure C-1. Conformance Testing

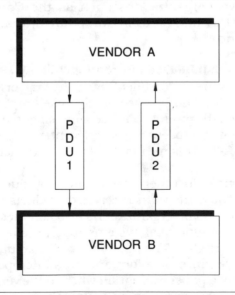

Figure C-2. Interoperability Testing

test the product against the X.25 specification. Also, some forms of testing evaluate how the product performs in accepting, using, and creating the relevant X.25 packets. That is to say, the tests typically do not analyze the internal operations of the product. Therefore, the tests can reveal when something goes wrong, but they may not reveal why the problem occurred.

ISO 9646. OSI Conformance Testing Methodology and Framework

In the future, X.25 will probably be tested according to the ISO 9646 standards. This specification (not yet finished) is divided into five parts:

- Part 1 describes the general concepts and architectures for conformance testing.

- Part 2 describes the Protocol Implementation Conformance Statement (PICS). This document is submitted by the manufacturer of the product and is used to evaluate compliance with the paper evaluation. Part 2 also describes in an abstract way how to structure tests and how to specify tests through special languages.

- Part 3 describes the relationship between abstract and actual test systems.

- Part 4 defines the output requirements of the tests.

- Part 5 defines the test laboratory operations.

X.25 Questionnaire

The questionnaire in this section can be used in an initial evaluation of an X.25 product. It provides a means to "break the ice" with the vendor and can lead to a more detailed analysis. While it does not take the place of conformance or interoperability testing, I have found it useful for structuring a company's initial analysis of X.25 products. In several instances, my clients have sent it to X.25 vendors to obtain information more detailed than what is contained in sales brochures.

I.   **Customer Interface Options (PAD Functions)**
   a. Do you support the X.3 PAD?
   b. If so, which version (1980, 1984, 1988)?
   c. Which of the 1980/1984/1988 X.3 parameters do you support?
   d. If you do not support the additional 1988 parameters, do you have plans to implement them? If so, which ones and when?
   e. Do you use X.28 fully or partially? Explain, if partially.
   f. Do you use X.29 fully or partially? Explain, if partially.
   g. Describe other protocol conversions options you offer (such as Bisync RJE, Bisync 3270, SDLC, etc.).

h. Do you have plans to enhance (or have you done so) your PADs with other user friendly features, such as electronic mail, user program storage, etc.? Please explain.

i. Describe your PAD-User interface. For example, is it menu-driven? Can an end user program the PAD?

j. Describe the port configuration options of your PAD. For examples, use of UART and USART chips and other programmable ports.

II. **Customer Interface Options (ISDN and X.25)**

a. Does your X.25 product support any ISDN interfaces? If so, please describe them and answer the other questions in this section.

b. Do you use any of the X.31 configuration options? If so, describe them.

c. Are any of your work stations configured with X.25 and (a) TE 1 functions, (b) TE 2 functions?

d. Does the X.25 use the LAPD link control? Explain.

e. Describe the data rate options, including the use (or nonuse) of the ISDN Basic and Primary rates.

III. **Furnish your latest rates/prices for all user/customer options.**

IV. **Use of X.25 (Layer 1)**

a. If a customer is connected directly to your system through a local interface, which physical level interfaces do you use? (For examples, RS-232-C, EIA-232-D, X.21, RS422, RS423, V.32, V.35). For what speeds are these interfaces used? (Exclude physical layer descriptions on ISDN, if described in section II.)

b. Please describe all non-local interface options such as dial-up, dial-up with dedicated port, leased line, etc.

V. **Use of X.25 (Layer 2)**

a. Which of the following do you use for link level control in your network: LAP, LAPB, SDLC, Bisync, others?

b. If you are using either of the HDLC Subsets (LAP or LAPB), describe any deviations you have made from the X.25 specification and your rationale for doing so.

c. Do you support the LAPB multilink option? (Any deviations?)

VI. **Use of X.25 (Layer 3)**

a. Are you using the 1980, 1984, or 1988 release?

b. Describe your plans to keep releases compatible with the current product line.

c. Several networks use some of the X.25 features slightly

differently (such as RESET, CLEAR, etc.) If your system uses any X.25 packet types differently, describe and explain your rationale for the differences.

d. Which of the X.25 facilities have you implemented? Which others do you plan to implement? (And when?)

e. Do you offer facilities other than those described in X.25?

VII. Use of X.75

a. Do you support as part of your product line the X.75 recommended standard?

b. Are you using the 1980, 1984, or 1988 release?

c. Discuss your implementations plans?

d. Several networks use some of the X.75 features slightly differently (such as RESET, CLEAR, etc.). If your system uses any X.75 packet types differently, please describe and explain your rationale for the differences.

e. Which of the X.75 utilities have you implemented? Which others do you plan to implement? (And when?)

f. Do you offer utilities other than those described in X.75?

g. How does your STE deal with the X.25 facilities that are mapped across the STE X/Y interface?

h. Describe the effect of X.25 flow control packets on your STE.

i. Describe how the STE handles the X.25 virtual circuit between networks.

j. Describe your X.75 addresses and how they are mapped between networks.

k. Describe how the STE provides for the integrity of the packets.

l. List and describe features of your X.75 software that can enhance network management and administration.

m. Does your STE require the input of X.25 packets? Explain.

VIII. Do you use the following standards with X.25? (Any deviations?)

X.1	X.92	X.213
X.2	X.96	X.32
X.10	X.121	TCP/IP
ISO 8473	ISO 8208	X.223
X.223	X.300	

IX. What is the address structure of your packets? For example, in a Call Request packet, what information is in a DTE calling field and a DTE called field (User ID, etc.)?

a. Do you support any of these CCITT/ISO identification standards?

X.121	ISO DCC
F.69	ISO 6523 ICD
E.163/E.164	The IP Internet address

X. Describe the procedure(s) by which a customer gains access to your network node (e.g. password requirements, user profiles, etc.).

XI. Describe your use of dial-up operations. Describe your authentication procedures. Describe if you use link level or packet level procedures for identification. Do you use the X.32 identification protocol?

XII. Provide a description of how your network actually routes packets from node to node.
   a. Is your routing centralized or distributed to the nodes?
   b. Are the paths through the network setup a (1) user subscription time, (2) user logon time, (3) during user session (dynamic), (4) other method?
   c. If you use routing tables/directories:
      1. Are the tables controlled by a centralized site or by each node or some variation?
      2. Does each node have complete or partial knowledge of the end-to-end path in the network?
   d. Do you use X.25 (level three) within your network in contrast to using it only at the DTE/DCE (network node) interface?
   e. Describe (in non-algorithmic terms) how the packet moves from node to node. For example, how does a node determine the best path out of the node for each packet. This question somewhat overlaps the other questions in section XI, but it provides an opportunity for you to state your "design philosophy" on network routing and management.
   f. How do you provide end-to-end accountability of user traffic?

XIII. Do you offer your X.25 products to customers on a non-network basis, on a point-to-point leased line for example?
   a. If so, how do you resolve the X.25 requirement that one of the nodes act as a network X.25 DCE?

XIV. Do you have local area network interfaces in X.25? Please explain.

XV. Do you have any PBX-X.25 interface products? Please explain.

XVI. Do you have plans for any ISDN/X.25 products? Please explain.

XVII. Describe how you determine loading on your product: for example, throughput and response time for users' traffic.

XVIII. Describe your service contracts.

XIX. Describe your procedures and agreements for the use of your product for a period of time to evaluate it.

XX. Do you offer billing packages or services for purposes of user charge-back and accounting?

XXI. Will you provide a list of other customers who use your products?

X.25 Check-Off List

This section contains a check-off list for evaluating an X.25 product. It serves the same purpose as the questions that are provided in the last section, but it is more detailed. Again, a check-off list does not take the place of conformance or interoperability testing, but it does provide a very useful tool for evaluating the product.

Physical Level	**Yes**	**No**
Uses X.21 Interface:	[ ]	[ ]
Uses X.21 *bis* Interface:	[ ]	[ ]
Uses V Series Interface:	[ ]	[ ]
If yes, which one(s):		
Any deviations from V Series RS?:	[ ]	[ ]
Uses EIA (Electronic Industries Association) Recommend Standards (RS)	[ ]	[ ]

If yes, respond to question PL2.

Follow-Up Questions

PL1. The V Series RS describe a great level of detail about modem characteristics. The Major V Series Interfaces Table in Chapter 3 is provided to guide you in responding to this question. Be aware that the table is a guide and does not cover all aspects of each V Series RS. What are the deviations from the V Series RS and what is the rationale for the deviations? Which options do you use within the RS (e.g., variable line speeds, alternative modulation schemes)?

PL2. What are the EIA interfaces you use (EIA-232-D, EIA-449, etc.)? What pins/circuits do you use? Do you use the terms X.21 *bis* and EIA-232-D synchronously?

	Yes	No
Link Level		
Link can be placed in active, idle, interframe fill, and abort states:	[ ]	[ ]
Bit stuffing/unstuffing and frame acceptance conventions are in accordance with LAP/LAPB. Whatever the answer, respond to question LL1.	[ ]	[ ]
DTE/DCE receiving a P=1, will set F bit to 1 in the next response frame that it transmits. Whatever your answer, respond to question LL2.	[ ]	[ ]
N(S), N(R), V(S), V(R) used in accordance with LAPB	[ ]	[ ]
FRMR frame used in accordance with LAPB	[ ]	[ ]
Logic of link level is performed in hardware and software. Whatever you answer, respond to question LL3.	[ ]	[ ]
Uses LAP:	[ ]	[ ]
Uses LAPB:	[ ]	[ ]
Adheres to HDLC subset BA2, 8:	[ ]	[ ]
Adheres to HDLC subset BA2, 8, 12:	[ ]	[ ]
Adheres to LAP/LAPB frame addressing rules:	[ ]	[ ]
Busy conditions can be cleared with either RR, REJ, SABM, UA, REJ:	[ ]	[ ]
Allows use of RR and RNR with P=1 to ask for status:	[ ]	[ ]
SABM/SABME or DISC action means previously unacknowledged frames remain unacknowledged:	[ ]	[ ]
Link setup with SABM/SABME requires DISC to be transmitted first:	[ ]	[ ]

Link setup with SABM/SABME requires DISC to be transmitted first with a UA or DM as a response: [ ]   [ ]

FRMR frame causes a DISC frame in response: [ ]   [ ]

DM frame sent with or without a DISC command: [ ]   [ ]

SABM/SABME always used with P=1:   [ ]   [ ]

Timers and Retries are used in accordance with LAP/ LAPB. Whatever you answer, respond to question LL4:   [ ]   [ ]

Follow-up Questions

LL1. Describe the sequence of events to perform bit stuffing and unstuffing, frame construction, and frame receiving. For example, a receiver might (1) unstuff 0s, (2) accept frame, (3) FCS check, (4) address check, (5) verify length, (6) verify sequence check, etc. Describe your systems logic. Also, if you responded no to the original question, state your rationale for not adhering to LAP/LAPB conventions for stuffing/unstuffing.

LL2. If you responded no to the original question, state rationale for not sending the next response of F=1. Also describe the specific P=1 frames (e.g., SABM, DISC, RR) and the specific response for F=1 that they invoke in your system.

LL3. Describe the specific tasks performed in software and/or hardware. If you have options of using either, describe these options.

LL4. Describe the parameters/thresholds for the timers and retries. Are they variable?

Network Level	Yes	No
Uses 1980 Version	[ ]	[ ]
Uses 1984 Version	[ ]	[ ]
Uses 1988 Version	[ ]	[ ]
Supports the following DTE-originated packets:		
Call Request	[ ]	[ ]
Call Accepted	[ ]	[ ]
Clear Request	[ ]	[ ]
Clear Confirmation	[ ]	[ ]
Data	[ ]	[ ]
Interrupt	[ ]	[ ]

Interrupt Confirmation	[ ]	[ ]
RR	[ ]	[ ]
RNR	[ ]	[ ]
REJ	[ ]	[ ]
Reset Request	[ ]	[ ]
Reset Confirmation	[ ]	[ ]
Restart Request	[ ]	[ ]
Restart Confirmation	[ ]	[ ]
Registration Request	[ ]	[ ]

Supports the following DCE-originated packets:

Incoming Call	[ ]	[ ]
Call Connected	[ ]	[ ]
Clear Indication	[ ]	[ ]
Clear Confirmation	[ ]	[ ]
Data	[ ]	[ ]
Interrupt	[ ]	[ ]
Interrupt Confirmation	[ ]	[ ]
RR	[ ]	[ ]
RNR	[ ]	[ ]
Reset Indication	[ ]	[ ]
Reset Confirmation	[ ]	[ ]
Restart Indication	[ ]	[ ]
Restart Confirmation	[ ]	[ ]
Diagnostic	[ ]	[ ]
Registration Confirmation	[ ]	[ ]

Adheres to all packet formats of each packet type. If no,   [ ]   [ ]
respond to question NL1.

Adheres to all DTE timeouts and DCE timers. Whatever   [ ]   [ ]
the answer, respond to NL2.

Enters and leaves X.25 states based on timers and   [ ]   [ ]
timeouts.

Uses X.121 in Calling and Called Address fields.   [ ]   [ ]

X.25 logic is in separate, independent logic modules   [ ]   [ ]
than that of other layers (physical, link, transport,
session, presentation, application).

Failure on Physical or Link Levels prompts DCE to   [ ]   [ ]
clear virtual calls and reset permanent virtual circuits.

For virtual call service, the DTE can indicate clearing   [ ]   [ ]
by transferring a Clear Request packet.

Clear Confirmation has end-to-end significance.   [ ]   [ ]
Whatever the answer, respond to question NL3.

The user data field must be an integral number of octets.   [ ]   [ ]

The D-bit option is used.   [ ]   [ ]

The D-bit mechanism is used in the Call Request and   [ ]   [ ]
Call Accepted packets.

The M and D-bit combined use conform to the X.25 A   [ ]   [ ]
and B categories.

The Q-bit option is used.   [ ]   [ ]

The A-bit option is used.   [ ]   [ ]

One Interrupt packet per DTE is allowed.   [ ]   [ ]

X.25 level uses modulo 8.   [ ]   [ ]

X.25 level uses modulo 128.   [ ]   [ ]

Packet numbering scheme is the same for both   [ ]   [ ]
directions of transmission.

Packet numbering scheme is the same for all logical   [ ]   [ ]
channels at the DTE/DCE interface.

DTE/DCE resets call or circuit for a duplicate or gap in   [ ]   [ ]
the P(S) numbering.

P(R) used to inclusively acknowledge.   [ ]   [ ]

Follow-up Questions

NL1. Describe any deviation of bit and octet use of any of the packet types.

NL2. If all time-outs/timers are not used, describe those that are not. In addition, describe the parameters used for all time-outs/timers.

NL3. The DTE Clear Confirmation packet may have local or end-to-end significance. Describe the technique used and rationale for choosing the alternative.

General Questions

NL-G1. Describe the manner by which the link level windows are set (fixed, dynamic, system generation, on-line).

NL-G2. Describe the scheme used to assign logical channel numbers (LCNs). Do logical channel groups signify specific user types, for example?

NL-G3. List the allowable user data field lengths. State the effect of (a) the communicating DTEs using different user data field lengths, (b) procedure (if any) for negotiating the lengths.

NL-G4. Describe the transit delay feature of the system (X.135). If this question will be answered by the questions on X.25 Facilities, then ignore.

NL-G5. Describe how overall network traffic influences the flow control into/out of user DTEs. For example, are flow controls usually DCE-initiated? Also, what is the effect of a local site-initiated RNR (or other 'choke') on the remote site?

NL-G6. Describe how X.25 product internetworks with TCP1IP-based networks. Describe the relationships of X.25 DTE addresses, logical channel numbers and IP addresses and TCP sockets.

NL-G7. If the evaluation is on a vendor, will the vendor give a consignment contract? That is, can you evaluate it for a period without a purchase requirement?

Diagnostic Codes

Introduction

Chapters 5 and 6 provide information on the use of diagnostic packets and diagnostic and cause codes. These codes are placed in a diagnostic packet or in other nondata packets, such as clears, resets, and restarts. Chapter 5 summarizes the X.25 rules for the disposition of Data and Interrupt packets that are affected by clears, resets, and restarts. These rules are repeated in this section with some explanatory graphics.

- Data and Interrupt packets generated by the local DTE before its (or the DCE's) generation of a Clear, Reset, or Restart packet will be delivered to the remote DTE before the remote DCE transmits the corresponding indication to the remote DTE, or be discarded by the network (see Figure D-1).

- Once the local DTE/DCE has issued a reset (or a restart for a PVC), any subsequent Data or Interrupt packets will not be delivered to the remote DTE until the corresponding reset procedure is complete at the remote DTE or the network discards the packets (see Figure D-2).

- Any outstanding Data or Interrupt packets from the remote DTE will either be delivered to the initiating DTE by the DCE before it issues a confirm, or will be discarded by the network (see Figure D-3).

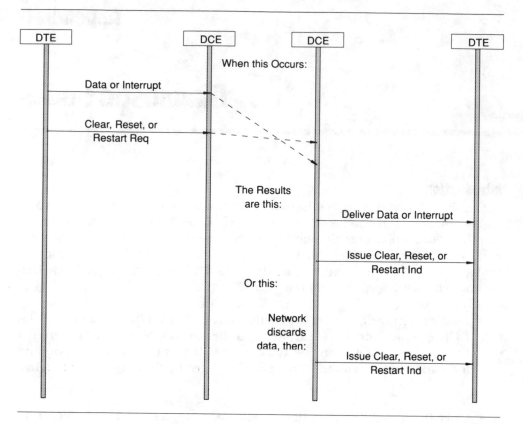

Figure D-1. Possible Consequences of Clear, Reset and Restart Packets

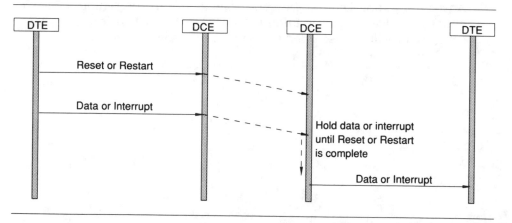

Figure D-2. Hold Data or Interrupt Packets Until Reset or Restart is Complete

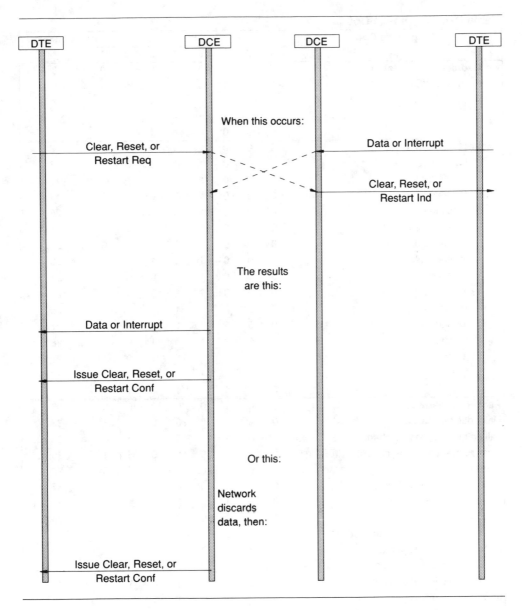

Figure D-3. Data or Interrupt Packets from Remote DTE

List of Diagnostic Codes

Table D-1 contains all the X.25 diagnostic codes specified in the 1988 Blue Book. Notice that codes 128-255 are reserved for the use of the specific network.

Table D-1. Diagnostic Codes

Diagnostic Code	Bits								Decimal
	8	7	6	5	4	3	2	1	
No Additional Information	0	0	0	0	0	0	0	0	0
Invalid P(S)	0	0	0	0	0	0	0	1	1
Invalid P(R)	0	0	0	0	0	0	1	0	2
	•	•	•	•	•	•	•	•	••
	0	0	0	0	1	1	1	1	15
Packet type invalid	0	0	0	1	0	0	0	0	16
for state rl	0	0	0	1	0	0	0	1	17
for state r2	0	0	0	1	0	0	1	0	18
for state r3	0	0	0	1	0	0	1	1	19
for state p1	0	0	0	1	0	1	0	0	20
for state p2	0	0	0	1	0	1	0	1	21
for state p3	0	0	0	1	0	1	1	0	22
for state p4	0	0	0	1	0	1	1	1	23
for state p5	0	0	0	1	1	0	0	0	24
for state p6	0	0	0	1	1	0	0	1	25
for state p7	0	0	0	1	1	0	1	0	26
for state d1	0	0	0	1	1	0	1	1	27
for state d2	0	0	0	1	1	1	0	0	28
for state d3	0	0	0	1	1	1	0	1	29
	•	•	•	•	•	•	•	•	••
	0	0	0	1	1	1	1	1	31
Packet not allowed	0	0	1	0	0	0	0	0	32
Unidentifiable packet	0	0	1	0	0	0	0	1	33
call on one-way logical channel	0	0	1	0	0	0	1	0	34
invalid packet on a Permanent Virtual Circuit	0	0	1	0	0	0	1	1	35
packet on an unassigned logical channel	0	0	1	0	0	1	0	0	36
Reject not subscribed to	0	0	1	0	0	1	0	1	37
packet too short	0	0	1	0	0	1	1	0	38
packet too long	0	0	1	0	0	1	1	1	39
invalid General Format identifier	0	0	1	0	1	0	0	0	40
restart with nonzero in bits 1–4, 9–16	0	0	1	0	1	0	0	1	41
packet type not compatible with facility	0	0	1	0	1	0	1	0	42
unauthorized interrupt confirmation	0	0	1	0	1	0	1	1	43
unauthorized interrupt	0	0	1	0	1	1	0	0	44
unauthorized reject	0	0	1	0	1	1	0	1	45
	•	•	•	•	•	•	•	•	••
	0	0	1	0	1	1	1	1	47
Time expired	0	0	1	1	0	0	0	0	48
for call request	0	0	1	1	0	0	0	1	49
for clear request	0	0	1	1	0	0	1	0	50
for reset request	0	0	1	1	0	0	1	1	51

continued on p. 269

Table D-1. Diagnostic Codes (cont.)

Diagnostic Code	Bits								Decimal
	8	7	6	5	4	3	2	1	
for restart request	0	0	1	1	0	1	0	0	52
	•	•	•	•	•	•	•	•	••
	0	0	1	1	1	1	1	1	63
Call setup problem	0	1	0	0	0	0	0	0	64
facility code not allowed	0	1	0	0	0	0	0	1	65
facility parameter not allowed	0	1	0	0	0	0	1	0	66
invalid called address	0	1	0	0	0	0	1	1	67
invalid calling address	0	1	0	0	0	1	0	0	68
invalid facility/registration length	0	1	0	0	0	1	0	1	69
incoming call barred	0	1	0	0	0	1	1	0	70
no logical channel available	0	1	0	0	0	1	1	1	71
call collision	0	1	0	0	1	0	0	0	72
duplicate facility requested	0	1	0	0	1	0	0	1	73
Non zero address length	0	1	0	0	1	0	1	0	74
Non zero facility length	0	1	0	0	1	0	1	1	75
Facility not provided when expected	0	1	0	0	1	1	0	1	76
Invalid CCITT-specified DTE facility	0	1	0	0	1	1	0	1	77
Maximum call redirects or deflects exceeded	0	1	0	0	1	1	1	0	78
	•	•	•	•	•	•	•	•	
	0	1	0	0	1	1	1	1	79
Miscellaneous	0	1	0	1	0	0	0	0	80
Improper cause code from DTE	0	1	0	1	0	0	0	1	81
Not aligned octet	0	1	0	1	0	0	1	0	82
Inconsistent Q bit setting	0	1	0	1	0	0	1	1	83
NUI problem	0	1	0	1	0	1	0	0	84
	•	•	•	•	•	•	•	•	
	0	1	0	1	1	1	1	1	95
Not Assigned	0	1	0	0	0	0	0	0	96
	•	•	•	•	•	•	•	•	
	0	1	1	0	1	1	1	1	111
International problem	0	1	1	1	0	0	0	0	112
Remote network problem	0	1	1	1	0	0	0	1	113
International protocol problem	0	1	1	1	0	0	1	0	114
International link out of order	0	1	1	1	0	0	1	1	115
International link busy	0	1	1	1	0	1	0	0	116
Transit network facility problem	0	1	1	1	0	1	0	1	117
Remote network facility problem	0	1	1	1	0	1	1	0	118
International routing problem	0	1	1	1	0	1	1	1	119
Temporary routing problem	0	1	1	1	1	0	0	0	120
Unknown called DNIC	0	1	1	1	1	0	0	1	121

continued on p. 270

Table D-1. Diagnostic Codes (cont.)

Diagnostic Code	Bits								Decimal
	8	7	6	5	4	3	2	1	
Maintenance action	0	1	1	1	1	0	1	0	122
	•	•	•	•	•	•	•	•	**
	0	1	1	1	1	1	1	1	127
Reserved for network-specific diagnostic information	1	0	0	0	0	0	0	1	128
	•	•	•	•	•	•	•	•	••
	1	1	1	1	1	1	1	1	255

The 1980, 1984, and 1988 X.25 Releases

The 1980 recommendation of X.25 was the first release that achieved world-wide use. Today, however, the vast majority of systems use the Blue Book 1988 Recommendation, which contains a substantial number of changes to the 1980 version. The most significant changes from 1980 to 1986 are summarized below:

- The datagram was deleted.

- The fast select facility is now essential, and user data can reside in both call setups and clearings.

- The Interrupt Data packet user-data field was increased to 32 octets.

- Facility fields in the call-management packets were increased to 109 octets.

- The transit delay facility allows the negotiation of delay: it was added as an essential facility.

- Additional error and diagnostics codes were added.

- Several telephone and PBX-type services were added:
  Call redirection notification
  Hunt groups
  Local charging prevention
  Network user identification
  Called line address modification

- The RPOA facility was added to allow the selection of transit networks.

- The registration facility was added and timer (time-limit) T28 was added to facilitate registration facility timer operations.

- Several end-to-end services were added:
    Address extension
    Interrupt procedures
    Minimum throughput class negotiation
    End-to-end transit delay negotiation

- A DTE can now belong to up to 10,000 closed user groups.

- Services were added to facilitate the interconnection of public and private networks.

- Several additions were made at the link level:
    Extended sequencing (modulo 128)
    Multilink procedures (MLP)
    Idle timer (T3)

The 1988 recommendation published in the CCITT Blue Books also has some changes, but they are not as significant as the 1984 changes. The major changes are as follows:

- Notations on the use of X.31 have been added to the physical layer.

- Transit delay definitions have been made more explicit.

- Discussions on throughput considerations have been amplified.

- Section 4.6, physical- and data-link failures, has been expanded.

- The long-address A-bit format (bit 8 of the first octet) in the call-management packets and facility has been added.

- The call deflection facility has been added.

Appendix F

X.3 Parameters in More Detail

This appendix provides more detail on the X.3 PAD parameters. The permitted values for each PAD parameter are provided, along with examples of how the PAD parameters could be (and often are) used.

X.3 Parameters and Name	Description	Values	
1 possible Pad Recall	Escape from data transfer mode to command mode	0 1 32-126	Is not possible DLE character User-defined characters

Parameter 1 is used to allow the user terminal to send commands to the PAD. If the value of the parameter is 0, the terminal is not allowed to send commands. This restriction might apply to users that are not (and should not be) aware of the PAD detail. Typically, a terminal sends the DLE, receives a reply from the PAD, and then enters X.25 commands.

X.3 Parameters and Name	Description	Values	
2 Echo	Controls the echo of characters sent by the terminal	0 1	No echo Echo

Some terminals use echo to detect transmission errors. Parameter 2 requires the PAD to echo the terminal's characters back to the terminal screen. This service may also be used if a terminal does not have local (internal) echo capabilities.

X.3 Parameters and Name	Description	Values	
3 Data forwarding	Defines the characters to be interpreted by the PAD as a signal to forward data	0	Full packet only
		1	Alphanumerics
		2	Carriage return (default)
		4	ESC, BEL, ENQ, ACK
		6	Carriage return ESC, BEL, ENQ, ACK
		8	DEL, CAN, DC2
		16	ETX, EOT
		18	Carriage return, EOT, ETX
		32	HT, LT, VT, FF
		126	All other characters in columns 1 & 2 of IA5 (ASCII Code)

Parameter 3 tells the PAD how to complete character assembly and forward a packet into the X.25 network. A carriage return (CR) is often used by the PAD vendors, but many choices are available. A zero value means only a full packet will be forwarded.

X.3 Parameters and Name	Description	Values	
4 Idle timer delay	Selects a time interval of terminal activity as a signal to forward data	0	No timer
		1-255	Delay value in twentieths of a second

Parameter 4 selects a time interval between successive characters in which the PAD will terminate assembly and forward the packet. It can be useful if an operator leaves a workstation during the session.

X.3 Parameters and Name	Description	Values	
5 Ancillary device control	Allows the PAD to control the flow of terminal data using XON/XOFF characters	0	Not operational
		1	XON (DCI).XOFF (DC3)-data transfer
		2	XON/XOFF data transfer and command

Parameter 5 is used by the PAD to flow-control traffic coming into it from the attached terminals. It prevents excessive traffic from saturating a PAD's buffers.

X.3 Parameters and Name	Description		Values
6 Control of PAD service signals	Allows the terminal to receive PAD service	0 1 5 8-15	No service signals Transmit service signals Transmit service and prompt signals Network dependent formal service signals

Parameter 6 is useful for controlling the use of service signals. However, for an average user it should be set to 0, since the service signals may be confusing.

X.3 Parameters and Name	Description		Values
7 Operation of the PAD on receipt of breaking signal from DTE	Defines PAD action when a break signal is received from the terminal	0 1 2 4 5 8 16 21	No action Interrupt packet Reset packet Indication of break Interrupt & indication of break Escape from data transfer state Discard output to start/stop DTE 1+4+16 combined

If the terminal user wishes to break a dialogue with the PAD, then Parameter 7 defines what action the PAD is to take. Some systems will interrupt the break to construct an X.25 Interrupt packet (value 1). Some possible choices are

Terminal → Break → PAD → Interrupt → Host
Terminal → Break → PAD → Interrupt → PAD → Break → Host

X.3 Parameters and Name	Description		Values
8 Discard Output	Controls the discarding of data pending output to a terminal	0 1	Normal data delivery Discard output to start/stop DTE

Parameter 8 is ordinarily used with Parameter 7. It instructs the PAD either to deliver the data that are stored at the PAD (upon receiving a break) or discard and do not deliver the data. Typically, this parameter is set to 1 after the receipt of a break from the terminal, and then set back to 0 when the host computer sends back a message that the parameter should be set to 0 (this is the set and read message explained in the X.29 section of this chapter).

X.3 Parameters and Name	Description	Values	
9 Padding after carriage return	Controls PAD insertion of padding characters	0 1-7	No Padding Number of padding characters inserted

Parameter 9 determines how many padding characters are to be added after a carriage return. It is useful on older terminals, but most modern terminals do not need padding, so this parameter is usually set to 0.

X.3 Parameters and Name	Description	Values	
10 Line folding	Controls PAD folding output line on terminal	0 1-255	No line folding Number of characters per line

Different devices use a predetermined number of characters per line of output. The parameter is useful for, say, changing a host's 132-character line to a terminal's 80-character line output.

X.3 Parameters and Name	Description	Values	
11 Binary speed of DTE	Indicates the speed of the terminal	0	110 bit/s
		1	134.5 bit/s
		2	300 bit/s
		3	1200 bit/s
		4	600 bit/s
		5	75 bit/s
		6	150 bit/s
		7	1800 bit/s
		8	200 bit/s
		9	100 bit/s
		10	50 bit/s
		11	75/1200 bit/s
		12	2400 bit/s
		13	4800 bit/s
		14	9600 bit/s
		15	19200 bit/s
		16	48000 bit/s
		17	56000 bit/s
		18	64000 bit/s

Parameter 11 requires the PAD to transmit at the terminal's receive speed, regardless of the input speed to the PAD. For example, a host could transmit to the PAD at 9.6 Kbit/s, and the PAD would then buffer the data and transmit to the terminal at, say, 1200 bit/s. This parameter cannot be changed by the DTE.

X.3 Parameters and Name	Description	Values	
12 Flow control of the PAD	Allows the terminal to flow control data being transmitted by the PAD	0 1	Not operational Use XON (DCI) XOFF (DC3)

If the terminal is receiving too much traffic from the PAD, then Parameter 12 can be used to "throttle" the traffic flow.

X.3 Parameters and Name	Description	Values	
13 Line feed insertion	Controls PAD insertion of line feed after a carriage return is sent to the terminal	0 1 2 4 5 6 7	None After carriage return to DTE After carriage return from DTE After echoed carriage return Values 1+4 Values 2+4 Values 1+2+4 (data transfer only)

A line feed control character is not always inserted by a device after a carriage return. Parameter 13 allows a line feed to be sent to or from the PAD or terminal in several combinations.

X.3 Parameters and Name	Description	Values	
14 Line feed padding	Controls PAD insertion of padding characters after a line feed is sent to the terminal	0 1-7 8-255	None Number of characters inserted (data transfer only) Optional extension

Parameter 14 provides for extra characters to be inserted after a line feed. The value depends on whether the terminal needs some time to do line feed before other data arrive from the PAD.

X.3 Parameters and Name	Description	Values	
15 Editing	Controls whether editing by PAD is available during data transfer mode	0 1	Off On

Parameter 15 can be used with Parameters 16, 17, and 18. If its value is set to 1, then data stored at PAD can be edited before being sent to the receiving station.

X.3 Parameters and Name	Description	Values	
16 Character delete	Selects character used to signal character delete	127	DEL character, other characters from IA5 (optional)
17 Line delete	Selects character used to signal line delete	24	CAN character, other characters from IA5 (optional)
18 Line display	Selects character used to signal line display	18	DC2 character, other characters from IA5 (optional)

Parameter 18 allows the terminal to get back the data from the PAD for verification.

X.3 Parameters and Name	Description	Values	
19 Editing PAD service signals	Controls the format of the editing PAD service signals	0	No editing
		1	Editing for printing terminals
		2	Editing for display terminals
		8	Editing using characters from IA5

The PAD service signals can be edited with the use of Parameter 19.

Parameter 20 gives the terminal user a wide range of options as to what is echoed back from the PAD. For example, the value of 0 can be used during system testing or during a trouble-shooting session. On the other hand, a nontechnical user would not want to see the control characters echoed back to the user terminal.

X.3 Parameters and Name	Description	Values	
20 Echoed Echo Mask	Selects the characters which are not echoed to the terminal when echo (Parameter 2) is enabled	0	All characters echoed
		1	No echo of carriage return
		2	No echo of LF
		4	No echo of VT, HT, FF
		8	No echo of BEL, BS
		16	No echo of ESC, ENQ
		32	No echo of ACK, NAK, STX, SOH, EOT, ETB, ETX
		64	No echo of editing characters

X.3 Parameters and Name	Description	Values	
21 Parity treatment	Controls the checking and generation of parity on characters from/to the terminal	0 1 2 3	No parity detection or generation Parity checking Parity generation Value1+2

Parameter 21 can be used to do parity generation and/or parity checking. When this parameter is set to 0, the PAD inspects only the first seven bits of the character. The actions of the PAD when a parity error is detected depend on the values of parameters 2 (echo) and 6 (service signals):

Parameter 2	Parameter 6	Action
0	0	Reset virtual circuit
1	0	Discard character; send BEL
1	≥ 1	Discard character; send BEL; may send parity error service signal

X.3 Parameters and Name	Description	Values	
22 Page Wait	Specifies the number of lines to be displayed at one time	0 23	No page wait Number of line feed characters before waiting (mandatory value) other optional values

Parameter 22 is useful when the terminal user wants a specific amount of display. The parameter specifies the length of a page when the terminal user needs to read the output of the screen as it arrives.

Index

Set normal response mode (SNRM), 66
Set normal response mode extended
    (SARME), 66
Shortest path, 14, 16
Signal(ing)(s)
    clocking, 37
    control, 37, 52, 225
    rates, 162, 164
    regeneration, 47
Signaling terminal exchange (STE), 18, 19
Single link procedure (SLP), 183
Sliding window scheme, 247
SLP, (See single link procedure)
SNA, (See Systems Network Architecture)
SNAP, (See subnetwork access protocol)
SNDCP, (See subnetwork dependent conver-
    gence protocol)
SNICP, (See subnetwork independent
    convergence protocol)
SNRM, (See set normal response mode)
SNRME, (See set normal response mode
    extended)
Source routing, 211
Speed of service (delay and throughput),
    169
State(s), 74, 75, 229
    diagrams, 111–117, 169, 229
    transition diagrams, 28, 83
    variables, 247
Statistical time division multiplexing, 5, 8
STE, (See signaling terminal exchange)
STE-to-STE communications, 192–193, 195
    interface, 169
SVC, (See switched virtual call)
Subnetwork, 179, 192
    types, 204–205
Subnetwork access protocol (SNAP), 182
Subnetwork dependent convergence
    protocol (SNDCP), 181–182
Subnetwork independent convergence
    protocol (SNICP), 180–181
Subscription facilities, 148, 150
Supervisory format, 61, 63, 68, 78
Supervisory packets, 100
Switch(ed)(es)(ing), 7, 10, 56
    channels, 54
    logical channels, 108–110
    virtual call (SVC), 86, 88–89, 162
Synchronous line controls, 242–243
Synchronous data-link control (SDLC), 51,
    56, 73, 78–79, 117, 129, 213
SDLC, (See synchronous data-link control)
Systems Network Architecture (SNA), 183–
    185, 233–235
    Interconnect (XI), 184
Systems services control point (SSCP), 184,
    185
SSCP, (See systems services control point)
TEI, (See terminal end point)
Terminal end-point (TEI), 78

Time limits and time outs, 111
Time sequence, 28, 80
    diagrams, 26, 83, 88
    functions, 244–245
Timers (T1, T2, T3), 66–67, 78, 92, 111, 229,
    272
    X.25, 92–93
Throughput, 9, 167
    class negotiation, 137, 142–143
    default, 137, 142
    rates, 142
TOA, (See type of address)
Trailers, 24, 25, 34
Transit delay facility, 271
Transit network, 183–185, 210
Transmission errors, 32
Transmission integrity, 16
Transmission link (wire), 5, 7
Transparent profile, 215
Transport layer (level)(#4), 32, 34, 103, 180,
    244
    protocol, 115
Two-way alternate (aka half duplex), 54, 56
Two-way simultaneous (aka full duplex), 13,
    49, 54, 56, 79, 108–110, 118, 245
Type of address (TOA), 97, 123, 206
    facilities, 154
UI, (See unnumbered information frame)
Unbalanced configuration, 54, 60
Unbalanced links, 68
Unbalanced normal response mode, 68, 78
Unnumbered format, 62, 63
Unnumbered frame, 68, 78
Unnumbered information (UI) frame, 78,
    183
Upper layer protocols, 87, 211
User classes of service, 161, 162
User data, 96, 97, 98–100
User facilities (X.2), 161, 162
User identifier (address), 24
VAC, (See value added carrier)
Value added carrier (VAC), 8
VAX PSI, 185–187, 188
    access, 185–187
Virtual call(s), 83, 90, 100, 106, 113, 114,
    132, 136, 143, 167, 185
    circuits, 192
    switched, 88, 88–89, 162
Virtual circuit(s), 6–7, 10, 83–85, 91–95, 112,
    147, 186, 229
    connections, 169–170
    ISDNs, 198–199
    manager (VCM), 184
Virtual private network, 133
Virtual terminal, 32
WANs, (See wide area network)
Wide area packet networks (WANs), 2
Wide area networks, 77, 228–229
Window,
    concepts, 117–118

Author's Profile

Uyless Black is associated with Information Engineering, Inc., a Virginia-based telecommunications consulting firm. He has designed and implemented many data communications systems and X.25-based networks. Black consults and lectures throughout the world on voice and data networks and international communications standards. He is the author of eight books on data communications systems, as well as numerous articles on the subject. His *Physical Level Interfaces and Protocols* is one of the IEEE Computer Society's best-sellers. Black is also the advisor for McGraw-Hill's *Uyless Black Series on Computer Communications.*

Uyless Black's undergraduate degree is from the University of New Mexico. He has graduate degrees in computer systems and banking and finance from the American University and the Stonier Graduate School of Rutgers University.